In the morning we are glass

/

Am morgen sind wir aus glas

Andra Schwarz

Translated from German by
Caroline Wilcox Reul

Zephyr Press | Brookline, Mass.

Printed in Michigan by Cushing Malloy, Inc.

Zephyr Press acknowledges with gratitude the financial
support of the Massachusetts Cultural Council
and the National Endowment for the Arts.

The translation of this work was supported by a grant
from the Goethe-Institut.

Zephyr Press, a non-profit arts and education 501(c)(3) organization,
publishes literary titles that foster a deeper understanding of cultures
and languages. Zephyr Press books are distributed worldwide
by Consortium Book Sales and Distribution [www.cbsd.com].

Cataloguing-in publication data is available from the Library of Congress.

ISBN 978-1938890-83-3

ZEPHYR PRESS
www.zephyrpress.org

Table of Contents

37   *Ich komme aus den wäldern / I come from the forest*

Ich komme aus den wäldern / I come from the forest
Du gehst hinein / You step out
Das wars / It's over now
Ein letztes / One final
Du lässt alles zurück / You leave everything behind
Dort bleibst du nun sitzen / You remain sitting
Es beginnt die blaue stunde / The hour of twilight begins

53   *Gespinste aus luft / Woven from air*

Wie wenig luft / How little air
Ich weiß nicht wo sie sitzt / I don't know where it lies
Ich war nicht da / I wasn't there
Sag mir, wer krieg spielt / Tell me, who plays at war
Seit gestern / A cross stands
Wo fing es an / Where did it start
Im hinterkopf / An image of cats
Wie lange schon / How long
Es hielt nicht stand / Your inner machine
Mit einem mal / Suddenly
Jetzt wache ich / I keep watch now

77   *Wir bauen zurück ins leere / We build backward into emptiness*

Wir bauen zurück ins leere / We build backward into emptiness
Fünfzig kilometer von hier / Thirty miles from here
Du kommst aus den lichten gestalten / You come from the luminous

Hier verschwinden worte / Words disappear from houses
Das ist die letzte station / This is the last station
Sieh dich um / Look around you
Meine hände greifen ins leere / My hands reach into emptiness
Ich kann sie nicht finden / I can't find them

Nächtliche trabanten / Nighttime satellites

Es berührt mich nichts / Nothing has touched me
Ich vergesse meine stimme / I forget my voice
Ich bin noch hier / I am still here
Sieh diesen riss / See this tear
Ich starre vor mich hin / I stare into space

Das ist das ende / This is the end

Das ist das ende / This is the end
Wir gehen über schwellen / We cross thresholds
Hier wird alles verschlungen / Everything is devoured here
Wir sind am nördlichsten punkt / We're at the northernmost point
Unter uns kristalle / Under our feet crystals
Ich stoße mich ab vom rand / I push off from the edge
Zieht sich das eis zurück / When the ice recedes
Das ist der letzte versuch / This is the last attempt

Translator's Introduction

Think about a place you went to long ago, somewhere meaning-ful not for an event, but for its sensual nature and the way the location contains a primary feeling like safety, relief, wholeness, or maybe home. Which elements of that place do you remember? The number of steps you took to get there or the crunch of your footsteps on the gravel path? The striated patterns of the rock walls or the coolness they exuded? The hypnotic churn of the stream or the damp air filling your lungs? The diffuse, time-less light or the dapple of warmth on your skin? Certain details remain while others have faded or disappeared. The full picture has been replaced by the essential one.

This is the first thing that strikes me about the poetry of Andra Schwarz—how place as revealed by individual, unadorned elements embodies fundamental emotions so resonantly that the reader can feel them without ever having visited her landscapes. She calls her poems *Reisegedichte*, travel poems, but for the reader as well as Schwarz, they are less of a trip through the exotic, and more a journey within the familiar yet estranged. Lines such as *du kommst aus den lichten gestalten der birken* "you come from the luminous figure of birches" capture the qualities of both nature and association in their very lack of embellishment. These worlds engage in conversation but never quite arrive at an agreement, with the space between them a borderland that Schwarz's speaker explores, seeking out a hidden and unreachable understanding.

The poems take place in various locations throughout Europe, but all hark back to Schwarz's home region of Lusatia, an area in eastern Germany about the size of Massachusetts along the Polish and Czech borders. The region is historically populated by the Sorbs, also called the Wends, one of Germany's ethnic minorities, who speak the sibling Slavic languages of Upper and Lower Sorbian. The name Lusatia derives from the Sorbian word *Łuži* "swampy or marshy meadows," and it is telling that the Sorbs named their land after its geographical features, and not after themselves. This bond between geography and population was historically expressed through traditional farming culture. For Schwarz, the rolling hills, pine forests, and wide marshland of alders and birches offer a sense of renewal and reconnection. They represent a place where one can pursue wholeness.

* * *

Schwarz was born in 1982, just seven years before the fall of the Berlin Wall, and a century after the steady loss of Sorbian language, culture and topography had begun. During the nineteenth and early twentieth centuries, the German state had forced Sorbians to assimilate with the majority German culture, intensifying during the Nazi years when Sorbian language instruction was banned from the schools, traditional practices were forbidden, and the villages were given new German names. During the decades of the German Democratic Republic, Sorbian cultural institutions were promoted by the government, perhaps in an attempt to control them, while the state contradictorily permitted coal production to flourish in the area unchecked. Large swaths of forest and marsh as well as entire villages were seized and bulldozed through eminent domain to access the coal beneath the ground. Some inhabitants, many young and seeking a future, took the relocation money and moved to metropolitan areas, while others were "re-settled" into concrete-slab apartment blocks in new towns. In addition, coal production attracted job-seeking Germans, which diluted the population of the remaining Sorbians. Today, Upper and Lower Sorbian are endangered languages with about 20,000 speakers, down from triple that number when Schwarz was born.

This is the context for Schwarz's poetry of land and self. She does not speak Sorbian, nor does she consider herself a Sorb. She did grow up in a historic *Vierseitenhof*, a farmstead consisting of four buildings—home, barn, stall and granary—connected as a square with a center courtyard. Through a grandparent, she became acquainted with Sorbian traditions such as weaving willow branches into baskets and brooms, but until an incident in college, she was unaware that she had an inherited history. To suddenly recognize that one is part of a historical narrative must be a destabilizing experience, and while the speaker in this book has returned to the physical homeland, their eyes must grope for *konturen & schärfe* "silhouettes and sharp lines" in the absence of them, drawing as close to resolution as that absence allows.

das nachziehen der fährten im grubensand geflutete wege
laufen durch unsere hände ins nirgendwo: weit weg

to retrace the trail in the pit sand flooded paths
running through our fingers into nowhere: far away

There is no anger to be found in Schwarz's work. In fact, there is no perpetrator in these poems, no denunciation, and this redirects the conversation radically toward a resilient and indifferent nature, and an observer who is subsumed in it, who moves as one of its elements. Witnessing a changed landscape without naming an aggressor, turning toward aesthetic beauty and spirit instead of anger is a way of refusing to affirm a system that allows a language to fall into oblivion, deems a culture expendable, and provides its youth with a path to self-erasure. Schwarz writes:

Was ich verschwieg ist diese landschaft
aus stehenden gewässern

What I withheld is this expanse
of silent wetlands

and

wenn es nass wird im winter kommt das wild
zu den häusern bleiben die geheimnisse für uns

in the wet of wintertime wildlife comes
to the houses our secrets remain our own

For her, anger in poetry has a limited reach, but a premeditated, deliberate silence goes far. Rage is expended quickly, but a precise measured image can transport emotions and reflect at multiple depths, just as the land with its individual elements can call up layers of memory and sentiment for the observer. These poems step out of the cycle of unjust action and subsequent protest by refusing to play on the oppressor's terms. Instead they center the land, the lost villages and the absent people from whom all this was stolen, and provide a space for the speaker to reckon with the past and reestablish their connection with the land and thus the self.

* * *

At the time I was translating the bulk of this book, I was reading out loud with a friend Robert Fitzgerald's translations of *The Odyssey* and *The Aeneid*. The meter of his translation, as well as its poetic beauty, merged with the melody and loveliness of Schwarz's German as I worked. The potentialities of sound come alive in her writing—rhythm and where it is broken, rhyme and its placement, neighboring assonance and dissonance. The longing for and the journey toward home, be it Odysseus's attempts to return or Aeneas's search for the one he was promised, accompanied me as I thought about Schwarz's speaker, who also moves in this space of transition.

Unlike the heroes of classics, what this speaker seeks no longer exists. The bulldozed villages of Lusatia became open pit coal mines, and in an additional layer of erasure, those mines, once expended, were transformed into large man-made lakes by an environmentally-minded federal German government. Tourists come and swim, boat and fish on top of the place of injustice and destruction. What must that look like to someone who remembers weaving baskets in the courtyard of a *Vierseitenhof* in that very same place? To someone from the next generation who heard the old stories but traded them for the jobs the mines provided? To someone of the current generation whose inheritance is only postmemory and the threat of future destruction?

Ich kann sie nicht finden in den restlöchern kleinere meere
aus wasser & kalk łužiska jězorina *liegen dörfer auf grund*

I can't find them in abandoned pit mines scattered lakes
of limestone & water *łužiska jězorina* villages on the land

This seeker, unable to find, operates in a border region; a complex, ever-changing, fundamentally unstable place where history is a palimpsest, constantly scraped away and replaced with each political change. I see the intersection of memory and place as the same type of location. Schwarz's speaker is stuck in a no man's land between what is and what was, where you can sense an answer but can never do more than cut the distance between you and it in halves, never arriving . . . quite.

. . . ich fasse mich an
doch ich berühre mich nicht . . .

. . . I reach for myself
but cannot feel me . . .

and

bis zu den knien stehst du gelähmt
am grenzstein zur nacht

you stand there paralyzed to your knees
at the border stone of night

Schwarz says that borders are deeply moving to her. As I travel with Schwarz's speaker through the transitory space between the boundaries embodied in these poems, I understand that searching allows a sensual knowing; that the heart of our memories lies in the elements of place—in Schwarz's case the features and objects of the natural world—which become containers of our emotions; that the more the divisions between seeing, speaking, and feeling fade, the closer we come to agency amidst uncertainty and an unknowable future.

—*Caroline Wilcox Reul*

Von hier gibt es keine bilder

/

There are no pictures of this place

Von hier gibt es keine bilder nur grau
gezeichnete landschaft und schilder die warnen
im dorf sitzen die alten halsstarrig & eng in den lungen
im abseits die jungen spielen backgammon
würfeln um glück: *hier gibt's nichts zu holen*
außer den blick den flusslauf hinauf in die berge
gewächshäuser streuobst rot über den wiesen
dahinter die GRENZE gesperrtes gebiet milizen
hier endet alles, auch unsere sicht
wir schließen die augen und gehen zurück
ins dorf zu den andern im rücken kehrt wind

There are no pictures of this place just landscape
traced in gray and signs that warn
the old sit in the village stiff necked & tight in the lung
off to the side the young play backgammon
toss the dice for luck: *there's nothing to be had here*
except the view of the river's rise into the mountains
greenhouses scattered fruit trees scarlet over the meadows
beyond them the BORDER no mans land militias
everything ends here, even our view
we close our eyes and return
to the village to the others behind us wind sweeps

Über kyrenia liegt ein knistern in der luft
pulsiert ein halbmond mit stern an den hängen
alles kniet oder richtet sich auf auch die hunde
ihr eingeschüchtertes jaulen während der gebete
ist keiner zu sehen nur in zeitlupe bewegtes
hinter den gardinen niedergesunkene körper
in sich vertiefte gesten fünfmal täglich die rufe
in alle richtungen *nichts ist hier größer* als diese
fünf finger aus kalkstein entlang der serpentinen

A crackling hangs above kyrenia in the air
the star and crescent pulses on the slope
everyone kneels or rises up even the hounds
their chastened yowling during prayers
no one is there to see only a slow motion shifting
behind curtains bodies that fall prostrate
gestures absorbed in themselves five times daily the call
in every direction *nothing is greater here* than these
five fingers of lime across the serpentines

Am anderen ende im osten windschief über dem meer
das andreaskreuz die karpaz noch unberührt *wir gehen
soweit wir können* restwärme unter unseren füßen
über den buchten fallwinde die strände liegen leer
kurz nach dem aufschäumen trübe flecken
das meer das alles auswäscht jahrhundertelang
zeit auf der wir gehen sprachlos und fremd

At the other end to the east slant over the sea
saint andrews cross karpasia still untouched *we go*
as far as we can a remainder of warmth under our feet
fall wind over the bay the beach stretches out empty
a foaming up then cloudy patches
the sea which for centuries has washed everything away
time upon which we tread foreign and mute

Hier bist du gewesen als kleiner junge über dir wolken
geruchlos & unsichtbar wie die schwere im schnee
unterm gaumen iod zu spät geschlossene fenster
regenfälle anfang mai geschossene tiere
und zuletzt das ausbluten der landschaft
im tiefland polesiens trockene sümpfe
dörfer mit unvollendeten geschichten
von spielzeugwaisen in den häusern
unterm tisch erinnern kyrillische zeichen
an namen die für immer hier sind & schweigen

This is where you were a little boy clouds above you
odorless & invisible like heaviness in snow
windows shut too late iodine on the tongue
rainfall early in may animals shot
and finally blood draining from the landscape
in the flatlands of polesia dried swamps
in the houses unfulfilled stories
of toy orphans in the village
under the table symbols in cyrillic
recall names that are forever here & silent

Zeig deine hände es ist kein krieg mehr jahre später die
alte brücke trägt wieder eure lasten eure körper es ist
zeit sich zu befreien von den löchern in den häusern
in den köpfen stecken noch kugeln granaten & splitter
zu entschärfen die minen im umland hochoben das kreuz
im rücken die stelen *alles ist gerichtet auch du* von kind an
verpflichtet zu sterben in der mitte vom fluss *narenta*
kopfüber der sprung ins fremdgewordene wasser ins loch
einer kindheit aus steinen & scherben du trägst sie herum
wie munition in den taschen *wer zeigt seine hände,*
wer öffnet die finger es ist kein krieg mehr *lass los*

Show your hands the war is over after years the
old bridge can bear your loads again your bodies it's time
to liberate yourselves from the holes in your houses
in your heads there are still bullets lodged shells & shrapnel
to disarm the mines in the surroundings high above the cross
the stelae behind you *everything is brought to an end, even you*
from birth on meant to die in the middle of the river *narenta*
somersault leap into forgotten waters into the hole
of a childhood made of stones & shards you hold them close
like weapons in the pocket *who will show their hands*
who will open their fingers the war is over *let go*

Schon morgens brennen die dörfer
sie legen haufenweise kleine feuer
an den rändern zur stadt nestelt hitze
augenflimmern füllen sich lungen mit teer
im hinterland jaulen wölfe endlich hündisch
geworden *es gibt kein fortkommen mehr*
in den östlichen gebieten schleicht ein fuchs
und verbeißt sich nächtlings im geraubten tier
auf der karte rote streifen: *wir waren hier*

In the morning the villages begin to burn
they heap small fires along
the perimeter of town heat riles
eyes flicker lungs fill with tar
in the back country wolves howl once again
like dogs *there is no way out now*
in the eastern lands a fox prowls
and sinks its teeth nightly into stolen prey
on the map lines in red: *we've been this way*

Was ich verschwieg
/
What I withheld

Was ich verschwieg ist diese landschaft
aus stehenden gewässern
hinter dem dorf der wüstenteich
der grund der dich hier umtreibt
wie karpfen unter schaumgrünem wasser
blasen aus luft *sie zittern wie du, wenn du atmest*
das pulsierende gemisch in deinen adern
dich trägt und du nichts denkst
außer birken kiefern und
bis du sie aufspürst ihnen nachgehst
den verwachsenen pfaden
dich heranwagst an die frühen verluste
nistplätze welche noch immer aufleuchten
unter den säumnissen der zeit

What I withheld is this expanse
of silent wetlands
barren pond behind the village
ground that haunts you
like carp under the water's green froth
bubbles of air *they shiver, like you, when you breathe*
when that throbbing mix in your veins
carries you and your thoughts are empty of all
but birches pines and
until you can hunt them down
pursue those overgrown paths
dare to summon the early losses
they are nesting grounds still glowing
beneath the failings of time

An der B97 langgestreckte dörfer
ein auf und ableuchten der wege
die baumrippen vom nachfrost vereist
zieht nebel hinauf hinter dem acker
ein stehendes gleiten im spiegel
die leere im rücken und unser gesicht
vor uns überstrahlt licht den asphalt
spuren weiße streifen an uns entlang
es geht immer tiefer hinein in den wald
am rand hirschkühe mit übergroßen augen

Along the B97 villages stretch
the roads flash and darken
ridged bark glazed with late frost
rising fog behind the fields
a constant glide across the mirror
empty space in the back and our faces
before us light sprawls across the asphalt
lanes white lines shuttle past
the way leads ever deeper into the forest
on the shoulder a doe with huge eyes

Endlich wieder störche im ort hohe masten *erinner dich*
an den dorfanger die vergessene kirche den spielplatz
überreste von damals *das was war hinter dickicht*
schwarze erlen am grund *vergiss nicht* die trägheit
beim wachsen flirrendes gras an den ufern
pilze an morschen bäumen sie schwemmen auf
wenn es nass wird im winter kommt das wild
zu den häusern bleiben die geheimnisse für uns

Finally storks again in the village the masts tall *remember*
on the green the forgotten church the playground
remnant of what was *the back then behind thicket*
black alder across the ground *don't forget* inertia
during growth rippling grass along the banks
mushrooms on the sponge of decaying trees they swell
in the wet of wintertime wildlife comes
to the houses our secrets remain our own

Das, was du aufgibst hunderte meter
bis zum waldrand dein jahrelanges wachsen
die erlen und eschen hinterm haus
hier bist du schon immer gewesen
in der brusttasche das messer ich schnitt
durch die wurzeln & schnitt durch die zeit
durch deine kindheit in deinen ohren
das maunzen der katzen im laufen nässe
wind der dich umtreibt noch einmal
sammelst du blicke vom hochstand
über der steppe treibgut und sand

You surrender everything the open stretch
to the forest line your long years of growing
the ashes and alders behind the house
here is where you've always been
knife in the breast pocket I've cut
through roots & cut through time
through the childhood in your ears
the meow of cats walking in rain
wind that once again tosses you about
you gather up views from the lookout
across the steppe flotsam and sand

Hier gibt es nichts mehr: kein schaukeln
kein heben & ausstrecken der füße
kein auf und abschwingen bei tag
die verschwimmenden lichter vom haus
an den händen die kühle und weiter oben
der schrei von tarzan in der luft das seil
sich wendend abrupte wechsel der spannung
dein hörbarer puls in der schwebe beim aufstieg
beim blick über die ebene graue ballen und dann
absprung schürfung *das sind die blessuren der kindheit*
auf dem boden anlanden wie beim allerersten mal

There is nothing left here: no pumping
no rising or stretching the legs
no swinging back & forth all day
the blur of lights from the house
cool breeze on the hands and at the rise
a tarzan roar in the air the rope
turning abruptly change in tension
your audible pulse as you climb moment
of suspension view across the plains bales of gray then
launch scrapes *these are the wounds of childhood*
to land on ground again like the very first time

Im landgang gefälle dein straucheln
verschobene gründe im auslauf der wege
es gibt keine geraden in diesem wald
nur dichte fein gerippte stämme
dazwischen deine augen sie tasten
entlang der gänge spüren nach licht
suchen nach konturen & schärfe
durchzieht ein flimmern den raum
du siehst die horizontale dort draußen
unterhalb der bucht die stege
im ausrausch schwankende see

Ashore on the slope you stumble
ground displaced where trails emerge
in these woods there is no straight line
only dense trunks with fine ridges
amidst them your eyes they grope
through rows strain toward light
search for silhouettes and sharp lines
flashes of light traverse the space
out there you see horizontals
below the cove the docks
fall back the sea sways

Vom fluss kommen wir an der nahle entlang
wo das wasser flach ist durchsichtig & hell
wachsen grasnarben schon siebenjährig
unter unseren füßen laufende meter
schotterflechten vernetzte natur
mittendrin güterverkehr fünfmal täglich
läuten signale fahren züge vorbei
ins blaue hinein gerät eine schwalbe
sie flieht vor dem abwind *was war*

From the river we reach the nahle
where the water is shallow & bright
seven year scars of thatch spread out
under our feet braids of gravel
by the running yard nature connected
right through the middle the hauling of freight
five times daily signals sound trains plow past
into the blue a swallow veers
it flees from the downwind *what had been*

Von osten kommt wind ortsfremde gerüche
das schwelen der laubfeuer vorm haus
und wie sie ersticken unter der decke
verschränkte füße die arme gekreuzt
da ist nichts unterm bett kriechen spinnen
nisten motten in ritzen durchlöchern alles
bis auf die haut *wir frieren schon länger*
auf dem acker die letzten heiligen tiere
und irgendwo da draußen lebt vishnu
er ist und ist hier nicht zu finden

From the east comes wind foreign smells
the smolder of burning leaves in the yard
and a smothering under the roof
crossed legs arms folded
nothing is there under the bed spiders crawl
moths nest in crevices bore holes through everything
to the skin *we've been cold so much longer*
on the fields the last sacred animals
and out there somewhere vishnu lives
he is and is here nowhere to be found

Wer weiß, wo du herkommst du schläfst
mit offenen augen dein schauen im halbdunkel
angedeutete schemen aus balken & schrägen
im dachraum das gurren der tauben *wer weiß,*
wo du hingehst alles scheint offen & weit
unter den ziegeln staut sich die luft
zieht vorüber die erste kühle vom regen
durchflutet die rinnen zahllose wege
sein beharrliches laufen über dächer
die fänger im saum deiner augen

Can anyone tell where you're from you sleep
with open eyes stare into the half dark
hinted patterns of beam and slant
in the attic room the pigeon's coo *can anyone see*
where you go everything seems open & far
under the roof tiles the air is thick
the first coolness of rain passes over
floods through the drain in countless paths
persistent wash across the roof
the catch at the rim of your eyes

Von hier aus geht es nirgendwohin
endet das licht am scheunentor
vor den graufasern der nacht
sinkt alles herab und verdunkelt sich
auch meine augen werden langsam & leer
breiten sich im tiefschlaf nebel aus
schieben sich vor bis an die ausfallstraße
der rand, der dich anhält
hier trifft es dich das endliche gehen
bis zu den knien stehst du gelähmt
am grenzstein zur nacht

From here the way leads to nowhere
light stops at the barn gate
before the gray threads of night
everything sinks and dims
even my eyes become slow & empty
deep in sleep they pour out fog
push forward to the road leading out of town
the line that brings you to a halt
this is where it finds you that final walk
you stand there paralyzed to your knees
at the border stone of night

Ich komme aus den wäldern
/
I come from the forest

Ich komme aus den wäldern so wie du
vor mir die niederung: das moorland
aus weichem moos & dichtem bewuchs
nie zu erreichen, weil es so tief geht
außer im winter frisst sich frost
in die lungen legt sich der schnee
und vergisst wer du warst
dein langsames atmen
über dir vögel sie fliegen
sie können das ohne verluste
ich sage: *es gibt nichts zu sehen*
dein ewiges verharren in der ortsferne
der horizont über dem boden
sinkt nie ab es wächst
wild um mich herum

I come from the forest like you
moorlands before me: bogs
of soft moss & heavy brush
too deep to ever be reached
except in winter when frost bites
your lungs snow lays itself down
and forgets who you were
your slow breath
your slow breathing
high above you birds they fly
they can without forfeit
I say: *there's nothing to see*
your eternal stillness in the distance
the horizon over the ground
never sinks it grows
wild all around me

Du gehst hinein in dieses land unter den hügeln
dein mühsames laufen im kreis neugierige blicke
sie wachen wie rehe über bewegungen am feldrand
die lichter im haus gespitztes lauschen hinter dir
gezogene linien die schritte im weggehen
sie hallen nach wie dein strahlen *zaudere nicht*
ich sehe den glanz deiner augen im ohr nur ein
rauschen von abwesenheit im nachklang die vögel

You step out into this land among the hills
your labored circular pacing curious gazes
like deer they track the field's edge for movement
lights in the house listening hard behind you
drawn lines the falling steps of departure
they echo out like your radiance *don't falter*
in your eyes I see a brightness the rush
of absence in your ears birdsong in the fade

Das wars da draußen das wendland
und drinnen läuft wasser in die lungen
du bist weit, weit zurück in der kindheit
unter den vielen röcken & schürzen
versteckt im heuschober zur nacht
dort liegt es sich im stroh bei den katzen
von unten das schaben & scharren der tiere
du bist am ende wie ich mała staruška
nichts was dich aufhält außer die augen

It's over now outside the wendish lands
and inside water fills your lungs
you are far, far back in your childhood
among the many skirts & aprons
hidden in the haystack of night
lying here in the straw by the cats
the scrape & rasp of animals rising from below
you're at your end like me mała staruška
nothing keeps you here but your eyes

Ein letztes berühren & begreifen deiner hände
mit ihnen der wald sein geruch der mich aufreibt
in deinen lungen sein atem eingeprägt ins tiefere holz
nach dem anschnitt eine wunde aus der alles herauswill
ein baum und sein leben *dein erstes vergehen*
entlang der maserung eingesprengte risse
brechen auf und geben nach mit der zeit
in den wurzeln ein letztes: wir wollen zurück
ins feuchte wir wollen zurück unter moder & moos

One final touch & grasp of your fingers
and the forest with them its scent that undoes me
its breath engrained in your lungs deep in the wood
once cut a wound from which all wants to pour
a tree and its life *your first demise*
along the grain seams split open
widen and with time give way
in the roots a remainder: we want to retreat
to the dampness to return beneath moss & decay

Du lässt alles zurück: dein herzstück deine lunge
wald bei den mooren der so alt ist wie du und
deine augen die sich schließen vor dem hiersein
vor dem puls & dem atem der durch uns hindurchgeht
wie durch diese landschaft aus wasser erde und gras
bis er dich anhält dein körper: jetzt wesen andere darin
nagen sich durch deine räume nisten hinter deinen rippen
während alles von dir abfällt dein körper dein wesen *du gehst*

You leave everything behind: your heart of hearts your lungs
woodlands as old as you lining the bogs and
your eyes which close faced with your presence here
with your pulse & your breath that flows through us
like it moves through this landscape of water earth and grass
until it stops you your body: now others dwell here
gnaw their way through your rooms nest behind your ribs
while all of you slips away your body your being *you go*

Dort bleibst du nun sitzen im toten winkel und manchmal
geht mein blick zu dir hinüber als sähe ich dich flüchtig
hinter meinem rücken als spürte ich dich dort sitzen
im grenzland und nicht nur mich ganz verbrannt von drüben
mein schattenich mit der hand an der schläfe *es zuckt*
dann wieder nicht vielleicht berührst du mich an der schulter
damit ich mich drehe wie etwas entferntes ein längst
verschwommenes gesicht als hätte ich dich erkannt

You remain sitting in the blind spot and sometimes
my gaze wanders over as if I caught you in a glimpse
behind my back as if I sensed you sitting there
in the borderlands and it's not only me burned by the beyond
also my shadow self with a hand on the temple *it pulses*
then rests maybe you touch me on the shoulder
so I'll turn like something distant like a long
forgotten face as if in recognition

Es beginnt die blaue stunde da wir es begreifen als ob
etwas fällt zwischen uns irgendwo kreischen katzen
wir streifen seit stunden umher in uns die letzten dinge
und die frage *was uns noch hält, warum wir bleiben*
an diesem ort verlieren sich stimmen verschwinden wege
von uns wird nichts bleiben außer dieses gedicht
im kopf des anderen die suche nach gewissheiten
ob es uns trägt übers gefälle bis ins offene licht

The hour of twilight begins now that we grasp it as if
something fell between us somewhere cats caterwaul
we traipse for hours within ourselves final things
and the question *what holds us here, why do we stay*
in this place voices become lost the paths disappear
nothing will remain of us except this poem
in the mind of the other a search for certainty and
whether it can carry us over the downslide into open light

Gespinste aus luft
/
Woven from air

Wie wenig luft noch in dir war zum schluss
dein zappeln als wärst du ein fisch
am haken blau angelaufen
mit großen überdrehten augen
was dachtest du da noch, an wen
den veitstanz in der schlinge
ohne sauerstoff dein blut im kopf
kein luftstrom mehr kein fließen
du drehtest dich minutenlang betäubt
wie ein gefangenes tier als etwas
hinter dir in deinen nacken fuhr
ein rabe vielleicht auch eine krähe

How little air remained in you at the end
you thrashed like a fish
on the hook skin turned blue
eyes wild and huge
what were you thinking of, and whom
saint vitus dance in a net
without oxygen the blood in your head
no coursing air no flow
for minutes you twisted dazed
an animal trapped while something
from behind swept into your neck
a raven or maybe a crow

Ich weiß nicht wo sie sitzt vielleicht im hirn
vielleicht auch hinter dir im nacken die stimme
die in kurzen wellen zu dir spricht dich verbindet
mit den riesensternen den pulsaren deine quelle
schickt signale aus den sphären züchtet schlangen
in deinen kapseln röntgenblicke dringen tief
bis hinter stirn & lappen du durchschaust mich
als wär ich nur ein schatten auf deiner linse

I don't know where it lies maybe in the brain
or maybe close at your nape the voice
speaks to you in shortwave binds you
with the giant stars the pulsars your source
casts signals from realms breeds snakes
in your capsules x-ray sight plunges
beneath brow & lobe you look past me
as if I were nothing but a shadow on your lens

Ich war nicht da sah deine spuren nicht
sah nicht den spiegel der zerbarst
als wärst du in seinem innern aufgesprungen
und dann von grashaut überzogen
fiel schwarzes licht auf deinen bauch
imaginär sein strahlen die stelle
über die ein schatten ging
fiel kohlestaub dazwischen
fiel durch dein suchen fragen
um mich herum ein schal von dir
der mich frösteln macht
als wär darin ein knoten

I wasn't there didn't see your signs
didn't see the mirror that shattered
as if you had burst inside it
then were covered with a skin of grass
black light fell on your stomach
that imagined place glowing
as a shadow passed over
coal dust fell in between
questions fell as you searched
around me a shawl of yours
that gives me chills
as if a knot lay within

Sag mir, wer krieg spielt soldaten stehen auf
und kämpfen gegen wächter mit schild
an deinen grenzen panzer sie krabbeln
wie käfer durch geschlossene kanäle
schießen auf alles was sich bewegt
ich sehe im traum ihre glanzlosen augen
und auch die krater in deinen gefäßen
während du schläfst dahinter wirds finster
jetzt stehen sie still die maschinen gewehre
hör auf zu laufen das suchgerät ohne signale
nicht mal ein flüstern unter der ebene
ein haufen asche der gefallene rest

Tell me, who plays at war soldiers rise
and fight against shielded guards
along your borders tanks they crawl
like beetles through closed canals
shoot at anything that moves
I see their vacant eyes in a dream
and the craters in your veins
it grows dark behind you while you sleep
they stand still now the guns of your machine
stop marching forward a detector without signal
not a whisper beneath the plains
a pile of ashes the fallen remains

Seit gestern steht dieses kreuz auf dir
ich seh dein bild und hör dich reden
es schnürt mir hals & kehle zu wie dir
seit wann, wie lange schon warst du markiert
und am ende nur eine stelle ein platz im hirn
für kleine spatzen die nicht aufhören können
herum zu hüpfen und ins loch zu piksen
die gemeinen fratzen als wär es nicht genug
ihr hüpfen zetern im kopf die schnabelstiche
mit jedem mal nehmen sie ein stück von dir
während ich noch vor dir stehe

A cross stands over you as of yesterday
I see your image and hear you speak
my nape & throat tighten like yours
how long, since when have you been marked
and ultimately one place a single spot in the brain
for the sparrows that cannot stop
their nervous flitting pecking that hole
relentless demons as if their hopping
weren't enough a clamor in your head
each peck of the beak carries off a piece
of you while I stand here looking on

Wo fing es an die wundersame stelle hinter deiner stirn
das graue ding *ich kanns nicht sagen* es war schon da
und machte faxen noch nicht laut genug noch nicht groß &
ausgewachsen der drache in deinem mund darin gelähmt
die zunge schon infiziert da wars noch eine kleine helle
im system ein funken erst später dann das phantom
das dich verbunden macht im raum die dunkle energie
noch unbestimmt das vakuum in das wir stürzen

Where did it start that uncanny place behind your brow
that ashen thing *I can't tell* it was already there &
playing tricks not yet loud enough not yet large
or fully grown a dragon in the mouth the tongue
gagged infected it was only a bright spot
in a system a spark then later the phantom
that held you bound in the room a dark energy
still vague the vacuum into which we tumble

Im hinterkopf das katzenbild drei kleine graugetigert
saßen still vor uns in tausend teilen und du entrückt
nahmst jedes stück in deine hände streiftest katzenhaar
mit deinen kuppen fast schon zärtlich war dein blick
hier hielt das bild nicht stand: war gaukelei
ein hirngespinst aus pappe der kleine kiesel im getriebe
darin ein federvieh ganz verkrötet & verkracht
flog auf und hielt dich fest im nacken

An image of cats on your mind three gray tabbies
quiet before us in a thousand pieces enrapt you
took every piece in your hand brushed fingertips
over feline fur your expression almost tender
the picture did not hold firm: it was a sham
chimera of paper the pebble in the gears
from which a bird all ruined and cursed
flew up and took you by the neck

Wie lange schon lebt dieses kind in dir
das dich müde macht
es atmet ein und aus in jeder zelle
als wäre es noch nicht abgehoben
wie ein ballon aus luft
mit glitzersteinen in den augen
manchmal spielt es verrückt in dir
und kichert leise in dich hinein
das kind das müde macht: das fratzenkind
es kitzelt dir im nacken und geht vorüber
als wärs nur luft die hasche spielt
und sich vergisst dabei
es hockt in dir wie ein klumpen
ein wulst der nie vernarbt
in deinem bauch es träumt
so lange schon von hier

How long has this child lived in you
depleting you
in every cell it inhales exhales
as if waiting to lift
like a balloon chasing air
with brilliant eyes
it often runs riot in you
and giggles from inside
the child that drains: a gremlin
it tickles your neck passes
like air plays tag with you
and forgets it's only a game
it sits like a knot in you
a lump in your stomach that won't
scar over it's been dreaming
of this place so long

Es hielt nicht stand dein inneres getriebe
aus rotoren manchmal überdreht
manchmal wars nur müdes laufen
im wechselfieber erst das glühen
später stürze kalte wechselfälle
entzündungsherde in deinen zellen
dein blick auf tauchstation begannst du
dich zu verstellen zu entkabeln
um am ende den strom zu kappen
mit mauern um deinen rippen
und an den füßen schwer gewichte
und nochmal lief dein motor gegen wände
lief und lief zu heiß zu laut zu schnell

Your inner machine could not hold up
with rotors racing high at times
and sometimes barely turning
fevered sweats and chills first a flare
then the crash cold sequences
hot spots in your cells
thoughts of seclusion you began
to dissemble to disconnect
and at the end capped the current
with walls around your ribs
and leaden weights on your legs
and your motor pounded into walls again
pounded too hot too loud too fast

Mit einem mal durchzuckt es mich als ob
du vor mir stündest die hände ausgestreckt
berührt das trifft und macht mich wach
das pochen unterm schläfenrand elektrisiert
dich sehen und sehen wie du verschwindest
im innenraum der zellen das weiße band
verspielt um deinen hals verliert kontur
das wiegenlied im kopf verdreht
du schläfst jetzt traumlos ohne takt

Suddenly it shoots through me as though
you were standing here arms outstretched
touching it jolts and wakes me up
the throb in my temples electrifies
seeing you then to watch you disappear
into the interior of your cells the white cord
in play across your throat becomes indistinct
the cradlesong in your head twists
now you sleep without a beat dreamless

Jetzt wache ich wie ein mond um dich
ganz ohne schlaf vor mir das seil
ich kanns nicht fassen es reißt
mit einem lauten knall im kopf
da bist du schon ein gespinst aus luft
ein augenblick vernarbt vom licht
in mir dein ruheloser raum

I keep watch now like a moon around you
no sign of sleep the rope before me
I just can't grasp it in my head
the rope snaps with a crack
you were there woven from air
a moment of time scarred over with light
and in me your restless space

Wir bauen zurück ins leere

/

We build backward into emptiness

Wir bauen zurück ins leere vor dir der abraum
im auge die ferne *niemand kommt hierher zurück*
sie gehen rüber zu den andern *jeder weiß das*
unter ihnen versanden wege im gelände die
schwärze von damals das ende in den gesichtern
ein landstrich am verbrennen über & unter der erde
čorna pumpa je row serbstwa schon weit vor der wende
ausradierte flächen fliegt kohlestaub über den feldern
verliert sich die wärme hinter uns verdunstet das licht

We build backward into emptiness before you the overburden
in your eyes the distance *no one comes back this way*
they go over to the others *everyone knows that*
under them paths in the compound fill with sand the
darkness from the past the end visible in faces
a swath of land burning over & under the earth
čorna pumpa je row serbstwa long before the wall fell
erased expanses coal dust flies over the fields
the warmth dies behind us the light dissolves

Fünfzig kilometer von hier zur polnischen grenze
granica sehr weit im osten die andere grenze *śmierć*
ich suche in den hölzern das sorbische wendland
die gefallenen kiefern und birken
was wäre gewesen, was wäre aus uns
verwachsen im grasland in diesem geflecht
unter euch kohle die ausschabung der dörfer
zuletzt euer zahlreiches verschwinden
an diesem ort wächst alles: *noch hier*

Thirty miles from here to the polish border
granica so far to the east the other border *śmierć*
I search in the timber the sorbian land of the wends
the razed pines and birches
what could have been, what could we have become
grown over in the grasslands in this plaiting
under you coal the scraping out of villages
and finally your mass disappearance
in this place everything grows: *here, still*

Du kommst aus den lichten gestalten der birken
nach dem aufbäumen im märz verjüngte rinde
steht saft in ihren höhen über dem wollgras
sterne im hintergrund die kamenzer berge
es bleibt diese sicht inmitten der topografie
jener landschaft sie wächst nach in deinen zellen
im torf abgestorbene gründe es staut sich darin
ein lichtbild aus früherer zeit das sich hineinprägt
in deinen spuren risse: *wenn alles verschwimmt*

You come from the luminous figure of birches
after they've risen tall bark rejuvenated in march
sap high in the treetops above the cottongrass
stars in the background the mountains of kamenz
this view will remain at the center of the land's
topography it takes seed in the peat
of your cells decayed ground it pools there
a vision of light from the past instilling itself
fissures in your tracks: *where everything clouds*

Hier verschwinden worte aus den häusern
bleiben die alten *baba* und *šeda* auf den zungen
in den mündern hohle klänge keiner weiß mehr
die zeichen auf den schildern sorbische namen
wir zählen sie auf *brětnja, michałki* seit jahren
gehen wir durch straßen die wir nicht kennen
nur manchmal die wege zwischen den teichen
bis zum flussbett der elster ziehen sie kreise
in unseren köpfen kommen sie wieder zu dir

Words disappear from houses here
to the tongue the old remain *baba* and *šeda*
vacant sounds in the mouth no one understands
the symbols on the signs anymore sorbian names
we count them off *brĕtnja, michałki* for years
we've been walking along streets we don't know
but sometimes on paths through the marshland
to the river bed of the elster they ripple out
in our heads circle back to you

Das ist die letzte station bevor wir da sind & halten
wir stehen mit unseren füßen auf diesem erdreich
aus lehm im umkreis von tausend quadratkilometern
immer seltner züge entblößte schienen aus eisen
noch laufen hier drähte zusammen in der luft
wachsen löcher zwischen den ortschaften die
drückende hitze über den köpfen schiebt sich vor
und zurück sammeln sich mücken in schwärmen
auf der suche nach warmblütern in den ställen
ihr stöhnen & rufen über den höfen brandstufe vier

This is the last station before we arrive & halt
we stand with our feet firm on this earth
of clay a thousand kilometers across
fewer and fewer trains exposed tracks of ore
still run through here wires bundled in the air
the holes grow broader between locales the
oppressive heat above our head thrusts
and retreats mosquitoes gather in swarms
searching for the warm blooded in the stalls
across the grange their groans & calls danger of fire high

Sieh dich um erkennst du es wieder fünf kilometer
streifen wald das mäandern der straßen schlieren
aus kohle & schwefel *damals waren hier striche*
grenzsteine & drähte die einsicht verhangen es
flickt sich zusammen das netz mit den andern stiche
in den böden zurückgebliebene gräben & löcher es
fallen die mauern zu allen seiten ringsum entblößte
ohren & augen unter asbest lagert schmutz aus vier
jahrzehnten noch tickt die stechuhr hinter den rippen
lauern wanzen die im stillen an euch saugen

Look around you do you still recognize it three
mile length of forest the curl of the road cords
of coal & sulfur *back then it was lines of*
boundary stones & wire that curtain the view
the net patches itself together in the ground
with a different stitch abandoned graves & pits
the wall descends on all sides everywhere naked
ears & eyes under asbestos the dust of four
decades the stopwatch still ticking behind ribs
bugs hide and suckle in the quiet at you

Meine hände greifen ins leere *was bleibt unter der erde*
ich laufe bis zur schwarzen mühle am rande die quelle
alles steht still ich höre noch das schleifen der räder
das schleudern von wasser wie sie sich drehen
jahrzehnte im mahlwerk der auf & abbau die wende
am ende das kind von damals *keiner weiß, was wäre*
jedes jahr nachwachsende ringe streifen wölfe in den
wäldern seit ich fort bin wird alles wieder groß & wild

My hands reach into emptiness *what is left under earth*
I walk to the black mill at its edge the spring
nothing moves I still hear the grinding of wheels
the spray of water and how they revolve decades
in the millworks the building the dismantling the change
finally the child from then *no one knows what might have been*
every year another ring grows wolves prowl in the
forest now that I'm gone everything is large & wild again

Ich kann sie nicht finden in den restlöchern kleinere meere
aus wasser & kalk łužiska jězorina *liegen dörfer auf grund*
enteignete schätze eure stimmen aus kohle & stein gebrochen
als gäbe es euch nicht aus dem blickfeld geschwundene dinge
wir graben noch immer untertage darüber renaturierte flächen
auseinandergerissene seilschaften *es gibt nichts, was euch hält*
das nachziehen der fährten im grubensand geflutete wege
laufen durch unsere hände ins nirgendwo: weit weg

I can't find them in abandoned pit mines scattered lakes
of limestone & water *łužiska jězorina* villages on the land
seized treasure your voices of coal and rock crushed
as if you'd never been there everything dwindled from sight
we dig and dig below rehabilitated nature above
bonds torn *there is nothing that is holding you*
to retrace the trail in the pit sand flooded paths
running through our fingers into nowhere: far away

Nächtliche trabanten
/
Nighttime satellites

Es berührt mich nichts seit tagen betrachte ich meine hand
nur taubes gefühl in den fingern darin drei sinne die
meine blicke schärfen doch dringt nichts zu mir durch
in mir klettert eine spinne über hunderte nerven vernetzt
mit dem mittelpunkt für den fall alarmgesichert & überwacht
von nächtlichen trabanten die mich vorm springen schützen
über dem augenrand die blinde stelle die mich nicht kennt ich
starre auf die flecken an der wand alles andere ist entkabelt
von innen eine minute zu lang kurzgeschlossene drähte

Nothing has touched me for days I observe my hand
only numbness in the fingers where three senses
sharpen my view but nothing can break through to me
within me a spider crawls across hundreds of nerves spun
from the center in readiness alarms secured & monitored
by nighttime satellites that protect me from jumping
beyond the rim of my eyes the blind spot that won't know me
I stare at marks on the wall everything else uncabled
from inside a minute too long short-circuited wires

Ich vergesse meine stimme im halblaut rede ich
für mich und zu den wänden die manchmal zittern
als wäre jemand hier und würde sich verstecken
wie eine dritte hand verstellt er dinge nimmt etwas
und lässt es fallen im kopf als säße er im trommelfell
hinter den kulissen und spräche durch das geräuschefeld
im ohr aus dem refugium im hintergrund das ticken

I forget my voice to myself I murmur
and to the walls which sometimes waver
as if another were here and concealing themselves
like a third hand they rearrange things pick them up
toss them in my head as if crouching in my eardrum
behind a curtain speaking through the field of static
in my ear from the refuge of the background a ticking

Ich bin noch hier an diesem tisch und suche nach
nach worten die in mir greifen bis ins mark
und taste alles ab mit augen was mich berührt
das netz der spinnen tote fliegen auf dem rücken
sie liegen da die beine hoch geschraubt erstarrt
schimmel in den fensterritzen & staub legt sich im lauf
wie schnee auf alle flächen doch schau wie tief die
messer sitzen ich schwitze kalt an meinen händen
die härchen aufgestellt im angesicht der klinge

I am still here at this table and I make an appeal
seek words that can pierce my core
my eyes grope for something to move me
spider webs dead flies on their backs
they lie there with legs twisted frozen
mold in the window cracks & dust gathers quickly
like snow on all surfaces just look how deep
the knives lie I'm cold with sweat the hair
on my hands rising faced with the blade

Sieh diesen riss der durch mich hindurchgeht
das abtasten des körpers: beugen gelenke
hinunter zum schambein wo ich mich verstecke
hinter den tauben empfindungen die leere stelle
an der alles verbrennt auch die sekunden
die mich bedecken ödnis zwischen den beinen
und drinnen das schaudern ich fasse mich an
doch ich berühre mich nicht hinten im raum
schauen spiegel geradewegs in meine augen

See this tear crossing through me
feeling out the body: joints bend
downward to the groin where I hide myself
behind the numb sensations the empty place
where everything combusts even the seconds
that lie over me wasteland between the legs
and inside a tremor I reach for myself
but cannot feel me from the back of the room
mirrors look straight into my eyes

Ich starre vor mich hin die pupillen aufgebläht in mir
arbeiten tausende spione verdeckt winzige blender
unter der netzhaut laufen impulse durch informanten
über millionen fasern *bis alles vergeht* auf meiner linse
ein wachraum aus verspiegelten fenstern in denen
es sich bewegt auch meine träume schwanken wie
nächtliche tänzer unter den lidern hockt ein käfer
mit schwarzem panzer er zieht sich zurück & schläft

I stare into space my pupils swollen inside me
countless spies undercover at work tiny imposters
under the retina waves travel through informants
over millions of fibers *until all is lost* on my lens
a secured room of mirrored windows where
everything moves even my dreams sway like
nighttime dancers under the lids a black-shelled
beetle crouches for now it retreats & sleeps

Das ist das ende
/
This is the end

Das ist das ende: letzte vogelschwärme
sibirische kälte legen sich weiße netze um uns herum
dursichtiges gewebe zögerndes erstarren der landschaft
wir ziehen uns zurück in unsere räume träges verharren
im dunkeln die langsamkeit der pupillen im schatten
erblindete spiegel *körper und wie sie verschwinden,*
wenn wir danach greifen am morgen sind wir aus glas

This is the end: trailing flocks of birds
siberian ice all around us a lace of white descends
invisible fabric the landscape's grudging freeze
we retreat to our rooms languid wait
in the dark our pupils slow in the shadows
blinded mirrors *bodies and how they vanish*
when we reach for them in the morning we are glass

Wir gehen über schwellen wie über wasser
steine den flusslauf hinauf hinunter
markierungen gezählte meter über jahre
jede schwelle ein rand der uns bricht
die gegenwart von schneereichen tagen
dahinter liegt schwärze wir schleichen
vorbei an den graten vexierbilder im kopf
dürre auf den zungen sehr langsam
das an und abschwellen der geräusche
im hinterland stehen die zeiger still

We cross thresholds like walking on water
stones along the river's meander
markers miles counted over years
every crossing is a border that breaks us
snow filled days ever present
beyond lies blackness we climb
past the ridges janus images in mind
a parching of the tongue so slow
the rise the fall of sound
in the back country the clock is still

Hier wird alles verschlungen: die geräusche der wald
das trippeln & rutschen der pfoten die tropfen
von oben und zapfen fallen sanft zu boden
auch deine stimme verliert sich im dickicht
lauern tiere ihre ohren im anschlag sie wittern
fremde geruch und lauschen wie ich nach innen
ins unregelmäßige pochen unter den rippen
als wäre alles verschwunden die geräusche
der wald der laut deiner stimme du & das licht

Everything is devoured here: the sounds of the forest
the prance & shift of paws the dripping
from above and cones drop softly to the ground
your voice also becomes lost in the thicket
animals in wait ears at the ready they catch
unfamiliar scents and like me turn inward
to the irregular thumping beneath the ribs
as if everything were gone the sounds
of the forest the ring of your voice you & the light

Wir sind am nördlichsten punkt: fünf schritte vor dem eismeer
wir wissen nichts, auch nicht von uns bleibt nur diese spitze
auf hoher see der rest liegt verdeckt im dunkeln & verharscht
unter der oberfläche zirkuliert das blut nur noch langsam
der horizont ist bloß eine rhetorische figur für anwesenheit
am himmel unfassbar in dieser luft aus glas unter unseren füßen
werden spuren zu zeichen: hier an dieser stelle zählt das gewicht

We're at the northernmost point: five paces from arctic waters
we know nothing, even of ourselves this headland is all that remains
in the high sea the rest lies hidden in the dark below
the surface & crusted over the blood circulates slowly here
the horizon is merely a rhetorical figure for presence
elusive in the skies in the glass air under our feet
tracks become signs: in this place it's weight that counts

Unter uns kristalle winzige kometen du siehst
ihren stillstand wenn sich nichts mehr bewegt
lichtjahre entfernt von unseren bahnen die wärme
du spurst hinein in den schnee *es hält uns nichts mehr*
in dieser verwaisten gegend außer die sicht auf die sterne
erscheint ein nordlicht über der atmosphäre schwebe
solange der puls schlägt zaudern wir vor der tiefe: *geh*

Under our feet crystals tiny comets you see
their stillness when nothing else moves
the warmth light years away from our paths
you feel the way of the snow *it can't hold us anymore*
in this region abandoned by all but the stars
a northern light appears over the atmosphere floating
as long as the pulse beats we pause at the depth: *go*

Ich stoße mich ab vom rand schollen in bewegung
westwärts bis hinter die baumgrenze verwehtes
das land gibt sich nicht zu erkennen chimären
chiffren in schnee du siehst nur zwei drei meter
durch diese trübe schwankende teilchen
kaum hörbar die rufe vom anderen ufer
knacken gelenke in den fingern steife die
abschattung ins weiße & jemand der spricht

I push off from the edge floes in motion
westward beyond the treeline driftings
the land refuses to be known chimera
ciphers in snow you see just two three meters
through these clouds of roiling flakes
muffled shouts from the other shore
joints crack the fingers tight shadows
falls across white & someone who speaks

Zieht sich das eis zurück aus unseren augen
im wendekreis lawinen *hier sitzt das fieber*
schon lange in den ritzen aufgeschlitzte rücken
seit jahrzehnten versinken schritte in der schmelze
gletcherzungen *ein nachort für erzähltes* wer misst
das gleiten über flächen glaziale hände wovon sie reden
sich selbst vergessen bis auf das eigene schwinden
in der wehe nur ein laut von wasser überschwemmt

When the ice recedes from our eyes
avalanches in the circle *the fever lies here*
long dormant in crevices slits in the crests
for decades footsteps have been sinking in slush
tongues of ice *an afterplace for stories* who gauges
the flow across surfaces glacial hands what they know
to forget oneself to the edge of disappearance
in this drift the sound of water is drowned

Das ist der letzte versuch: weit hinter uns
aufgerauhtes land im kiefer sitzt seit tagen die
eingefrorene zunge ich trete hinaus bis an den rand
stürzt licht hinab wir schwanken schürfen nach
im untergrund was hier versickert *wer geht,*
wem folgen wir zieht sich das netz zusammen
angewachsene füße die fährten ausgespäht
das watt der saum von dem du lebst und
eine hand die lange danach noch zittert

This is the last attempt: far behind us
furrowed land the tongue frozen locked
in the jaw for days I walk out to the very edge
light falls downward we sway and dig below
the surface for what has trickled away *who goes,*
whom do we follow the net is closing tight
rooted feet the footprints spied
the tidelands is a seam on which you rely
and a hand that won't stop shaking

Notes

B97: a heavily forested highway between Dresden and Cottbus that runs through Upper Lusatia.

baba and šeda (*Sorbian*): grandmother and grandfather.

Brětnja, Michałki: Sorbian villages in Upper Lusatia, Germany. In German the towns are called Bröthen and Michalken.

čorna pumpa je row serbstwa (*Sorbian*): a saying in Sorbian that means "the Black Pump Power Plant is the death of the Sorbs/Sorbdom." Through this lignite power plant and the German federal government's use of eminent domain, many Sorbian villages were seized and demolished. Many Sorbian people left the region while many Germans moved in to the area to work at the plant, all of which had a devastating affect on Sorbian language and culture.

granica (*Polish*): border.

Karpasia: northeastern peninsula on the island of Cyprus.

Kamenz: town in the rolling hills of upper Lusatia.

Kyrenia: harbor city on the island of Cyprus.

łužiska jězorina (*Upper Sorbian*): Lusatian Lake District, a region of artificial lakes the German government created by flooding many decommisioned open pit mines.

mała staruška (*Sorbian*): little old (lady).

Nahle: the Nahle is a tributary of the White Elster River in Leipzig, Germany.

Narenta: also known as the Neretva, this is a river that runs through the town of Mostar in Bosnia, where heavy fighting occured during the Bosnian War.

Polesia: historical region in Poland, Belarus and Ukraine. Large portions of this marshy land were rendered uninhabitable by the accident at the Chernobyl nuclear power plant.

śmierć (*Polish*): death

Wendish lands: in the German original "wendland." This refers to the land of the Sorbian people, not the geographic region in northern Germany near Hanover.

the Wends: in general, these terms refer to the Slavic peoples living in Germany. Here, the Wends are the Sorbian people living in Upper and Lower Lusatia along the border with Poland and the Czech Republic.

Acknowledgments

Many thanks to the editors of the *Michigan Quarterly Review, Tupelo Quarterly, Bomb Cyclone, Columbia Journal, LIT Magazine,* and Action Books *Poetry in Action* blog series for publishing translations from this collection.

Thank you to Lauren Paredes, Andrew Chenevert, Dan Wiencek, John Hellermann, Michael Shay, Emily Smoke, Andy West, and others from the Eastside Poetry Workshop. You are my poetry best friends. Your work inspires me. I can't imagine what these poems would look like without your ability to read past early drafts and recognize where they could go.

Thank you also to Luna Albertini and Sophia Kongshaug for years of working and talking together, and especially here for including me in your academic worlds. Your interests helped me to see this collection on broader and deeper levels.

Finally, thank you to Hannu Töyrylä for sharing your evocative art, and to Jim Kates and Anna Maria Reck for your thoughtfulness, encouragement, and sharp eyes.

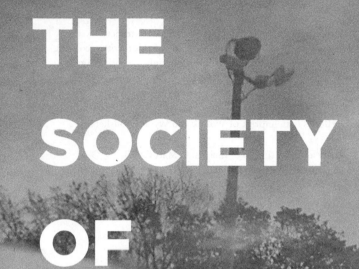

THE

SOCIETY

OF

EXPERIENCE

MATT CAHILL

Buckrider Books is an imprint of Wolsak and Wynn Publishers.

Cover and part title page images: © Matt Cahill
Cover, interior design, and cityscape image: Ingrid Paulson
Author photograph: Katia Taylor Photography,
www.katiataylorphotography.com
Typeset in Baskerville 10 and Gotham
Printed by Ball Media, Brantford, Canada

Canada Council   Conseil des arts
for the Arts   du Canada

ONTARIO ARTS COUNCIL
CONSEIL DES ARTS DE L'ONTARIO
an Ontario government agency
un organisme du gouvernement de l'Ontario

Canadian   Patrimoine
Heritage   canadien

The publisher gratefully acknowledges the support of the Canada Council
for the Arts, the Ontario Arts Council and the Canada Book Fund.

Buckrider Books
280 James Street North
Hamilton, ON
Canada L8R 2L3

LIBRARY AND ARCHIVES CANADA CATALOGUING IN PUBLICATION
Cahill, Matt, 1970–, author
The society of experience / Matt Cahill.

ISBN 978-1-928088-04-2 (paperback)

I. Title.

PS8605.A4S63 2015   c813'.6   c2015-905094-4

For Ingrid

"Time is no law of nature," she said. "It is a plan. When you look at it with awareness, or start to touch it, then it starts to disintegrate."

Peter Høeg, *Borderliners*

I WAS IN TWO PLACES. Half of me sitting up in my bed in St. Mike's Hospital, early March, waiting for something other than the certainty of my breath and the sound of footsteps outside my door to break the vacuum. Half of me was stuck in January.

The nurse was due; it was seven p.m. I tried to focus on whatever routines were available to me, whatever I could look forward to, as opposed to being whisked into the past. Her green eyes tracking me, wary when we exchanged glances. Being observed wasn't comforting, especially when it was just the two of us. I remember her dark, short hair, and her tenuous manner, as if figuring out what it was she was supposed to being doing.

Anyone could see what I'd done to myself. It was naive to wish otherwise, though I continued to do so. She'd been pleasant and attended to me efficiently. Sometimes I'd think I was alone, but she would be in the room, snatching glances at me in the mirror.

I'd arrived on a stretcher smeared with blood, unconscious, oblivious to the voices of people shouting out the details of what I'd done. I couldn't help thinking of the mess waiting for me when I'd get home, and I kicked myself for not being lucid through it all, as if I'd missed out on a good story to tell.

I couldn't remember her name. Did she even wear a name tag? All I knew was that she never mentioned my suicide attempt when she was tending to me, inspecting the stitches, never poking her fingers into my shame. But I wanted to be punished. A part of me wanted someone to walk in, slam the door and yell at me — give me what I deserved. I didn't feel like I merited the nurse's attention. She caught me once, crying, my sewn-up forearm exposed. Nerves under sutures, under cotton bandages, on fire. She'd come from behind the dividing curtain. I'd assumed my sobbing was out of earshot. My face was flushed and covered in sweat.

I wish I could be one of those people who could do terrible things without regret, or at least do them well enough that I didn't have the opportunity to look back and regret them.

"Are you okay, Mr. van der Lem?"

Her green eyes. I could barely look up.

I was under observation for obvious reasons. She stepped closer, tentatively, locking eyes with me, then she formed a word that never passed her lips. I couldn't figure out what it was she tried to say — maybe she did say it and my body was too busy processing the remnants of the pills. I smiled politely and waved her off with my good arm: I wasn't worth it. She hesitated, as if wanting to say more but unsure, glancing over her shoulder toward voices in the hallway. She left my room and I couldn't remember her name or whether I ever knew it to begin with.

All of the things I didn't want to think about worked themselves into my mind, crowding out the rest, past versus present. January versus March. Sometimes I sat up for hours, waiting for her — not the regular orderly, but her — to come and break the silence. And for the life of me I couldn't remember her name, or even her voice.

"Derrick."

I'm convinced it was a dream. I woke up on the second night and saw someone in the dark who I thought was her, leaning over, doing two things: sorting through my clothes and staring at me.

+ + +

5

I HAD ONE eye on the alley, the other minding the ice puddles dotting the asphalt. I sauntered along in the January chill, snapping photographs and collecting my thoughts. It was part of a network of tucked-away lanes stretching several blocks along the northern length of West Queen West. I was craving a cigarette, the little kick it used to give me. Nancy Sinatra's Bond ballad, "You Only Live Twice," played in my earbuds. I was scanning for new graffiti, new arrangements of debris casting shadows in the noon sun, away from the white noise of shoppers and brunchers. I was looking for answers. No matter that I came home with more questions. No matter that Karen kept asking for her Leica back.

I got a call on my cell. It was the daughter of the brother of my dad's second wife. I called them step-somethings.

I lost track of what I was doing in that moment, straining to understand what I was being told. Someone I barely knew was telling me something profound that I couldn't process. Her voice on the phone sounded pre-recorded. Then something inside me popped loose and all of my movements felt automatic.

A stranger turned the corner ahead, walking toward me, his dog on a lead. He was younger, maybe by five years, rimmed hat, unshaven. It was just the three of us and there was no way for me to turn around or look away without drawing more attention to myself. I would've preferred to be alone with my thoughts, whether or not I liked them, and not have people invade my space while I was on the goddamned phone, struggling to hear something I was trying very, very hard to both clarify and dismiss.

Tattoos. Tattoos on his neck. I bet if he took off his jacket his arms were inked like high school textbooks. We passed each other, inches from each other's shoulders, his shepherd obediently minding its business. Ink was cheap and tattoos were permanent. Not even my most basic beliefs felt assured. I hated him. I hated the permanence of his commitment.

The phone call ended. It was a completely mundane, completely forgettable conversation.

My dad had died.

I lost my footing on a patch of ice and nearly fell on my ass like Josée Chouinard. I recovered, knees awkwardly bent for balance, arms outstretched as if walking a circus tightrope. Karen's camera dangled from its thin leather strap, the tip of the lens inches from hitting the asphalt. After a moment of deep breaths I turned around. The dog walker hadn't paid attention. Nancy Sinatra was still singing in my ears.

Dad had died.

+ + +

INSTEAD OF CLARITY — or the nostalgic regret I assumed would organically materialize after he died — I felt a vacuum. The first thing I did was call the person who had hurt me second-most. We hadn't spoken in months, but we settled into post-coital intimacy like snakes coiling.

"I read his book, Derrick." Karen lying naked, spooning. She meant the new one.

I couldn't form words — my windpipe swollen. I'd called her as soon as I'd ambled home, and she invited me over too easily. "Little essays," she said. I hated the way she filled the silence. "Pieces about little... obscure locations in Europe and Southeast Asia. He was so good at that."

I preferred silence to her voice. I wanted to grab her copy of *Rosado's Atoll* and tear it in half. I lay numb beside her, my erection subsiding like a tantrum. I didn't have time to know what I was doing — good or bad — sex with the ex, staring at her flame red hair in the tungsten bedroom light, hoping that she wouldn't turn around, that I could leave her here whenever I wanted, encased in amber.

He travelled extensively. Had. Thirty-seven countries articulated in a store of notebooks and papers sought after by aficionados, and catalogued by York University and the National Archives. All said, they contained his musings on at least 138 cities, hamlets, counties and states across the world; places portrayed as alive, uneasily inhabited by less-alive people. Yet, over a forty-year career, Peter van der Lem rarely wrote about his hometown of Toronto, referring to it only as "the abandoned cathedral." He refused to explain what that meant. In our sporadic conversations, which I kept brief for my own sake, he sometimes tried to instill a conspiratorial notion: the city's shape and behaviour had been constructed by more than greed and circumstance, the same elements that underscored the creation of other major centres. He treated Toronto with suspicion, but was paradoxically unable to abandon it himself. He told me once there was a flow of power beyond city hall and the pink palace of the legislature at Queen's Park. Something buried long ago in a drunken mistake, like Garrison Creek forced into a pipe, active underneath the soil of everyday life but invisible. There was a star chamber, a group who dealt with the real business of the city. He neglected to go into detail, and I always found the topic off-putting, so I never pushed him to elaborate. I figured he was making excuses for his lack of belonging, and creating straw men to do his bidding.

It was his heart. They found him in his car, parked outside a grocery store. His leg was locked in place, his foot pressed firmly on the brake pedal for the better part of an hour before someone discovered him and called an ambulance. People thought he'd fallen asleep, his white Audi TT idling restlessly.

I remember the sound of my voice when I called Karen, the distracted urgency of the shock setting in.

"My dad's died," I said. You only get to say that once.

I couldn't remember what we'd talked about when I got to her place. I had to keep checking that I was breathing. She had herbal tea and managed to remind me that I still had her camera. In a fit of desperation I reached for her, I held her. Without him around everything felt unformed. Past, present and future walk into a bar, stunned.

+ + +

"EXCUSE ME, SIR?"

I turned around and this older guy approached me, a weathered face wearing a blue denim jacket. His hair swept back in a wave of grey and nicotine gold. He was unshaven and his lips were cracked and swollen.

"Excuse me," he said.

He'd caught me standing in the middle of a parking lot, on the outskirts of the Distillery District in the east end. I was holding two bags of office supplies. I can't remember what I'd bought. Toner? Paper? I was rooted, gazing into the distance, and must have looked like a performance artist. I was staring at an old warehouse; its archways, which once framed busy carriage ports, were censored with brickwork. I'd walked aimlessly, crossing downtown as if waiting for someone to stop me. I couldn't do it. I didn't have that sort of skill, the filters and instincts other people had.

"I've run out of gas," he said, pointing uncertainly beyond the parking lot. "Was wondering if you knew where the nearest station was."

He reeked of cigarettes and was holding a red plastic gasoline container. It looked like a child's toy in his hand.

"I don't know," I said, pointing as precariously as he had. "Probably twenty minutes' walk west?"

He followed the direction of my arm then turned back to me and smiled.

"That's gonna be a hike, eh?"

I nodded and shrugged as honestly as I could. The last thing I wanted to do was talk to anyone.

"Look," he said, "I've been on the road for the last fourteen hours — I'm goin' to a job — and I only have enough for the gas, so...don't suppose you have a dollar or so for a cab, so I could get to the station. It's gonna be a while if I have to walk there an' back and it's gettin' cold."

He flipped the collar up on his jacket, the plastic gasoline container awkwardly hanging from his fingers.

I had fifteen bucks. I was waiting on cheques.

As if tapping into my thoughts: "Please, sir. Anything... I'd really appreciate it."

I took out a five. "It's all I got."

"Thanks, sir. That's wonderful. Thank you very much," he said, raising his arm in a weak salutation as he turned around and walked somewhat obediently in the direction I'd pointed.

I spotted him later on my trudge home, in an alley off of Bathurst, beside a Vietnamese karaoke bar. He had his back against the wall but even then seemed like he couldn't remain standing. A shorter man in a Chicago Bulls jacket lit his cigarette. I kept walking.

Everything felt rehearsed. The stranger. Karen's tungsten bedroom. My dad.

I remember getting home and lying on the futon, the winter sun on my face as I stared blankly at a wall. Eggshell. A streetcar roared past beneath the apartment, its steely wake threading itself into my head.

+ + +

[Notebook excerpt | Derrick van der Lem | February 13, 2008]

There were so many people coming in and out of the café, their entrances and exits over the floorboards amplifying off the walls, like on a theatre stage.

There were many people coming in and out of the café, the floorboards amplified by the empty basement directly beneath, their entrances and exits sounding like a theatre stage.

Locals came in and out of the café regularly, footfalls on the floorboards amplified by an empty basement beneath; every entrance and exit sounding to him as if performed on a theatre stage.

Patrons came in and out of the café regularly. Footfalls on the floorboards amplified by an empty basement beneath; each entrance and exit sounding as if on a theatre stage.

People came in and out of the café regularly, their footfalls on the floorboards amplified by the empty basement beneath; every crossing sounding to him as if on a theatre stage.

People came in and out of the café, their footfalls amplified by the empty basement beneath; every crossing sounding as if on a theatre stage.

11

+ + +

"I'VE SPENT YEARS trying to avoid this question." I fidgeted with my stool, moving it first back then forward. "I didn't have to deal with it until now."

Paul and I were upstairs at The Rivoli, on Queen West near Spadina, ostensibly to shoot pool. I just wanted to drink and soak in the atmosphere. I couldn't avoid seeing the happy-go-luckiness around us. I couldn't unhear the shitty grunge rock someone had filled the jukebox with. For my own sake, I kept Paul within an arm's-length periphery; conversation safe, not looking directly at him, not exactly listening closely to what he had to say because the last thing I needed was advice-advice-advice, which people who might as well have been strangers had been attempting to offer me over the last week. Paul was a better friend than a stranger and, even though he could be odd, I valued his perspective.

"I've hit a brick wall, and everything in my life is being questioned right now. It's all up for grabs."

He nodded obligingly. He was taller than me, with a semi-permanent smirk.

"Derrick, didn't you say once that you wanted to open a bar?"

I stared straight at him, my spell broken. "What? Did I?"

"That's a cliché."

"W-what is?"

"Hitting a brick wall. Isn't that a cliché?"

I looked at him, confused, running my hands over my thighs.

"I remember you told me once that you wanted to open a bar," he leaned forward. "Just asking..."

"I think so?"

"Well, would you rather run a bar?"

I shook my head. "Rather than what?"

"I don't know. The music rights stuff. Writing."

He bent over and, with a swift jerk, struck the cue ball, which collided with the others at the far end of the table.

I didn't want to telegraph an answer so I didn't budge on my stool. I didn't even exhale until I could think of a proper response. Paul sank two stripes on his break, the bastard.

"I don't know," I said.

He nodded encouragingly, perhaps falsely; in brief moments he would glance back at me, smiling.

"Look," I said, staring at a few tables around us, making eye contact with whoever happened to stroll by. "Once upon a time. I don't know. I probably said something about a bar. Five years ago I wanted to do things. Start things. Hell, ten years ago. And then I just put things off and then there was... the back and forth with Karen and shit. It's like I just woke up one morning and discovered I'd gotten lost. All I have is writing. That's the only thing, I swear, that keeps me from becoming some sort of fucking psycho. But, with Dad gone..."

Paul put up his hand. It was also my turn.

"Derrick, I don't know anything about writing. I've read one of your stories once, but like, who am I? I'm just a guy who likes watching basketball and having a good time. In spite of this, I think I qualify — as your lawyer — to, you know, say you have some talent," he smiled and sipped his gin and tonic.

I was staring at a crowded mess near the corner pocket, as if all the other balls had decided to gang up on mine. Paul had a degree in law — JD/MA from U of T — even though he never took the bar exam. Instead, he abruptly changed course and decided to focus on an acting career. He lived with his common-law partner who, despite them being together for as long as I'd known him, he still referred to as his girlfriend. She was a lawyer.

With my cue stick angled high, I tapped my way out of the mess, pocketing one of Paul's in the process.

"One story," I said, taking a sip of my drink. "I've had just one story published...three years ago, under a fucking pseudonym because I was scared shitless my dad would read it. And then there was the stoner essay I wrote about camera lenses."

He looked at me critically. I remembered that look from when I told him I'd cheated on Karen.

"But you've started something lately, right? It's not like you haven't been writing, right?"

"The cowboy stories," I mumbled.

"The cowboy stories!" he said.

He was the life coach I never quite felt I needed. I stirred my glass. He dropped two more stripes into their respective pockets.

"You haven't really had a clear shot yet," he said, taking inventory of the game. "What's it called again? The Empty something? It's not a novel but a...thingy-thing."

I cleared my throat and tried to speak in a calm, deep voice.

"It doesn't have a name yet. It's a collection of stories."

"Yeah, but what's it about?"

A party settled at the table next to ours. Everyone was happy. The music got worse. Foo Fighters.

"Uh...They're about the...ah...Injured Cowboy. The Injured Cowboy."

"Go on."

"Well, it's a short story collection — it's not a novel. It's about a mysterious drifter in a kind of self-consciously clichéd Old West. He rides into town on a horse, or he comes in on a bush plane, or on a wagon with immigrants. That sort of thing. And in every story, he has to confront..." and then I paused, rolling around my words, "a sort of existential heartbreak." I waited, wondering if that phrase made any sense to him. "And there's a sort-of running tragedy as well: he has a handicap that keeps him from settling down and forging a newer, happier life."

"What's the handicap?"

"Well...you know, that's sort of a secret. I'd rather you read it in the book."

"Okay. Let's say I'm your editor. Let's say you just tell me what the handicap is."

"It's his heart. His heart was broken long ago when his bride-to-be disappeared just before they were to be wed."

He nodded and came over to fetch his glass. I could never read his face, which made everything he did unpredictable.

"She left him a note," I added.

"And what did the note say?"

"I don't know, Paul." I raised my arms helplessly. "It's not sketched yet. I'm not sure. All I know is that he's trying to kill himself over the course of the book. He puts himself in worse and worse situations with a kind of subconscious desire to find something that will obliterate him. But, after resolving each conflict, he only gets stronger. It's this weird, elaborate self-deception and at the same time he's only half-aware of it."

He nodded, staring off into space. "Well, it certainly sounds neat."

"If I can get it past the concept stage, yeah. But..."

Paul's attention turned to the table. "Wait...whose turn is it? Did you go? Did I go?"

I've tried this before — not just this, but other things: novels, short stories. They don't go anywhere. They sit on my hard drive like photographs of dead relatives. I considered how naturally I allowed that idea to appear in my head, without hesitation.

Paul shrugged and opted to take another turn, perilously leaning across the table to make his shot. It made me wonder if he was ever actually competing with me.

"Look, I think you're being a little hypercritical," he said, trying not to brush the 7-ball aside with his sleeve. "I know your father's gone..." he paused. "And I know from, you know, our previous conversations that he was, for better or worse, an influence, let's say," his eyes darting up to mine. "But it sounds to me like you're kinda chastising yourself. And these are classic symptoms — self-recrimination, guilt." He tapped the cue ball so that it banked off of the side table and knocked a striped ball into the opposite side pocket. "I know it's natural, but fuck, it's not healthy."

I let out another slow breath. I was looking at an empty glass and had forgotten what the hell I was drinking. I needed to answer him. I saw him looking at my glass. He raised his eyebrows, offering me another one. I nodded.

When he left for the bar I noticed a woman with short, black hair staring at me a few yards away, standing alone. I thought it was accidental because she happened to be behind

Paul and it was only as he stepped away that I caught her looking. Or I was making this up — maybe she was looking at something else, maybe at Paul. Her cheeks were flushed and she was dressed for the winter. She turned away and reached into a pocket. It occurred to me I was just as visible to her but doing nothing about it. She pulled a card out from her pocket.

"Derrick, sorry. I need you at the bar. My debit card's not working."

It was Paul, flustered.

"I guess I'm just realizing what an idiot I've been," I said, turning to follow him to the bar, craving a cigarette, the woman in the parka downgraded in my mind. "I convinced myself of so many things that required the constant orbit of his presence. It was the reason for so many decisions that I regret, Paul. And so many of them were reactive — meant to piss him off, or do the opposite of what he'd think was the right thing to do." When we got to the bar, I fixed a gaze on him. "Do you know how pathetic that sounds?" I asked. "Wasting so many fucking years?"

"It's okay," he reached over and put his hand on my shoulder. "My apologies if I'm bringing this up at a bad time."

I gave the bartender my debit card.

"You're not," I said, staring down at my shoes. "You're just saying the same shit everyone else probably says about me. Sometimes it feels like everyone is talking about me, and all the things they're saying are shitty, critical things. And then I feel like an idiot for not being more self-aware. It makes me feel immature, like I've spent years stuck on autopilot."

"Derrick," he turned to allow me to complete the debit transaction, "you should go get lost and get some perspective and stuff. It's not going to go away, for sure, but..."

"I know."

"Yeah, I know. I know you know. You scare me when you get like this, that's all. You've got this dark part to you. You're your own worst enemy like this, and I just hope you're not sitting at home stewing like a crazy guy, planning to destroy the world."

We picked up our drinks and went back to our table. The woman, whether she was coming or going, was gone. A buser was clearing our glasses. While he swept away some used napkins I thought I saw a white card gathered in the debris.

Paul paused in front of me, before I could get to the table, stopping me from figuring out what it really was. A card. For me? For everyone? Was she publicizing someone's gig? We looked in opposite directions: me leaning against our pool table, spying around the hall for her; Paul appearing to appraise the tip of his cue. He rubbed some chalk on it.

"In case you are interested in opening a bar, let me know," he said. "I'm looking for a tax writeoff."

+ + +

IT WAS THE beginning of March and people were traumatized from February. Winter's fury came later than normal and all signs of spring had been taken captive in the process. I walked along a side street to Karen's house, not far from my apartment in Little Portugal, staring down at the shadows of my legs against the snowbank, listening to the tick-tock metronome of my boot heels as if in a trance.

She wanted her Leica back.

The clearest, sunniest days are the most bitterly cold. It was easier to distract myself with the rhythm of my footsteps, dodging ice puddles. Today marked the point I experienced every year between winter and spring when I wanted nothing more than to throw the three sweaters I owned into an oil barrel and set them aflame.

My lungs were pinched by the freezing air, my mind buzzing with the pot I'd smoked before I left. It was the morning after her appearance on *She Says*, a local TV talk show. Her and two other women were invited to talk about singledom. I watched it, of course. It was Karen, a dancer and a something whatever. Unsurprisingly, the conversation came around to the subject of being single and dating.

"I've had a lot of dates," Karen had said, smiling modestly into the studio lights above, "and it's really...Well, there's no real science to it. I'm afraid I don't see a series of platonic meetings as any sort of necessary step toward sex, or some sort of relationship for that matter. I'm totally comfortable with the idea of sex on a first date. It's not like that's never happened." As if she knew I was watching her, Karen interrupted the dancer's attempt to respond: "But I also want to add, I don't really have boyfriends either, come to think of it. I honestly don't see it that way. What I've had — how I would prefer to see it in any case — is a series of partners."

That's when I turned it off. I'd felt my fingers digging into my leg.

It struck me as odd, considering how many times I'd been frustrated with her, that of all the people she could've prioritized — her parents, her friends, her "partners" — she had chosen to call me, to see if I'd seen the show after it had been broadcast. Mind you, a Leica is a very expensive camera. Once I'd finished my diplomatic comments, she'd asked for it to be returned.

I didn't understand why the camera was such a hang-up for me. I hated her half the time. I'd asked to borrow it after we last broke up, a loaner until I was able to afford one of my own. In the end, I enjoyed hers so much that I had no motivation to replace it. Furthermore, it had dawned on me that if I returned her camera I'd be giving up the last tether between us.

Her tone of voice over the phone was familiar. I didn't need to hear the words. I could see the colour of the conversation ahead.

+ + +

"I WORRY ABOUT YOU when you drink."

It came out abruptly, like the symptom of a disorder.

She'd mentioned the interview and I began to talk about it. I began by offering a piece of constructive criticism about how she tends to cut others off in conversations, then slowly, almost pathologically, I unwound until everything coming out of my mouth was completely offensive. I knew going in that the show — her appearance, her answers — was up for discussion. How could we not talk about it? I didn't understand why I wasn't able to simply talk about the obvious and do so in a way that wasn't opinionated. I marvelled at how, up to seeing her ten minutes ago, the last thing I wanted was conflict and yet...

"You end up this loud, confused person," I continued, my face blushing. I had my arms crossed. It sounded completely terrible as it rolled out of my mouth like a script.

She sat at her editing station, the cool glow from the monitors accenting her face as she stared me down, even though I was the one standing.

"Loud. Confused," she mimicked. She turned around in her chair. "How about rash? Am I rash, too?"

I stared at the floor, blanching at the sound of my words being repeated back to me. I could storm out at any time, but leaving peacefully was what I wanted, a logic that flew in the face of what I was spewing.

We were in her basement. It was half-finished, poorly insulated and damp. We both wore several layers of clothing. I don't know what had possessed her to insist on moving her editing equipment down here. I wished I'd postponed everything, at the risk of being taken to small claims court for the fucking camera. Every impulse was compounded by a grief that blanketed anything I had to offer.

"You're a fucking snob," she said.

She turned in her chair to shut down an application, shooting me a quick glance. I allowed the insult to flow through me without much immediate damage.

"Come on, Karen," I whispered.

I rarely spoke the first names of friends and loved ones. When I said her name, the foreignness of its sound struck me, as if I'd never been entirely sure about her name all this time. Karen's name had little mark on the present for me and I sensed somehow she tuned into this — her shoulders lowered as she stared at the monitor, seemingly at nothing.

"Why the hell should I take advice from you? You're aloof about everything so nothing has any meaning."

"Come on, Karen," I said, not believing I'd said the same sentence twice, in exactly the same tone.

She turned around, gripping the arms of her chair, as if she couldn't decide whether to sit or bolt toward me.

"Something is fucking wrong if you can't deal with me being on television, alright? I asked you to come here because you had my fucking camera and the first thing you do is accuse me of being an asshole when I drink? What the hell do you think I'm supposed to do with that?"

I shrugged helplessly and rolled my eyes, realizing I was stuck acting like a character in a sitcom. My cheeks burning, I turned and made for the staircase.

"Fine, fine. Fuck it," I said.

High school. This was high school.

The Leica was sitting on her desk. If it had been within arm's reach I would've grabbed it by the strap and run out.

"I mean, what do you want me to say, Derrick?" she yelled from behind me, her voice betraying a hurt I tried to deflect as I marched up the wood plank steps. I couldn't believe that for the last three months since we'd split I'd spent nearly every night thinking about her. The warm body I'd nestled beside in grief growing cold. A voice stripping me bare.

I felt covered with burning sores as I climbed up to the kitchen, her voice triggering memories of my parents fighting when I was young. My face was numb, my heart beating defiantly. There were stars in my eyes and it took me a while to find my coat and boots, all the time fearing that she was going to follow me up the stairs and kick my ass. I gripped the handle to the screen door and took a moment to linger over the familiar elements of the place we'd once shared — the main floor of a house on Euclid Avenue. There was a brief, absurd relief when I saw the same brand of rye bread we liked sitting on the kitchen counter, its familiar blue-and-yellow wrapper. I looked down. She'd bought new boots. Red.

The wind had picked up, and no matter which direction I turned — whether I chose the alley system or the sidewalk along Dundas — it lashed my face the entire way home.

+ + +

THERE WERE NO leaves on the fire escape. No songs coming from the stereo. Only the dim churn of someone cleaning plates somewhere — it was hard to tell in the hollow chest of the low-rise. When the lights were dimmed, the TV not humming.

It was the first time I thought: there wouldn't be another.

I stood above the kitchen sink, head bowed, trying to listen to the rumbling of pipes and not the hostage pleadings of my common sense.

I prepared in secret, knowing the turn would happen: the point at which my conscience would discover it was being tricked. I spent the day popping sleeping pills, but never so many at one time as to risk passing out. I was disciplined; it allowed me to preserve an important bit of strength I'd been searching for.

I stood staring at a serrated carving knife in my hand.

Thank God, I remember thinking, angling the blade in the incandescent light of the kitchen. Thank God it's not so reflective that I could see the look in my eyes. The stupid fever.

My knees were weak and drunken, pressed against the cabinet under the sink for balance. I was afraid my lower back would cave in and I'd fall back on the floor and mess it all up. It was like my brain had been stitched into a mannequin.

This time's for good. You can't undo something like this. You can't uneat that many pills. One for every poor bastard who remembers me.

I swung around, my elbows supporting my torso along the edge of the sink, the knife pointing away clumsily so that I could stare out the window at the other end of the narrow kitchen. Blackness. Nothing. I glanced at the half-empty bottle of wine on the table, humoured by the idea of a last swig, the pills making it harder to focus, stand. My lips were dead, my breath was burning. I turned and looked at the blade suspended in mid-air. It couldn't be cleaner.

Before I could find another distraction (the garbage bags were on the fire escape waiting to be disposed of, I'd forgotten to mail the misaddressed Canada Revenue Agency letter to the previous tenant) I did something magical. I watched myself slit open my left forearm with the blade while staring into the light bulb above me. Blind.

Split seconds. Surprised by how fast it happened, how fast I'd done it. Surprised by the resolve with which I'd finished it off: every tooth of the blade sunk deeper as if my arm were a turkey's neck. The drugs managed the pain, but the euphoria of what I'd done made me spin spin spin and fall to the floor.

My arm pulsed hot water all over my hand and leg and belly. Hot water, by God.

The knife was still in my hand. It took a second for my eyes to adjust, having been blinded in the light. I threw it to the side only for it to rebound off the wall, nearly back into my face. Adrenaline bursting through the blur. I rolled over onto the numb-armed side, gasping for air as if I hadn't breathed for hours, propping myself up with my good arm and using whatever I could reach for leverage. Hot water gushed all over me. I felt like I was floating above the floor.

RAISE IT ABOVE YOUR HEART.

I could barely stagger, leaning against the walls for balance like a stupid drunk, from the kitchen to the bedroom to the phone. Inflatable castle.

Phone.

I fell on the mattress like diving into a backyard swimming pool, rolling over, stars in my eyes like tiny cartoon fireworks, reeling with the want to roll forever like a seven-year-old on a day off from school.

PHONE.

Oh God...it's so soft.

PHONE.

PHONE.

I don't know whether it was the bleeding arm that reached for the receiver...

Red pillow...and dialled 9...

Rolling in red leaves...1...

Rolling in soft, red leaves, all over me...1...I...just...

I...just...

"911. How may I dir –"

+ + +

I COULDN'T REMEMBER her name.

When it was time for this abandoned dog to leave the hospital, two days after my arrival – after being intubated, stitched up, bandaged and made to think about what I'd done – I pulled on a shirt Paul bought for me at the gift shop: a long-sleeved black sweatshirt with *Toronto* printed on it in large block letters, with red maple leaves on either side. Anything for a laugh.

The nurse was nowhere to be seen. When I inquired, not knowing her name, only knowing that she was "the one with short black hair," the ward manager didn't seem to know whom I was referring to. Fair enough. I didn't have the will to pursue it, and I didn't want to let on that I was more unwell than I looked. Anything to avoid another psych eval. Elevator doors opened and I had just enough energy to find my way to the street and flag a taxi.

I was curled up on the futon in my living room, grazing on TV news with the sound turned down. It had a distorted rhythm that soothed me like white noise. Places and names washing over me in waves: up, down, across. Every light in the apartment was on. I kept thinking back to the night before I woke up in the hospital. How it wasn't, in the end, the end. How I was now given the task of putting that terror and sick sense of failure — and everything else — into perspective. The place below me played Lou Reed. Bad Lou Reed. Silly, indulgent Lou Reed. Even Lou Reed wasn't that Lou Reed anymore.

I could get up and stomp on the floor.

I could get off my ass and call the hospital and get the name of that stupid nurse, maybe under the ruse of privacy concerns.

Or I could just . . . rest.

Waking up and seeing someone who I thought was the nurse, in the dark, leaning over. Sorting through my clothes, staring at me.

In the rear pocket of my jeans I found a card. On one side was an ornate black insignia. I couldn't figure out what it meant. On the back was a name — Wallace Turner — and a phone number. It obviously wasn't hers.

+ + +

"LOVE IS AN ENIGMA, and, like all enigmas, it inspires religion."

I couldn't even say whether it had been quoted accurately but hearing it always gave me a cramp in my gut. What little my father had written about the city was toxic. In essence — how provincial it was. Perhaps he used a different word.

Whenever I used *provincial* I felt I had to explain that it didn't necessarily concern Ontario.

A voice recorded in my head. An old Scot in a pub sputtering, "He lives in a goddamned condo on Lakeshore. The fuck is he sore about?"

When did I hear that?

In short, Toronto the Good was not.

And people like Dad were prone to too much hope. When something he cared about strayed into mediocrity it was portrayed as if sabotaged by conspiracy, as opposed to the less dramatic orchestrations of circumstance. I wasn't sure whether he was being a provocateur or whether he actually believed Toronto had such a dark soul. Or none. Perhaps it was as a result of this that he found himself discreetly shuffled toward the periphery of cultural authority as, one by one, every ally he had either retired from making public appearances, went bankrupt or died. Every October he would complain about all the invitations he received for literary events — launches and talks — and how disorganized they all were, but as the winds shifted there came a point where he found himself managing his own agenda, making plans for himself, rather pathetically, in order to create the appearance that his life was too busy and he had no time for the publishing world anymore. More likely that he was sitting on a stool at Dora Keogh, an Irish establishment on the Danforth, waiting for someone to recognize him. His exclusion would've been a career dead end were it not for his international endorsements. Oddly enough, in spite of his exclusion from invitation A-lists and his briny obstinacy, he became a sort of martyr for local artists. And after his death his abandoned cathedral metaphor took on growing significance. Someone — a group? — had even extended a graffiti campaign across parts of downtown: an outline of a church with the text 484NDON stencilled underneath.

He died at the height of my apathy toward him.

+ + +

I SAW *THE ATLANTIC* beside me on the cheap side table as I sat in the waiting room. It lay open, the table of contents showing. I squinted to read the typeface.

"Do you want that?" a patient-in-waiting asked. She was leaning over me, pointing at the magazine. "Are you reading that?"

I'd been looking for an obituary. My dad's, possibly mine. I looked at her and didn't know what to say.

"Um, no. Please…" I said, nodding at it. She took it from the side table, staring at me warily, as if I was going to grab her wrist and not let go. I felt lost and was dressed appropriately.

"Derrick?"

I saw a nurse who looked like every public school teacher I ever had craning her neck outside the corridor. A timeless shuffle later I was sitting in Dr. McAlistair's examination room surrounded by framed diplomas and snapshots of her children. I stared at a poster that provided an illustrated cross-section of human lungs complete with exploded perspectives of chronic diseases, like emphysema — a collapsed bronchiole like a withering arm holding the fruit of hollowed-out alveoli. Dirty, sinful smokers. For a moment I found myself unaware of how I ended up here, the purpose eluding me.

The Tylenol was wearing off. I could feel the pulse of my left forearm, like blood rushing after a tourniquet was released.

Despite the wavering numbness in my fingertips in the first week, despite the hypersensitivity to any pressure put on it, they said there would probably be no permanent damage but it would need to be treated gently until the stitches came out. I couldn't take a shower, for fear of infection. And even after all that, I wouldn't have full use for a while. As a result, I didn't want to be outside. I just wanted to sleep, smoke pot and watch the news.

I appreciated being alone in her office, and hoped she would take her time, allowing my mind to swim in the atmosphere. I was staring at a bright yellow sharps disposal container when I heard her approach.

"Sorry for the wait, Derrick," Dr. McAlistair called out, walking through the doorway a few beats later and closing the door behind her. She held a thatch of folders under her arm, her itinerary for the day, I guessed. She added the stack to a pile on her desk, drawing one off the top and opening it up.

"It's busy," she sighed, sitting down beside me, her singsong voice tinged with motherly routine. Her eyes behind glasses, framed with thoughts.

"No problem," I said.

"So..." she began, smiling. Her hand rested on my folder. My history.

There could still be pleasantries between us, despite the darkness. It was like being at the unemployment office, except I was telling her about how I tried to kill myself instead of how there were no jobs available. I'm pretty sure it was in the folder. Her name had been given to the ER team after all.

"Darling, are you still employed?"

"For now," I said.

Barely. Between projects. Hoping I didn't have to beg anyone.

"And what is it, I'm sorry... I don't think I ever wrote it down. I know you work in television."

"I'm a music supervisor for TV and film. I track down music and do contracts for rights." I didn't want to get into it.

She nodded and amended something in the folder.

"I don't know if you know, but my dad passed away awhile ago. So, that's been..."

"I heard about it, dear. I read it in the papers," she said, smiling cordially.

I took her support without reservation. I was only recently used to people I hardly knew offering me their condolences: half-read emails from semi-strangers, journalists, people on Twitter. It was more of the same pseudo-celebrity I'd already been acquainted with, only reversed. Perverted.

I continued talking with her, regardless that I couldn't hear or process what I was saying. I felt like an actor playing me in a low-budget movie, discussing his fictional father's death alongside his near-own. Yet, for the first time, I could summarize my feelings and share them with someone who wasn't judging me. She didn't twist my words around. She didn't turn what I was saying into jokes, like Paul did. It didn't feel as if she were more interested in her own thoughts.

29

+ + +

I WAS LEANING on the edge of a tall bar stool at a place on Ossington, digging through my pockets while the head of my Pilsner settled. I flipped her appointment card over and under my fingers like a magic trick. Dr. McAlistair had asked me to come back in a few months. I stared at the hospital logo.

She had told me in her warm yet matter-of-fact way that grief, even depression, was a perfectly normal thing to feel.

I'd always been a somewhat moody person but never cared to talk about it, or alternately synthesize it as a part of me. It gave me a perfect excuse to avoid speaking with anyone who was more interested in my father than me.

"Do you have any place to get away to, for the spring?" she had asked, after examining my arm. She wanted to make sure I was doing physio; they had to reattach tendons. I didn't want to think about any of it. It physically sickened me, which might have been an association with what I could half-remember from the hospital after they wheeled me in. Despite all this, she felt that the stitches could be removed in a few days. It was almost as if I were being allowed to rewrite my mistake. Of course, there would be a scar, and there would still be discomfort for a while.

I'd told her I didn't know. Dad has a cottage that will be sold by the estate soon. A part of me wanted to go for old times' sake, but not in the middle of winter. The executor and estate lawyer had to figure out a number of items first.

"Another part wants to stay," I'd said, "and, you know, soak it in."

"That's perfectly natural," she had replied. "I can tell you that's exactly how I would feel," then she flipped through my folder. "But, you know, after you've soaked it in, it may be good to consider removing yourself from it. You know? Just to take yourself away from your situation, after your responsibilities are taken care of, that's all."

I took a long sip from my pint and flipped the card over.

"If you are interested in speaking with someone — a therapist, perhaps — I could..."

I'd told her I didn't know. It's not like I hadn't ever considered seeing one. I'd considered it lots, but it just seemed like a lot of work to do.

She had put my docket down and looked at me above the rim of her glasses as if bypassing a filter on her honesty.

"If you do arrive at a decision where you are considering seeing someone, would you mind if I recommended a professional, Derrick? Unfortunately, the waiting lists for people who practice therapy who also happen to be covered by the province are long." She wrote something on the back of one of her cards. "His practice is new and, you know, if you felt at some point that things were getting too much to deal with, perhaps it would help to give him a call. I've heard nothing but good things."

I didn't feel I had much of a choice in the matter.

"He's a shrink?"

"A psychiatrist? Not exactly, although he is a doctor. He's a psychotherapist." She then reached over her dockets and handed the card to me. "Strictly speaking, he doesn't prescribe medication or anything. It sounds to me like maybe you need someone to talk with. He has a good reputation with our clinic. Runs his own practice and he's perfectly accredited. Prefers not to approach things from a traditional analytic perspective. A little more progressive." Ah.

"His name is Wallace Turner — Dr. Turner. I'm giving you his number."

I stared at the card while Tracey Thorn's wounded voice drifted from the speakers above. I reached into my back pocket and pulled out the card the nurse had put in my bloodstained jeans. The other side had a name with a phone number written beneath it.

Wallace Turner.

There was a wave above me, staring down, menacing and undefined. I sat thinking of idle years that now seemed wasted: not drunk enough or too drunk; not poor enough to endear myself to amateur socialists, or else impoverished; of the almost illegible ambitions of what remained of my youth. I didn't want the wave to disappear. Nostalgia, even the painful kind, was therapy. Everything that didn't make me want to leave my bar stool and run in front of oncoming traffic was therapy.

+ + +

I HAD CALLED Dr. Turner, expecting a sense of destiny to be unveiled to me. But what I got instead was a plate of vagueness. His voice was breathy and almost characterless, as if it lived in the suburbs. He had kept coming back to what I thought about "the chronology of my narrative" and "the perspective of temporal shifting," not as in how I felt about my childhood, but rather how I felt about time itself. I'd told him I wasn't sure, because I honestly didn't care about the question. About everything else that had been lingering — how I got his name on no less than two different cards, how he knew Dr. McAlistair, how he knew me, what kind of therapy he practiced — I couldn't get a straight answer. When I had asked how much his rate was, he'd said it was a sliding scale, but didn't go into much more detail than that. Sure, I'd thought. What the hell. I might as well have worn a shirt these days that had *What the Hell?* written on it. Instead, I was wearing the Toronto sweatshirt. It was beginning to smell.

Paul sat in my living room. I was doing the dishes in the kitchen. He'd come over on a lunch break, which, for an unemployed actor, was pretty much any time. My blood was still on the carpet. Details. What the hell?

"You could've had a real hard-ass." He dipped into a bowl of salted nuts he'd brought as a (his words) happy-my-friend-didn't-die gift. The stitches had come out the other day. I didn't want to look at my arm or talk about my post-op prospects, which left me talking about the nurse. I didn't want to get onto the topic of the business cards and Wallace with him. I didn't need protection. I chose instead to talk about the fact that, whoever she was, she had paid a lot of attention to me.

"Catholic hospitals don't mess around," he added. The television was left on, muted this time. I still needed the comfort of its sonic hum. I could glance at it and have my thoughts numbed with images without dialogue and music. Thin people with tans, but deeply concerned about the world and its sports.

"Congratulations on meeting someone in the city who isn't just thinking about herself. You know, there's nothing stopping you from paying a visit to the hospital. That's usually a heartwarming moment."

I nodded, realizing that he could only see my back. A dishtowel was over my shoulder.

"Wanna go for a pint?"

"No thanks. Sorry," I said.

"No problem. I kinda figured you may want to get out."

All I had to wash were plates and glasses. I wasn't making any food. I ordered it in. Making food meant caring and I just didn't care about food.

"I do. I do, Paul. I want to go outside. But I go outside to relax. So I can't go outside. I can barely face myself. The thought of being out there and having other people see me like this..."

I couldn't see his poker face, but I imagined him nodding behind me.

I wanted to retreat from everything. That was my MO after all. Natural wants and needs grabbing the steering wheel and taking me wherever desire pointed. But that's what got me in a hospital, and now tracking down a therapist.

"That's a nice sweatshirt, by the way," he said.

I broke out in helpless laughter, and then tears flooded my eyes.

"No, really: black Toronto sweatshirts are really in, particularly if they have little red maple leaves. Because, you know, otherwise who can tell if you're Canadian. Right? You could be promoting that Toronto in Illinois. But seriously, I've seen models in Yorkville wearing that sweatshirt."

"Fuck off."

I turned and he was standing in the doorway to the kitchen, smiling. I chuckled for a while and noticed his glances at my arm. Who knew? Who didn't? Who needed to?

"Seriously, if you need anything – like, anything – please just let me know. Okay? I know you've got some time on your hands to think about shit, but just don't overthink."

"I'm okay, all considered," I said quietly. "But thanks. I just need to soak it all in."

"Sure."

I stretched out my arm and looked at it, rolling up the sleeve of the sweatshirt.

"I'm not in too much pain. I just gotta take care of it and get some rest."

"Are you left-handed? I can't remember..."

"No."

"Does your family know – am I the first?"

"Whether I'm left-handed?"

"No, I mean...the, uh..." he nodded.

I mopped up around the sink with the dishtowel.

"It's not something I want to advertise. I'd rather get healed and wait for questions after. There's gonna be a scar. That's not going to go away." I glanced at him. "Does Karen know?"

He stared at me blankly, then shrugged.

"Good. And she won't," I said. "I don't want her to be connected to this. I don't want her to get involved and think..."

"Sure."

Enough. Got it.

A streetcar passed below. An unknown song played quietly in the place downstairs. The hum of the mute television. All I was able to handle were ambient sounds. If an underpaid associate producer called and asked me to secure rights to a Lil Wayne track, I wouldn't psychically be able to listen to it.

Paul made his way to leave. "And, if I may, you should accent your kitchen walls with red blotches to cover the stains," he said. "Also, I would recommend replacing your silverware with plastic takeout cutlery."

I locked the door behind him, listening to his steps down the staircase to Dundas West. Having that one person with whom I could confide, even if he could be frustrating: like me, but somehow happier. I was not in the mood to thank my luck.

I thought of calling Karen, but realized it was pointless. It burned in me, fuelled by pot and Tylenol, by guilt. Air it out.

I'm too smart for my own good. It was something I remember saying to her on our first date.

As for chronology, Dr. Wallace Turner had been unable to pin down a date for an initial consultation when we spoke earlier. He kept saying he would get back to me, as if I were bothering him and he had six other more important things going on.

+ + +

[Journal entry | Seneca Lewis | March 13, 2055]

I got into trouble with security on the way to an f2f interview. I was in a civ-cab heading east-downtown when we hit a new construction zone near Jarvis. Someone behind us honked and the guy on duty thought it was us. My driver was sweating.

It was hot. Ssswell-ter-ing! as Mom would say. Another day for masks and gloves, making everyone look like research assistants: sad. The driver didn't want to lower his window, but I could see he was still upset that the cop was blaming him. He was waving his hands behind the window, trying to make his point. But it was tinted! Quite a sight...or from the officer's perspective, probably nothing.

"It wasn't me!" he said. He had some sort of Slavic accent.

I was running late and all I'd had for breakfast was a hand-ful of pills with fake pear juice. I was already suited up, not to mention running late, so I opened my door and slipped out to talk to the cop.

You know, they've really come a long way with masks. There are different colours and styles. High-density lenses, friction-free suction. But for the life of me, you'd think they could improve the speaker quality. I don't think enough people complain about things like that — it's like we're being taken advantage of.

I couldn't hear a goddamned word the cop said. All I heard was, "...back in your car..." When I tried to explain, he just stood there — and I knew my speaker was working, I could hear it. I don't know if he got a transmission or something because he turned and paused for a second, putting his hand on the side of his helmet. Before I knew it he pulled out his wand, fucking swiped me and walked away!

I got swiped for contextualizing his goddamn error!

And I flinched like a twelve-year-old, like a hornet had come too close to my face, which was silly because they only need four feet of clearance to catch your chip-ID on their system. Done and processed, post your questions with the City later please. No one called it by its name anymore. Just "the City."

After what had happened sunk in, I looked up and saw him having a dandy ol' chat with the construction supervisor, standing there looking at me like I was some cute movie character. You look at your daughter like that, asshole?

When I got back in the cab, feeling guilty for a number of crimes — least of which was sticking up for the driver — there was finally a gap in the traffic and the driver hit the pedal and got the hell out of there. During my failed negotiation we'd managed to bottleneck more traffic than the construction had. Neither of us talked for the rest of the trip, probably out of humiliation (me). Or pity (him). When he dropped me off at the interview (oh, that!) he tapped a code in his meter, turned around and told me that the ride was free. His expression in the rear-view mirror was apologetic. I saw in his face that he felt I'd asked for it. That's why he didn't roll his window down when the cop was giving him shit. So long as he stayed inside behind tinted windows he couldn't get swiped, just his civ-cab ID. I knew better than to make a scene and it was going to go on my record, if I didn't have one already. I guess you never really know. (At least I don't have to lie about having one now — I think.)

37

Walked into the office just in time for the interview and I had mask-face because I didn't have any time to freshen up beforehand. It was one of those interviews where everything becomes completely apparent after the introductory hand-shake. More apparent than the remaining good things in life. It was apparent that they didn't want me, my mask-face or my sweaty cheap interview dress that was three years old.

Fuck the world. Too late.

+ + +

[Journal entry | Seneca Lewis | March 20, 2055]

If only I was good at something that made money.

The latest interview. They got my name from an agency even though I can't recall using one in the last year. Privacy Movement, my ass.

They liked that I was interested in image collage. They asked me to bring a portfolio for the next interview.

A portfolio? It's a hobby! They're barely organized by date. But desperation, as I've learned, has a way of motivating order. Consoldebt's on my case, literally. Creditors are already messaging me. And I really want these sexy yellow boots at Cavulho's. The last thing I want is to call Mom for another loan.

I unarchived a few of the better ones: residential alleyways at sundown combined with staples protruding from old street posts, elderly women in face masks (imagining a time when they weren't necessary) mixed with diseased homeless people lying on asphalt. I brought them with me to the next interview and they — anonymous spook types — took their time looking at them while I sat there, waiting to hear that

I wasn't who they had in mind (you mean, like, a professional?). They shared some comments with each other, no telling what they really thought. There was a glass of water in front of me with a few drops of something floating below the surface like red smoke. Like the time I cut my lip when I was five, after Pino hit me, and I stared down into the sink.

After the presentation they asked me to run on a treadmill. I knew they wanted someone in "good physical condition," but I always figured it was just a phrase companies used to scare away the obese. They gave me a jumpsuit. (AND IT FIT ME!) The track wasn't even going that fast but I was nearly vomiting into the respirator by the end of it. Cathy — if that's not a fake name; how many people are named Cathy? — stood there watching from behind the equipment. Not endowed in the personality department, Cathy. Blood tests were next. The whole routine, like I was getting a municipal immunization check. I don't know what was going through my head — I don't know why I didn't get the hell out of there. I ended up being disease free, thankfully. I feared I'd been carrying something around in permanent remission. When they told me I was clean I even asked if they were sure.

They didn't answer. They were like that.

Getting a contract is hard work these days.

+ + +

THE SOUND WAS thin and silvery, but beneath it pulsed a warm bass with a long decay that gave the music danger with the strike of each beat. The heat of stage lights panning across my face. I didn't mind the odd strobe leaving me momentarily blind against the dark. I stood against a black wall with a bottle of Labatt 50 in my hand. I'd scrounged the last of my pot and, as if prepping myself for an impossible mission, proceeded to smoke half a joint before leaving home.

I came to the Dance Cave years ago, with friends when I had friends, only this time I wasn't looking for laughs or girls. I wasn't even there to drink. Everything was a prop, and this was my theatre. I envisioned how I would look now, how sad my photo would appear. When I needed to remind myself of a youth that passed too quickly, the Cave inevitably flickered in my memory. My reasons for not returning materialized as soon as I walked in. For one thing, I was too old.

But I needed light and heat and people. And life. I wasn't able to brood alone in my apartment any longer. And as the palette of life around me grew, so too did the need for a different sound. And I so desperately needed to be surrounded by very loud music, so that I couldn't think. About Wallace, about Karen. About Dad. About me. I wanted to experience the world as dark crowds and flashing lights, if only for the sake of nostalgia. Comfortable, empty surprises. I wanted the bass to pound through my skin like an auxiliary heart, to see people alive and moving, glittering, and talking about useless bullshit. I'd thought about this place while lying in the hospital, to keep myself sane. I wanted to smell sweat and perfume.

My arm felt better, but I kept it close to my body nonetheless. A part of me wanted to expose the scar. Another part didn't care. These people didn't know me. They'd never recognize me on the street. And if I couldn't bare myself to friends or family I needed to bare it to strangers.

Feed your eyes on this creep, please.

+ + +

[Excerpt from Exam #16 (page #1) | Seneca Lewis |
March 25, 2055]

Question No. 7) You discover that the squirrels in the park
are especially personable. They readily approach strangers,
looking for food. The park is peaceful and well shaded.
Which eventuality would you most likely see yourself picking
if this represented a place near where you lived? Please circle
the answer that most closely resembles your primary instinct.

(CIRCLE ONE)

a) Stay away. I don't like open spaces — I'd rather be inside
where the air is clean.

b) Bring a bag of peanuts for the squirrels, a thermos for
myself and a good book. I'll consider it the backyard I
never had. Where can I buy binoculars?

c) Neither of the above — I will incorporate it into my day-to-
day life and take note as I pass through it, but nothing
more interactive than that.

+ + +

[Journal entry | Seneca Lewis | March 25, 2055]

I couldn't find much on them. I could always dig up this
kind of info before — even with the Privacy Movement in
full swing. Ironically, this was one of the skills I highlighted
in the bio I gave them.

Truth be damned. I followed through with their suggestion
and applied for a position as image consultant. Not for the
Society, of course, but — as they instructed me — for an obscure
third-party agency: Perimeter One International. Odd, see-
ing as there were so few full-time employment opportunities

anywhere these days. Even my grandmother worked freelance. Free of thinking about debts, there's a question of principle: ultimately, who am I lying to by taking them up on their offer? With other potential employers I'm either too old, too smart or too stupid. Here, I'm paid for every visit, on every visit. Working with them weirds me out. They're too straightforward and nice. Every time I go there I feel as if our time is meticulously planned. It felt like giving blood, which I had already done. They had everything on me: government registration, bio/gen ID, my music playlists from the last six months.

When I came for the latest exam I had to level with Cathy.

Me: "Who the hell are you?"

Cathy: "We belong to a non-partisan coalition of citizens implementing new technologies and ideas in society."

Me: "What technologies? What ideas?"

What citizens?

Cathy: "You know what a Rotary Club is?"

Me: "Yes, sort of."

Cathy: "Philanthropic, community-based..."

Me: "Yes."

Cathy: "We're very similar: we incorporate aspects of that sort of infrastructure, among others. We seek out the best candidates to work on our ventures. As I'm sure was mentioned to you earlier, aside from the initial description in the ad you replied to, we cast our net wide. Wider than we have before, to avoid [I thought she said 'specialization traps,' whatever that means] that happen when you narrow the criteria too much."

This is when she leaned forward.

"We received four hundred thirty applications, sweetheart. We chose two people from those: someone else, and you."

Me: "I see."

What was I going to say to that?? I was stunned. A pain in the ass a minute ago was transformed into a personal best!

Cathy: "We understand that our process has been demanding, perhaps a little unclear and intrusive. We appreciate that you've been fair with us and in return we've shown good faith by compensating you throughout this process."

Me: "Okay — but, wait there. This process. What is this process? I hear what you're saying and I appreciate the payment transfer, but at some point I have an identity. And my job, or whatever it is, seems like a decoy; I need to know what I'm really doing. In my life, in general, for sake of dignity."

I'm making that sound much more polished than what I probably said, like Erica Wong from *Court: Adjourned*. They — Cathy and the two others who seemed to hover in the background whenever I was being tested — looked at me and then they looked at each other. Knowingly, as if they'd all had an aha! moment. Happy to oblige so long as at some point I'm told what's going on.

Cathy: "We'd like you to complete Exam #16. We're only asking this much more from you. It's long and complex, but in return we'll increase the payment for your work today."

There wasn't an Exam #15 — the exams were randomly numbered.

"And after this?"

"An answer," she said.

Her eyes were so intense I had no choice but to be convinced. And she was the nice one.

The test took two hours. They supplied cookies and water and a shower afterward.

At least they were interested in me.

+ + +

HEARING THE WOODPECKER in the distance seemed too perfect. Suspiciously perfect, as if the city had it playing through camouflaged speakers installed throughout the park. I imagined the entrance to a custodial room somewhere in the bowels of the brush, where — inside, cast off to the side — an old LP sleeve read: *Best of Intermittent Woodpecker (Southern Ontario)*.

I sat on a picnic table beneath two barren maples in the basin of Trinity Bellwoods, a sprawling park framed by Queen and Dundas. This was where I came to think, sometimes to jot down ideas. Only now, weeks after the fact, could I see evidence of spring's promise. Free of snow, the pungent scent of soil breathing, the relinquished business of robins and squirrels, all beneath the fading warmth of an April sunset. I sat far enough away from the parents playing with their children above, with only the dog owners down here to bother me. I kept calling it a basin, but everyone else called it the dog bowl.

Virgin greenery sprouted where earlier there had been ice and mud. I couldn't stay warm enough, despite the sun. No matter where I walked to or where I sat, it always felt five degrees too cool. Don't call your first-born April.

I had to start thinking about work, but every part of me pleaded not to be forced to return. I could only say no so many times before risking that my phone would stop ringing and my chequing account would dry up. The distraction of the industry was welcome, but the stress wasn't. I'd told anyone who needed to know that my unavailability was due to legal circumstances stemming from my father's death. Unlike the majority of people, it was handy to have an excuse corroborated by national newspapers. There were also requests for interviews that I needed to respond to.

A black Labrador trotted toward my picnic bench, followed at a distance by his owner who seemed stymied by his tireless energy. I reached out and brushed my hand over his thick coat as he scouted past me. He turned his head around, busy breath panting like an engine, happy to receive attention. I reciprocated, grinning.

The panting stopped. The dog looked at me. He stepped forward hesitantly, his black snout daintily isolating the source of curiosity. It sniffed my palm, but before I could attribute it to some food I'd handled earlier, his snout followed further up my wrist. There. Flesh. There. Sniffing delicately. Flesh.

"Rudy!" someone called out.

I didn't understand until I realized that my forearm was exposed. He continued to savour the scar.

"Rudy! Come on! *Come on!*" his owner pleaded, waving a long stick he'd picked up from the grounds.

Rudy looked me squarely in the eye, then back at the other man.

"It's okay," I whispered.

He began panting again and trundled off to his owner.

"Come here. *Come here.* Good boy! Good boooyy!"

I'd thought of obscuring my forearm with an elaborate Polynesian-style tattoo, but when I heard how painful it was to ink scar tissue I dropped the idea. I resolved to wear long-sleeve shirts while it healed. If it healed. There was a cream people recommended, which I still hadn't bought. I had blazers. Tweed could be a new look. In a sense, I already had a tattoo — one I had authored and which could not be removed.

Domestic accident, if someone asked. I lived in fear of having all of what had happened in the last few weeks somehow leaked to the press. Do I just leave the scar open to speculation?

45

I didn't want to do much of anything today except drink coffee, crave cigarettes and read the copy of *Steppenwolf* I had picked up at a used bookstore along the way. I didn't know what to do with it. I'd read it once before and it didn't make any sense. It made for a good prop in case anyone wondered what I was up to — it was hard to go out somewhere and just think. You have to bring proof that you are thinking.

A clamour of clumsy paw thumps on my picnic table behind me. I whipped around and found myself staring at a small Welsh terrier sitting next to me on the tabletop. It wasn't as interested in me so much as feeling pleased to be sitting there, panting happily, panning its head around as if all the Great Dog Accomplishments in its life had been met at that moment.

"Cory!" a man called. The dog's attention jerked instinctively toward the voice. I followed suit.

"Sorry about that," a man said, approaching. He was tall, with sandy brown hair. Glasses.

I smiled and shrugged. He nodded, then turned and pitched an orange ball across the field. Cory sprung from the top of the bench, rocketing after the ball.

"I'm Dr. Turner, by the way," he said. "You can call me Wallace, if you like."

One one thousand . . . Two one thousand . . .

I stared at him. I couldn't see through the plainness.

"What?"

"I'm Wallace Turner."

"Are you out of your . . . What?"

He smiled and held up his hand, as if expecting my confusion. Cory meanwhile trotted proudly around the larger dogs with the ball in his mouth.

"Sorry about that. Crossed signals," Wallace Turner said, looking into the distance. "Sheila – Dr. McAlistair, sorry – mentioned you were grieving for a loved one. I actually had your information sent to me earlier. In any case, my apologies. This is a little proactive. I could have set a date for us over the phone, but, well – believe it or not, this is the way I like to meet prospective clients."

I was stunned.

"I don't know what I should say. Perhaps the police can sort that out?"

His smile widened.

"You don't trust me?"

"Trust what?" I asked. "Who are you? Are you following me?"

"More or less," he said. "Yes."

Perhaps the woodpecker was just an album playing through speakers. Perhaps everything I'd heard until now was just footfalls amplified by the empty basement beneath; every crossing sounding as if on a theatre stage.

"I-I didn't expect you'd have a dog."

He seemed to weigh my comment good-naturedly. There was a good-naturedness with which he seemed to weigh everything. Within the two minutes I'd been exposed to him, it began to grate.

"If he smelled the park on me when I got home, he'd have me figured out and wouldn't forgive me. I'd be the bad guy."

He looked at my book.

"Hesse."

And now it felt like my reading habits were being judged.

"I read it a long time ago," I said. "It's just a prop, basically."

He nodded.

"I'd like to ask you a few questions, Derrick. My approach is pretty casual — I don't really care to use an office. What's the rest of your afternoon like?"

"Fairly open."

He asked to meet later, and whether I knew Rosa Branca at College and Ossington.

"I think so — it's a sports bar where old men hang out?"

"Not too busy during the workweek. An older, discreet clientele. Yes," he nodded.

"I've passed it a few of times." And by that I meant it was the sort of place I avoided, particularly during the World Cup.

"Meet there for two p.m.?"

The sound of a crying child beyond the ridge of the bowl could be heard crescendoing above us like an air horn. We stared in the direction it came from.

"Sure thing," I said.

+ + +

[Journal entry | Seneca Lewis | April 9, 2055]

I was having dinner with Mom and Sis when I told them I got a job: image consultant. We were sitting on a patio on St. Clair, shielded from the sun by one of those large, striped parasols with solarization responders on top. It was very Renoir. Always with the Renoir, my mother. And it was a perfect setting, considering the news I had to share.

They stopped in the middle of their business with each other and looked at me like I'd told them I was opening a digital tattoo studio.

Where? What company? Are they registered with the Provisional Government? She keeps calling it the Provisional

Government even though we've had free elections for a decade. Those were the first questions on their lips. Not "Are you happy," "Is this what you want?" Mind you, I didn't get "Is the owner's son expecting to date you," like with the place she set me up with last time.

And so I told them about Perimeter One International, the organization that fronts for the Society.

"They're a philanthropic organization that donates on behalf of large estates across the world. I'm going to be working closely with them to..."

I had this memorized, and I recited it like a well-practiced script. Thanks, Cathy.

"...administer how those funds are distributed. And manipulating photo images."

They probably didn't hear me past "large estates." They didn't even bother to ask me for more details. The looks on their faces. Forever. Forever I will remember the look of relief; no more loans to prop me up, no more excuses when their friends asked what I did.

Fuck them.

That I would be at this point in my life. Where I couldn't even feel some sort of sick vengeance in lying to them like this. I wanted the opportunity to embellish! I wanted to tell them it involved Ottawa and the feds. Hell, I would've poured it on thick – I had the Society's FAQ memorized – but I have to admit, I don't know if I made the right decision. The lie, my stupid petty lie to them, was just wallpaper to me. It was legitimate wallpaper because, in truth, I wanted to believe my own bullshit as much as they did.

+ + +

"SO, YOUR GP and I belong to the same club, would you believe that?"

We were waiting for coffees to arrive. There was only one other occupied table in the café, an older man in a tracksuit fidgeting with his cellphone and a pad of paper, as if one accounted for the other. The interior was dim, with only the waning April sun to provide light. Interference was provided by a couple of wall-mounted TVs broadcasting in Portuguese.

I waited for him to finish his point, but Wallace was staring out onto the street, seemingly content.

"When you say club, what does that ...? What is that? You work out at the same gym or something?"

"No, nothing like that. It's not one of those places where you get accepted because you can afford the membership fee. It's not even about connections. It's more like a Rotary sort of thing. Sheila — Dr. McAlistair, sorry — and I, we actually went to school together originally," he smiled. "Long ago. McGill."

"That's nice," I said.

He was taller than I remembered from the park. He'd changed into a dark suit. I'd decided on wearing a hoodie that originally belonged to Karen. Even though I was surrounded by soccer memorabilia and beer ads I still felt underdressed.

"It's funny. My wife is jealous. She thinks Dr. McAlistair has designs on me."

I wanted him to keep talking so that I wouldn't have to think too hard. I still couldn't believe I was sitting here having this conversation.

"I keep telling her: look, she's married, she has kids for God's sake. I think she does it to tease me."

"Your wife."

"Yes. Not Sheila."

"It's not a bad strategy."

"No, it's not," he conceded with a smile, nodding. "I guess the trick is to never let it be known that you're teasing. I think tension works wonders."

Our coffees arrived with the puffed out butter croissant I'd ordered. Wallace kept his eye on the waitress and stayed silent until she was far enough away. She tended to the man in the tracksuit who smiled and started writing something down on his pad of paper after she left.

"It's an interesting club we're part of."

"Yeah? How so?" I couldn't give a shit.

He leaned toward me, catching me off guard with a knowing smile. "Aren't you going to ask the name of the club, or do I have to initiate everything?"

"What's the –?"

"It's called The Society of Experience," he said, pausing for effect. "Interesting, eh?"

My hand stilled, holding onto one of the horns of the croissant. I looked at Wallace with my best poker face, hoping I wasn't conveying any enthusiasm. I remembered the card I found in the back pocket of my bloodstained jeans, with the ornate inscription.

"The Society of Experience has been around for over sixty years. It's comprised of lots of different types of people, from all walks of life," he said. "From the top to the bottom, everyone's represented."

I didn't like the way he spoke to me, or the words he chose. I didn't see the point in him talking like a human pamphlet if, as I slowly gathered, he'd spent considerable time trying to bring me here to talk in the first place.

"That's interesting," I said. "What do you... or this club... What do you all do?"

"Well, we involve our members by exposing them to situations that motivate them toward becoming better people through the agency of direct experience. Through direct experience people are able to integrate these new exposures and sew them into the larger fabric of their lives."

I smiled. I couldn't help it.

"I think that's a little more highfalutin than the Rotary Club."

"Yes. And we're not the Rotary Club," he said, leaning forward, staring at me with a light in his eyes. He matched my smile as if he was holding back more, as if knowing his pamphlet-speak was irritable. For a moment what laid within that light in his eyes seemed predicated on whatever followed.

"I'm afraid I don't get you."

"Your doctor — my friend — recommended you to me because of the Society. Not necessarily because I'm a therapist. But if you're willing to work with me, and work with us on what we're proposing, I think we can help you."

I wished I was recording this. My doctor? What about the nurse at the hospital psych ward?

"Tell me this isn't religious. Like, at all."

"Only if you want it to be, Derrick."

"What kind of an answer is that?"

"Think about what I've said just now," he replied in a clear whisper. "The Society aims to provide experiences based upon the individual needs of our members. If what they happen to require involves a religious framework, we provide it — carefully, of course. Everything we do is careful. Discreet. I should mention firstly that we are what you would call a secret society. We don't advertise. We have no official public presence. We don't look for attention."

"Interesting." I held the croissant in my hand, wondering what I was about to hear.

"It is interesting. It's a lot of things. But I'm not here as a salesman, Derrick. Sheila contacted me because she thought you were ready for this sort of opportunity. She mentioned you seemed...ready for a departure.

"I am a therapist, yes. But I also represent the Society, and I feel the Society is better able to help you than I can alone in the capacity of therapist. You could come sit down in my office and have some sessions, sure. You know, perhaps there's something in that which could eventually prove useful. You know, slowly tease out some of the material going on inside you. With the Society, however, I think we can offer new first-hand experiences, not just reheated leftovers, memories. And it would be designed with you, the individual, in mind."

He took a sip from his Americano while I waited for him to continue. It reminded me of my dad's penchant for manipulating the expectations of family guests by introducing similar dramatic pauses.

Talk about therapy.

Out of raw hunger, and because I hated eating in front of anyone I couldn't trust, I felt obligated to clarify things: "So...you — the Society — you customize experiences for people. Are they all members by default? Do I need to be a member first, go through some sort of initiation or something?"

Wallace smiled, amused. "We're not Freemasons, Derrick. It may all sound very odd, maybe old-fashioned, but it's progressive. We're also very protective, necessarily. As I said, we don't want attention, so, naturally, our methods of fishing for new members are pretty low key."

53

Low key, like having someone plant his business card in my pants. Subdued, like having my family doctor forward my information to him.

"Sorry, but it sounds as if you may...?" I hoped that he would jump in and explain everything that I didn't understand, which was a lot. "Do you have something...? In mind...?"

"We do," he nodded.

I had the feeling of being steered to this juncture. Nevertheless, I bit the horn off my croissant, circling my index finger for him to continue.

"What do you think about time travel, Derrick?"

A rogue flake of pastry travelled down my windpipe, causing me to cough, my face flushing while involuntary tears welled in my eyes. Unable to speak and — momentarily — to breathe. I put my hands on the table and didn't want to let go. When I was convinced I wasn't going to choke to death, red-faced and appearing to be crying, I lifted my napkin and attempted to restore dignity by carefully dabbing my lips, swallowing the rest of the mess in my mouth.

Wallace sat patiently, biding the passage of time, waiting for me to regain composure.

"I believe I missed something," I said, trying to offset the raspiness of my voice by sounding as intelligent as possible.

He smiled and waited while I worked to compose my words.

"There's a connection point of some sort," I said. "That, or I'm not getting it..."

"You haven't missed a thing, Derrick. It was a simple question."

I sniffed and snorted, trying to clear my sinuses, taking note of the pause that followed. I realized he was going to sit there silently for eternity, until I responded.

"You want an answer," I asked, trying to keep my voice low, "to what my feelings are about the question of time travel?"

"That's right."

I looked out the window. I didn't want to feel his attention on me. I grappled with the idea in earnest, intellectually – I even peeled off a new layer of croissant, weakly clearing my throat in an effort to restore a sense of decorum. But then I thought that maybe this was one big joke: somewhere there was a camera crew recording my strained reactions for a TV gag reel.

"Um, well, I'd say that it's not a great idea."

"Why's that?" He said it quickly, and I began to understand just how rehearsed this was. He was two steps ahead, and I had long ago been figured out.

"Because the chances of, you know, disrupting the natural balance of things is too great," I said, searching for whatever authority over the subject that I could. Karen could do this. She could answer questions without really answering them: "You know, I've been reading about that and I just don't know who to believe." She could pull that shit out of her purse at a moment's notice. I was too much a thinker. I couldn't deflect with her skill, or fake lacking an opinion.

"Look," I said, setting my hands on the table, "I've read some stuff here and there. Seen some movies. They're not wrong about that. I'm not a science geek, but... I mean, if you go back in time and disrupt an established pattern, what follows would need to adjust itself accordingly. Like..." I looked around, then onto the street. "Say you put spare change in someone's parking meter... picked up a newspaper that was sitting on the ground that was meant for someone else to see. These things could all have potential effects on the future. Blah-blah-blah."

"I see," Wallace nodded. "And if this were virtual?"

Pause.

"What do you mean?"

"I mean, what if the whole experience — at least on your end — were virtual. The physics being real, the experience being real, but your participation purely virtual. No physical contact whatsoever."

"Then... yeah, I guess. I suppose."

He leaned forward. "You suppose... what?"

"Ah, that... That it's interesting. And stuff."

I took a sip from my cup.

"That's good to hear," he said. "You're the type of person we're interested in."

I stared down at the table and widened my eyes, trying to discern whether or not I was caught in a dream where I was cursed to repeat the mistake with the parking lot con artist from weeks before.

"Dr. Turner..."

"Wallace."

"Wallace... no offence, but this sounds like a scam. It's a very interesting scam, but people don't just develop this sort of technology and then benevolently bestow it on strangers, let alone randomly drop it on people like me. Maybe I'm being cynical, but human nature says I shouldn't believe you." I pushed my plate forward. "The only reason I'm here with you is that my GP somehow knows you — that's it. And I gotta say, between that shit with the card stuck in my fucking jeans at the hospital, and what you're telling me now, this is getting creepy fast."

He nodded politely. He sat with a leg crossed over the other and his hands resting on his knee.

"Compared to other organizations," he said, looking aside, "because of privacy needs, our membership is small, but the talent and the quality is very deep. We're discerning about who we bring in. Some of the greatest minds in the world have collaborated with us because they trust our philosophy. We have someone in pretty much every sector of every industry, and each of these individuals — myself included — search from time to time for a candidate to join our ranks. Our strength is in our depth, rather than the thickness of our Rolodex. Not that anyone uses a Rolodex anymore; it's just a nice analogy. But in the end, you know, our goals are what ultimately attract the quality people. Ever heard of Vijay Abapathy?"

"Ah, nope."

"Exactly. He's about your age and one of the best quantum mechanics theoreticians in the West. We recognized his potential when he was a U of T undergrad — your alma mater, before you dropped out — and instead of losing him to private interests, which so often happens, we brought him into the Society so that we could develop his talents. In turn we provided facilities and considerable financial support for him to use at his leisure. So, instead of some multinational company poaching and cocooning someone like Vijay into designing yet another internal combustion engine for yet another family sedan, he's helping us — and the world, to some extent — with the sort of progressive R & D that will benefit a far more significant, broad-platformed goal."

I cleared my throat. I was done with the magic show.

"Look, Wallace...again, this is super interesting, but I'm not exactly spinning out award-winning contributions to science. I clear music rights for TV shows people don't watch. I can't stand most of the people in my industry."

"But that's just for money — you write also, correct?"

Pause.

"I can write, yes..." I said.

He stared slightly upward, as if looking for his words in the air above my head. "You wrote an anonymous article for a magazine a few years ago."

My face whitened.

"You applied a photographic term, a Japanese word — *bokeh* — to social philosophy. It describes the quality of out-of-focus areas in a photographed image. If I remember correctly, every camera lens manufactured produces its own bokeh, its own distinct pattern of how out-of-focus areas are rendered. You applied it toward self-reflection. You wrote that the aesthetic of bokeh applies equally to the facade we develop in order to obscure parts of our lives that we'd rather not see clearly. You argued that everything, even the most painful things, should be within reaching distance, but they didn't necessarily need to be in focus..."

I nodded, speechless, struck by how my own words sounded foreign to me. And better than I remember having written them.

"We thought it was interesting."

"I...was never happy with that essay," I said, my throat feeling dry. "I figured only five people read it."

"Look, we're hands-off people, Derrick. I don't want to invade your life."

"No, you just keep tabs on my life. And hire strange nurses to –"

"We collect information. Yours was persuasive."

"So what are you proposing?"

"Nothing. We want nothing to do with you if you aren't interested."

I threw my hands up. In my mind it was much more exaggerated than it might have appeared. I looked at him skeptically, shaking my head, hoping the subsequent puzzle pieces made sense. But nothing came. He sat there, waiting for me to respond.

"That's it? Some absurd song and dance and then you cut it short saying that it depends on my approval to go any further? And if I don't call you, does that mean the Society of Experience spy network stops?"

"More or less."

I wanted to throw my spoon at his head.

"Look," I said, "you're a very unique therapist, Wallace. Give me some time. I've got your number. If you hear back from me, great. If you don't, please don't call. Back off, in other words."

He looked onto the street through the café window.

"That's fair. You've probably heard enough."

He got the attention of the waitress, who was polishing glasses behind the bar. He pushed out his chair and stood up. After he donned his coat he extended his hand with abrupt cordiality.

"All the best."

I stood up and ambivalently shook his hand, unsure of the message behind his quick departure, still processing the content of our discussion. I turned to the waitress, expecting her to bring the bill. She smiled politely, as if having waited for my glance and continued setting tumblers on the shelf above her. She looked vaguely familiar.

"Cheque's taken care of," Wallace added, nodding politely before exiting.

In the awkward silence that followed, as I zipped up my hoodie and left, my footsteps echoed on the floor as if on a stage. I opened the door to leave and saw that the waitress was still smiling.

+ + +

[Article Excerpt: "Sharply, Softly, Deeply: When What's In Focus Isn't All There Is To Be Seen," from *Lens Lover Magazine*, vol. 14 | Derrick van der Lem | October 24, 2002]

It was of a yellow butterfly with black-dotted patterning on ornate wings — a tiger swallowtail — resting on a magnificent blue cornflower. Even for the experienced backyard photographer, the contrasting colours were a beauty to behold. And yet my friend made two decisions that serendipitously changed the way I looked at photography from that point onward. For one, she used a tripod; the ambient light wasn't reliable and she didn't want to lean too heavily on her Leica M6's shutter speed. She also chose to situate the POV in a style different from many hobbyists; whereas most people shoot top-down — that is staring down at your subject — she instead set her camera so that she was more or less eye to eye with the blue cornflower. This combination allowed me to notice how rich and ghostly the out-of-focus areas of the photograph's background were, dappled with May daylight, as if with a brush.

The green leaves and organic *mise en scène* of the garden seemed to have a heavenly weight and depth to them; they had definition and yet, vis-à-vis the combination of light and lens, appeared as a mesmerizing sea of shapes within shapes. You see, the blur, the less essential material you manipulate within the frame as a means to centre the viewer's attention upon the focused object itself had character. The term for this is *bokeh*, from the Japanese *boke*, which means *blur*. It's the way in which each different lens — through a combination of optics and manufacturing — imparts an idiosyncratic shape and texture to the out-of-focus areas of a photograph. Quite often this effect is more evident in photos with a more dramatic contrast between foreground and background.

I have a great admiration for bokeh. It teaches us that there is depth in everything; that the clearly focused foreground, like the isolated mind of Descartes, may be the centre of our subjective universe, but it is only that way because it finds itself supported on the surface of a less-focused sea of background. Not only that, but the lack of focus itself has characteristics that enhance and compliment the whole.

It also makes me question my assumptions of photographic composition. I've since attempted to play with the dominance of my middle- and backgrounds, juggling lighting conditions that favour the sort of bokeh I'm searching for. Notice I use the word *searching*. This word has a great deal of significance for me because my approach to photography, even though I admit to being more of a hobbyist than a professional, has always been about self-discovery. What are my values? How have I equipped myself (or been equipped) to follow the rules of society, and how have I interpreted those rules?

+ + +

[Journal entry | Seneca Lewis | April 23, 2055]

I didn't have any problems with what they were saying. Technically.

I tried writing "I trust them" in this log. I couldn't. I thought that maybe I'd fucked up once again. I thought that I was now part of some cult. The end of the road for fuck-ups.

Today they told me straight-faced, "We have an experiment."

All this training. All this testing. And then they tell me that they have — wait for it — a TIME MACHINE. I can't believe I wrote that. Trust me, I was looking for hidden cameras when they spat that out.

They have, or claim they have, an honest-and-for-real time machine. They've tested it, and they want me to be the first person to try it.

I nearly threw up. I couldn't believe I'd gone through such a complete and supreme episode of gullibility. I expected my credit account to be empty when I got home. It was like being in an old David Mamet film.

Cathy said, "We like you, Seneca. We've been watching you for a while. We wouldn't approach you with this if we didn't think you were ideal."

Not to be neurotic, but I noted the fact that they didn't say that I was perfect. *Ideal*: yes. But why didn't they say something like *perfect*? There is a difference.

In any case, I can feel my mother rolling her eyes already, pre-emptively ready to admit what a moron I am. And our lack of shared genes becomes coldly apparent; the ease with which I once again feel put on probation as her daughter and the tentativeness of that existence.

I don't think I said anything intelligible to Cathy. It was just after a treadmill session, so I was tired. Maybe they chose that moment intentionally. It always seemed like they chose the moments where I was most vulnerable to spring some new exercise or test on me.

I was led into a boardroom and it was like an intervention. A bunch of people smiling cautiously. All of them standing. Standing up as if preparing for an ovation or to keep me from sprinting for the door. I am proud of the fact that I didn't flinch or show my fear. When Cathy walked me out afterwards, I called their bluff. I told her I wanted to see it. I wanted to see the fucking thing and see a test for myself before I even considered it.

What bugs me is that my demand — and I was absolutely trying to be difficult — seemed to make her happier. I thought she was going to give me a hug when we separated at the exit to their "municipal waste dispersal station." Everything so cloaked and hidden.

Strange people.

I started revising my resume and cover letter templates.

I will not cry.

+ + +

I SAT ON my picnic table in the dog bowl of Trinity Bellwoods, staring at Dr. Wallace Turner's card.

The man can't be sane, I thought.

I needed more: information, context, reasons to believe that this wasn't a reality show I would end up being asked to source stock music for later. Something massive seemed unresolved. I couldn't explain for myself what it was. Everything seemed to be moving forward with inevitability, as if I'd been placed on a conveyor belt after Dad passed away. Walking along Queen West on my way over, I passed a black-and-white flyer for a local salon stapled onto the poles of several street lights in a row. In large sans serif type the headline read:

SO LONG AS MAN

WANTS GOD ON EARTH

THERE WILL ALWAYS

BE A HITLER

It burned itself into my mind, obliterating whatever it was I'd been thinking, as if I'd stared at the sun.

There was a lot I didn't want to be concerned with: Dad's estate and my subsequent inheritance at the top, and somewhere in the middle there was returning to a career I'd never embraced beyond an affinity for music and short-term commitments. And I had no patience for the new breed of junior lawyer/film producer looking to license Alicia Keys tracks they knew they couldn't afford, if only they slowed down and thought about it, for productions that would be lucky to find distribution.

I couldn't figure out what I wanted to do and the aimlessness was alarming because it reminded me of where my head was prior to landing in a hospital. To keep myself occupied, if only to give me time to process Wallace's offer, I focused on a short queue of magazine and radio interviews I'd stalled on. Maybe *flaked out* is the best term. Most of the requests that had come in since Dad's death were cold because their filing deadlines had passed. I kept saying I'd get back to them, I'd get back to them. I told them I was recovering from grief, and to them that meant my father. To me it meant so many more things. It still does.

"Reflections on an Icon" was the working title of a proposed magazine piece. I did not return that person's email. I was also suspicious of anyone probing the circumstances of my extended time away. Otherwise, I didn't figure my fussiness was a great concern to the interviewers because, compared to the other people who played a larger role in Dad's life (friends, writers, lovers), I simply wasn't at the top of the list. Fair enough. It's not like I tried to compete for a spot on that list. I anticipated the tone of how I would be portrayed: the anonymous, slightly ungrateful (if not bitter) first child.

"And do you write?" one of them had asked.

"Yes. Fiction. Sometimes non-fiction."

"Derrick, was your father an influence on you?"

I couldn't respond to the question; the truth of how I felt blocked the door to polite exchange. My silence responded for me. The interviewer thought our wireless connection had been lost.

What do I say to that when whatever I have to say becomes categorized either as a commemoration to the man, or the admission of callousness on my part. What do I say when I pause to consider one legacy he left: his disparagement of Toronto. With its "limitless potential stifled by the chains of an inexplicable and painful earnestness." Toronto, with a "compulsive sincerity so paradoxically naive and corrupt as to render even the most mundane local community achievement an emancipation from the jackboot of the Family Compact." Pressing "the faces of young talent into the asphalt like cigarettes. The faithful search in vain and end up expatriates — conflicted gypsies."

"Sorry, are you still there?" the man on the other end asked.

"I honestly don't know," I'd said, shaking my head. I was relieved he couldn't see my expression.

+ + +

"HOW DOES IT WORK?"

"Well, it's not like in the movies. Again, no one is being physically transported anywhere, so you don't have to do much," Wallace explained.

"But...Okay? I don't understand."

We sat in a lounge close to where I lived. I'd set the condition, based upon our first meeting, that the Society of Experience pick up my bar tab wherever we meet, whether I was drinking club soda or Johnnie Walker Blue. I would at least bleed them of as much petty cash as possible.

"It's entirely virtual, synthetic, and for you it's even less of a concern. For you it's completely logistical."

"How's that?"

"Because you would be on the receiving end. You wouldn't be going anywhere, in time that is. Rather, you would be hosting. You would be hosting a projected traveller."

It contradicted everything I thought I was going to hear, regardless that part of me still thought it was probably all a joke.

"So I'm not going to be the time traveller."

"God, no. No, you wouldn't be a time traveller. We thought you'd be better suited as a host," Wallace said, holding his bottle of beer. "Besides, we're specifically interested in a subject from the future going back in time. If it were reversed, if we sent someone into the future, well, you could imagine how potentially shocking that could be. There's too much chance of the traveller...getting a bit overdosed, if you get my drift. With this sort of technology, with its inherent implications on the philosophical, not to mention psychological, direction of the participant — well, you only really want to go backward."

I looked away, searching darkly through my reactions.

"The past is known," he continued. "It's been recorded. It's done. What remains to be sorted out are the contextual details. From the viewpoint of those in the future, there's a predictability to the past that is obviously more accurate than any prediction we can make of their future. We can only make estimations and probability forecasts of the future, and those can only be constructed using existing and historic recorded data. It's complex. Lots of theory — some conflicting. Even in explaining this I'm doing more interpreting than informing, I know."

Was I supposed to nod? I took a sip from my Glenlivet. It almost felt like he was explaining this partially for his own clarification.

"Let me put this in different terms. Transporting someone from the 1800s to the present, you can imagine how shocking that would be, coming from an era that – technologically and intellectually speaking – was only on the cusp of theorizing about space and time they way we do now. That is, when they weren't busy killing or enslaving each other. You would have to explain to that person all of the leaps and bounds of thought that have occurred over the last hundred or so years just to keep their heads from exploding, and at the end of the day not only might he or she never truly understand what it is they are seeing, but when they go back to their original timeline they're like a ticking bomb, filled with facts and scientific information that – if unleashed to the world prematurely – would alter history for good. And we wouldn't be having this discussion, to say the least.

"Now, you would make a great host; you happen to be alive at a point when society's technological progress is such that the idea of hosting someone from a future where time travel is being actively developed is conceptually feasible. You are capable of understanding and accepting this, at least on a basic level. You wouldn't think the time traveller is a witch or an alien, I guess is what I'm trying to say, Derrick. Getting back to your comment about being a traveller, what can I say? You were born at the wrong time, experientially speaking, to go travelling back into the past. And your science marks in school were terrible, so that rules you out even if we had the technology in the present. So no, you're not going anywhere I'm afraid."

I stared at the space between Wallace and the votive candle that sat between us, flickering.

"You've obviously thought this through," I said. My mind was trying to keep pace with the logic, punctuated by flourishes of imagination and humour inspired by the subject matter. "So...what would I be agreeing to if I agreed to any of this?"

"As I've said, the Society is all about allowing people to experience opportunities to make their lives more fulfilling. You would sign the same contract anyone else would."

"Okay, contract. You still haven't answered my question: what am I agreeing to?"

"To share reality – the reality of now –" he pressed the tip of his finger on the table, "with someone from a future reality."

"Okay, but why me?" I blurted out. The argument had been building within me for days. "I don't understand...you've got this sci-fi breakthrough and you're picking me. Why not a scientist? Why not the latest Gandhi?"

"Understand, Derrick...We didn't decide on this quickly. It's taken well over a year to find a candidate. Our primary choices were, as you say, scientists and Gandhis. But experience, personal experience, is our speciality. We realized that sometimes it's just as valid to have, and pardon my saying this, unexceptional people participating in this."

I turned my glass around on its coaster contemplatively. "I suppose it also helps you to keep a low profile."

He smiled. "That too, sure. Remember when I asked you if you'd ever heard of Vijay Abapathy? I didn't exactly expect you to know of him."

"And tests. You've done tests on this?"

"Yes, of course: animal, vegetable, mineral. All appear perfectly with no long-term affects."

What about short-term?

"So who's being sent, or transported, or whatever the term is?"

"We can't really reveal that information now. This is a preliminary discussion. I can tell you that the visitor is as well-chosen as yourself."

I started chuckling. It was a painful, revealing laugh that came from the bottom of my belly.

God help the poor bastard.

"So, are you...Will you agree to go to the next level on this?"

"Which is what?"

"Sign the contract and the non-disclosure agreement and get more information."

+ + +

"TELL ME ABOUT your father."

It sounded more like Karen and not someone from CBC Radio. I was so tired of hearing about him. I was so tired of hearing how I must be so tired of hearing about him. Mind you, he was the one who died; I couldn't even get that much right. Early days, Derrick.

The reporter sat with me on a corner bench at a local patio. She came with a list of questions and a strategy that occasionally flattered my ego with sympathy. My loss. The weight on my shoulders. She should be my therapist. But the more attention I paid to her questions the more superficial they seemed. The thing is, what she didn't know is that I had this question burned into my head already; I'd quietly dared anyone previous to ask it.

Tell me about your father.

"No."

69

"May I ask why not?"

"Because if you had asked him the same question about me when he was alive, he'd give the same answer."

"So you feel he wasn't a ... Was he not a presence in your life?"

I felt like rolling up the sleeve on my left arm and unveiling his presence.

"Look, all writing is deception. Writers counterfeit reality. Whether it be a travelogue, or a poem, or something you jot down in your diary and forget about. It's a forgery. The fact we put things in writing doesn't auto-reckon them authentic or true."

Despite my defensiveness, I was surprised at how easily it came out. She was still, for a moment staring just past me, then began jotting down some thoughts. I was sure that whatever I said next would decide whether or not I would be portrayed as a sociopath.

"I mean, of course he was a presence," I said. "He existed, and on his terms. One of those terms was to leave me out of his life. As a son, a person, also a writer. I have no affection. I really didn't have a lot of affection for him."

"In light of how you describe your relationship, have you kept track of his work?"

I gritted my teeth, listening to the little angel inside my head pleading for me to understand that this interview, for a national broadcaster, wasn't about me but him. It would never be about me until I did something to warrant it.

"Yes," I said. "I believe I've read all of it."

Her eyebrows arched questioningly.

"Everything?"

"Yup."

It was mostly everything. It stacked two rows of my bedroom bookshelf.

She looked at her notepad as if someone else had been writing on it.

"Well, forgive me for pointing this out, but for someone who claims to have no relationship, that's... that's certainly interesting."

"I didn't have a relationship with him, but I tried. I tried very hard for a while, and in the end it became about reading his work. That was how I stayed in touch."

"That's fifteen books."

I nodded

"And as many of the magazine articles as were available."

"And what did you find?"

Good question. I paused, staring at my drink.

"A wanderer. A very good writer. Except when it regarded individuals. If you read a piece like the one from *Benelux*, you'll notice how he never really enters the subjective space of the people he encounters in his travels. He's at his best when he's surveying empty terrain." I began to think of his idea of the abandoned cathedral. "I think empty environments spoke to him," I continued. "I think he was much happier being an outsider. Even if it meant forcing himself into that position."

+ + +

[Notebook excerpt | Derrick van der Lem | May 5, 2008]

Our — that would be mankind's — attempt at time travel reflects our limited ability to imagine it in practical terms, and paradoxically our ideas are choked by that perennial baby step called virtualization. Even though the Society tells me it's real, it's not. In the same breath, I am told it works.

Considering the advanced levels of science, mathematics and engineering involved, the process is surprisingly approachable. According to Wallace – if indeed it works – they planned it over a very, very long time, knowing that time itself was their putty.

Rather than projecting a complex vertebrate organism through time physically, they rely on an advanced prototype, which blends nanotechnology and quantum advanced-spectrum wireless communication. I don't exactly know what this means, but I am told it is this what serves as a gateway between future and present. Except, of course, their present is my future and their past is my present.

Someone fits into a harness – a bodysuit – which is inlaid with these microdermal sensors that can communicate with your nerve endings and transmit incoming and outgoing info to them. At the base of the volunteer's cerebral cortex an additional cluster of sensors are attached. Signals from the harness are sent to a capsule. Inside the capsule is a nanoscopic sheath, which picks up signals from the human subject/volunteer. Being nanoscopic, the contraption cannot be perceived by the human eye.

Height and width. Thoughts and emotions. Everything is transmitted from the bodysuit to the nanoscopic sheath – I wish I could think of a better term for it than nanoscopic sheath because it looks obscene on paper.

It can rearrange itself through a combination of signals from the human harness and directions from lab supervisors sent via wireless signals into a physical shape – even that of the human host. It is the probe or "sheath" that is projected into the chosen time period. It picks up and transmits sensory information on an intimate level from the future-local volunteer; it communicates bidirectionally with the suit harness and thus relays information back to the human subject. I was told a lot more, but this is all I could manage to scribble down after my chat with Wallace.

Or so I am told. A part of me thinks I'm a born sucker. I may be right.

+ + +

"CAN I SEE IT?"

I pushed the signed contract across the table toward Wallace.

"See... the machine? No, it doesn't exist yet."

"Interesting," I said, watching him tuck the papers into his leather case. I realized I should have asked that question earlier.

"So how do you know it works? How do you know where and how this all happens if you don't have the machine? I don't get it."

"We know what we know because the Society – its membership in the future at least – has verified it with us. This has been successfully tested, Derrick. Trust me."

"So... what, a piece of paper appeared in your office one day. 'Everything's cool,' signed The Future?"

"No. An orange, actually," he said. "One year, many years after we started this particular venture, we discovered that an orange had appeared on our table. We'd set aside a specific table, in a specific room, in a specific building as a point of communication between us, here and now, and whatever our speculation at the time figured was out there. We used some cheap card table that had been sitting in the basement since the '50s. It was monitored constantly. This went on for a number of years."

"Why an orange?"

"Don't know, really. For all their genius, scientists can be goofy. We don't talk much between here and there — or then, as it were — because of energy concerns. Energy is very precious, there as well as here."

"So, the traveller is going to appear on your table."

"No, but we're hoping it will be somewhere near you. I'm not convinced your apartment will suffice due to a slew of reasons, least of which is your personal convenience, unfortunately. The deal as I understand it is that someone will call you at home just before the projection procedure is started. You will then be given instructions, with coordinates. From there, you will proceed to retrieve the projected traveller's nanoscopic sheath. And again, like I said, though it's in everyone's best interest to transmit the probe somewhere near you, where is up to them ultimately. They own the toys."

"Understood."

"We come to our most important topic now."

"And it's not a flesh-and-blood person who's coming, it's…"

"It's the sheath, yes. Correct, Derrick. A nanoscopic sheath."

"Can he move?"

"Yes. They move and the sheath moves. As I was saying earlier, it senses on behalf of the instructions sent by the person on the other end. I think we've discussed this."

"And I'll be able to see it."

"Yes. A little fuzzy at times though. Now," he looked around us carefully, "the important topic…You've read the part in the agreement about non-disclosure?" He looked at me as I collected my thoughts. "In particular, you've read the section 'Duties of The Host'?"

"Yeah, sure." I shrugged. "I went through most of it." Half of me still thought I was on a reality show and that at any time, with an exuberant chorus of SURPRISE, this would all be revealed as an elaborate ruse. For the first time I saw something akin to anxiety in Wallace's eyes. I saw him swallow it, and then, feigning polite offence, he squared me in his sights.

"Okay. Derrick, you have to work with us on this one. We're allowing you in on an incredible opportunity and in return we need some assurances. Sober assurances." He leaned in closer. "Reverent assurances."

"Sorry. Okay, yeah."

"We know about the suicide," he said, averting his eyes to the ceiling. "Sorry, your attempted suicide."

He looked at me as if he held a gun under the table. "We know more about you than you do. We know you can be trusted, yes, but it doesn't mean we don't also expect you to proceed with your full attention and respect for those who have worked very, very hard to make this happen. Do I make myself clear?"

"Um, yeah."

"Sorry?"

"Yes. I understand."

I know they knew about the suicide – the nurse was their plant, after all. But I didn't expect Wallace to place it on the table like that: a bargaining tool. I'd never seen him angry, and the shock shot through my head like a drug. Realizing that there wasn't a fourth wall with an audience behind it. Realizing what I'd just signed and handed over, from every caution I'd heard growing up: if it's too good to be true, it probably is.

It probably was. And yet, despite it all, it still seemed more fun than reality.

+   +   +

[Notebook excerpt | Derrick van der Lem | May 12, 2008]

The duties of the host, contained in the two-page document I was handed, are more complex than the phrase implies. You are called a host, yet you are not there to serve Manhattans or display your etiquette skills. You are not required to know a form of ballroom dance.

A certain Isaac Asimov once remarked that time travel was proven impossible by the lack of artifacts. By artifacts, he meant garbage. Human nature and human limitations dictate that something inevitably would be left behind by any time traveller. A clue in the form of litter. A mistake. And there is simply, literally, no proof.

Think of the last vacation you spent somewhere far away, or in, say, a local park. Having something as inoffensive as a cup of coffee. You pass by, not rustling a feather, and yet the smallest absent-mindedness and you make an impression that can be measured afterwards. Every communication and interaction leaves physical traces, if only in the memories of strangers. People see you on the street. And if one of those strangers should talk to you? And if that talk should alter the orbit of that person's thoughts that day? A left turn when they were supposed to take a right? If it stops them ordering the magazine they were fated to buy, to read that article they had bookmarked?

Wallace tells me that it's all part of what they call the block universe concept of time travel. He tells me that the structure of time is fixed and you're just going back and forth on a fixed course, like moving a craft along a canal.

(But inevitably there must be a reaction to something, right? Something that shouldn't naturally have happened at a particular time, even if the interloper can't be seen?)

Anyhow, just as a precaution, it's the job of the host to minimize the risks. I do not:

1) Discuss the future, for idle interest or for profit.

2) Expose the projection/traveller to third parties unless sanctioned by the Society.

3) Allow them to be photographed, their voice or image captured, be positioned in front of windows or access unrestricted data networks.

You know, light stuff.

I can only assume the person who drew up these rules was promptly shot, thrown into a cab and then dumped in the lake, the cab subsequently set on fire and the driver drugged and sent to live in a village in Nepal.

Noticeably lacking from the rules are positive things. Suggestions, for example, of approved conversation topics, card games, etc....

My fear is that I'll be stuck with a weird, semi-electronic flickering thing that just wants to sit and watch television all day — in other words, someone like me and not someone different.

+   +   +

IT WAS TOO WARM for ice, yet too early and dreary for flowers and fountains at city hall. Downtown had a purgatorial complexion: expansive and blandly concrete. I sat on one of the benches by the drained skating rink in Nathan Phillips Square. It took only a few minutes for me to realize how dim-witted I'd been in choosing it: would it not have been harder to be tracked in any one of the hundreds of lesser-known bars and cafés across the city? But Nathan Phillips meant not drinking and for once I didn't want alcohol to help me talk, whatever the words ended up being. There was too much to say and so much of that I was contractually bound not to repeat. I hoped to keep it vague, for Paul's sake and mine. I called him on a pay phone down the street from my apartment. If I decided to snitch on them, I didn't know the extent of the Society's preparations; nor their disciplinary measures. I tried to recall ever hearing of some-one – anyone – involved with or talking about a "society" of anything. All I could think of were musicians' guilds. Nothing came up on Google, save for the fact that I could reserve the web domain should I wish to start a site.

"Comrade!"

It was Paul, smiling, suitably dressed in a black wool trench coat. He approached, waving, as if trying to catch my atten-tion above a throng of imaginary tourists, drawing attention to the fact that we were the only two people in the area.

"Thanks for making it out."

"No worries," he said, taking a seat beside me on the bench, folding his hands into his coat. "I was at an audition in the east end! Some sort of TV special or something. They wanted a tall, Italian-looking guy." He smiled and shook his head in disbelief.

"Then why did they call you?"

Paul's hair was dark, but his eyes were blue-green. His parents were Irish. Put a beret on him and he'd barely pass for French.

"Beats me, but we clicked: they liked me, I liked them. Maybe they'll be nice and let me add more lines for my character."

His idea stuck with me. I wondered what it would be like to have that kind of power; to change the script I seemed to follow, not just a coordinate in someone else's larger, smarter plan.

"That's great news. That's the most excited you've ever been about an audition. You normally beat yourself up after them."

"I know."

"Actually, you hate auditions."

"I know!" he said, sticking his chest out proudly. "So, what's going on with you? What's with city hall?" He smiled curiously, nodding to the parenthetical towers behind us. "Running for city council? Got some dirt on the mayor?"

I found myself stalling, wondering if anyone was listening.

"I'll try to shorten a long story for you. It's a bit odd."

"I've come to expect odd things from you."

"So, I'm... I've volunteered for something."

Paul smiled and nodded, noticing a small tour group pacing around the other end of the rink. He looked back at me. "So, like, what then?"

I couldn't answer.

"Adopting a foreign baby?"

"No."

"Reality show contestant?"

I chuckled, trying to preserve the seriousness.

"No. Look, there's this group, okay? They arrange things very elaborately. And very discreetly, or at least that's what they tell me."

"Escort service?" He leaned in and whispered, "Prostitutes creep me out."

"No. And they're called sex workers."

"I'll stop, sorry."

I looked at him, irritated. "They're... a sort of group, society... fellowship." I wanted to be vague, but I realized I wouldn't be able to convey much of anything if that were the case. It was beginning to snow. White petals began drifting down around us.

"That's interesting."

"Yeah, they are that. They're very interesting. Very secretive too." I looked at him and raised my eyebrows, attempting to pantomime my concern.

"Freemasons?"

"No. No, not Freemasons. I don't know what they are..." I took a deep breath, and with that last sentence stuck in my head: "I'm going to be involved in a...a sort of study. A sort of scientific...uh, thing."

I was never going to say what I actually wanted to say. The snow was falling more heavily, in larger wet flakes.

"Wow. No shit?" Paul's smile became a scrutinizing smirk.

"Yeah." I rose to my feet. I needed to keep walking but I wasn't sure whether it was because I was getting cold or that I was a sitting target if anyone wanted to spy on us. We walked north, passing city hall on our way up to Dundas. Paul was dotted with snow, which began to bind into clumps in his hair.

"Like, is this like – and I know that you can't talk about it, or at least that's the impression I'm getting..."

"Yes. Thanks."

"...but is this thing, like, some sort of government thing. Is it a university thing?" He parodied my facial expressions of concern.

"Yes and no. It's an experiment, basically...It's a secret experiment. There are machines and things involved." I caught myself motioning with my hands and felt once again like an actor.

"Wow."

"Wow, yes. Very wow...I'm kinda risking a lot telling you. That kind of wow."

Paul leant toward my ear.

"What are you risking?" His tone was serious.

Glancing at each other, it became sadly clear that the only guidelines we knew for these sorts of situations were provided by espionage movies. I said nothing for a long while.

"What am I risking...?" I stared at some playground equipment, mindlessly noting their bright colours. "Possibly the most interesting opportunity in my life, Paul. Possibly...? I don't know."

He dipped his chin against his chest as if to conjure something delicate.

"But...no one's going to beat you up or anything...For telling me, right?"

I needed to hear this part of him. The big brother. Someone who cared about my welfare.

"I'm not sure," I said. Then, reluctantly, "I signed a contract..."

His expression shifted dramatically.

"Oh boy," he shook his head. "Oh boy. Most horror stories include the line 'So, I signed this contract.'"

"I know. I know. But it could also be a big fucking joke."

I was relieved to say this to someone. The more I believed that I was just a contestant on a weird reality show the calmer I became. I turned to him: "But that's why I'm telling you. I haven't broken any rules telling you what I have just now. I just need to tell someone in case it is some sort of scam...or trap, or something."

"I see," he said. Given the scarcity of information I'd provided, it seemed he was unable to say much more than that.

"I know, I know. It's silly bringing you here and pretending we're in *Three Days of the Condor*. But I need a witness. I've gone through so much crap — and, trust me, I'm getting tired of saying that — but I have been through a lot of crap. I need a witness. I end up walking away from things, whether it be out of a hospital, or an apartment I can't afford, or a relationship. I'm tired of being the only person who witnesses things, with only myself to prove that those things actually happened." I looked at him quizzically. "Does that make sense?"

Paul nodded, looking around as if for a cause for doubt.

"I respect that. I mean, I wish I could help you directly — i.e., you telling me flat out what's going on so that I can be something more than what I am right now, which is, no offence, a bystander. Maybe an accomplice. Who knows? But no, I understand. You're trying to be fair to...whatever menacing cult they may be."

"Yeah."

A breeze drifted in from the lake and gave us pause, taking turns glancing at the pulsing weather beacon atop the Canada Life Building.

"Are you at least getting paid?"

"Believe it or not, I haven't asked." Then, as if wishing for a way to remove myself from how moronic I felt, a nagging note of business occurred to me. "It goes without saying, even though you probably have no clue what any of this is about or means: no one can know what we're talking about. Not you, not your barber. And Karen can absolutely never hear about this."

"I knew you were going to say that." He was shaking his head.

"About it being a secret?"

"No, about Karen. For fuck's sake..."

I snatched glances at him, trying to keep from flinching. I had a sense of what was coming.

"Let's get something straight: for the record, I don't actually speak to Karen, right? She and I weren't friends before you met, and since you guys broke up the first time, I've had no reason — nice person though she seemed to be — to contact her. You know this, right?"

"I know, I know. Maybe I don't know. I'm sorry."

"It's just...look, don't worry about me. As for Karen, that's none of my business. Not my pig, not my farm."

"Okay. Sorry."

I hadn't thought much of her, not since meeting Wallace. It made me feel good. Paul raised his hands, as if to wave away any ill will between us.

"No worries. So, when does this thing...er, whatever it is, start?"

"Soon. Next few days. Someone's going to call me, and then..."

"And then the fun begins, right? Right?" He grinned, nudging my shoulder with his elbow. I smiled, feeling ten years younger, but I was still worried. It all confirmed the extraordinary: the experiment was happening soon. I needed to clean the apartment. Buy soap. Pretend someone lived there who was alive.

+ + +

"I'VE HAD A communication from our associates."

Wallace sat behind me on the park bench in the dog bowl, our backs to one another. His demeanour seemed deflated, hard as it was for me to read him under normal circumstances. I'd been sweeping the apartment when I received his call. There was a tinge of annoyance in his voice on the phone; it was normally very calm. I'd even practiced it to myself many times when I did the dishes. It was a model of measurement and balance.

"A couple of things for you," he began, looking away, a Styrofoam cup of coffee in front of him. Cory, the terrier I'd met weeks earlier, was absent. "First: the experiment commences tomorrow night – I hope you're prepared."

Oh, there you are, heartbeat.

He reached into a small canvas hiker's bag hanging from his shoulder and produced what looked to be paperwork with graphics on it. I reached over and took them, adjusting my eyes as I scanned them, realizing they were copies of someone's notes.

"Your guest," he began, staring at the horizon, "keeps a journal."

I flipped through the pages quickly, surprised at what I'd been handed, yet fascinated by the evidence. For the first time, I was beginning to believe this wasn't a joke.

He continued while I scoured over the pages: "For the record, I object to this. Handing out people's personal things. I don't think it's right that you have this privilege. However, rules are rules and hierarchies are hierarchies, and a sub-council chair decided that, for sake of your..." he seemed to swallow his displeasure over the matter, "curiosity, it was best that you knew about your guest in advance."

"Best that I know what, exactly?"

"Well, what you're getting into," he said, as if it were apparent. "To be honest, Derrick, there was a crisis of confidence in you. Within the upper ranks. I had to level with them, tell them that you were, shall we say, hesitant in the beginning, but worth the investment overall. I had to do some soft-shoe. Somehow – and this is above my pay grade – they must have ended up bending some rules and requested something to prove the reality of all of this to you. So, yes, please rest assured if you are not yet convinced: you are real, your guest is real. This is really happening. For real."

I looked off to the side in astonishment, listening intently to the echo of what Wallace said, the journal entries rolled up in my hand like a scroll of ancient spells.

"And if you fuck this up, I will hunt you down myself."

I froze and slowly turned around to look at him.

"That's a joke," he said, barely breaking a smile. "I don't tell jokes well. My wife reminds me of this whenever we have company."

I was speechless. He kept me on edge, between fear and curiosity, as if by intent. If he hadn't admitted it was a joke I would've called the police.

"Anyway, this is a day off for me. I've got guests coming for a barbecue. Have a read." He nodded to the pages. "And again, keep all of this to yourself. What we do involves a careful dissemination of privileged information. It's kept this way so that your experiences in the coming days are untainted by expectation. I want you to appreciate the magnitude of the exception we have made for you."

With a disconcerting nod, Wallace stood up from the picnic table and made his way up the sloping lane that led out of the dog bowl. With the papers rolled under my arm, I rubbed my face with my palms. The skin of my face felt like it hadn't been touched in years. Slowly, I looked around as if I'd just woken up. There were no dogs or people, no birds sang. The voices of children above were silenced. The wind was missing.

+ + +

[Excerpt from "The Injured Cowboy and the Sheriff of the Mesa Jumanes" | Derrick van der Lem |September 17, 2006]

The Injured Cowboy was by no means a stranger to the sight of a town in fear, but when he approached Jicarillo, emaciated from his travels through the barren Mesa Jumanes, he had second thoughts about entering. There might as well have been a storm cloud over the town. Two wagons he'd passed, and two sets of miserable townsfolk looked at him as if the sight of him only added to their misery.

If there was anything less sought-after in the cowboy's life on that scorched New Mexico plain, it was being the wrong stranger at the wrong time in a town that lynched to cure its ills. But he needed rest, and his everlasting wounds needed their due attention.

Sheriff Cogill sat on the porch of a grain merchant, perched at a bend in the main road so he could view both of the main entrances to town. Seeing the stranger hunched in his saddle, over his mare, Alabelle, his clothes bleached by the sun, the holster on his belt, the sheriff came out and blocked their path. Not wanting any trouble, the cowboy tugged lightly on the reins. Alabelle resisted. She wanted to get out of the sun as badly as he did.

"You here on business, stranger?" the sheriff called up to him, his eyes squinting past the brim of his hat.

The cowboy stared at him and saw his badge, the gestures of anticipation in his pistol hand, and the marriage ring on the other. Raising his arm carefully, he tipped his hat to the sheriff, a show of caution on his face.

"Sheriff, I can't say I'm here on business. I've come a long way — through the Mesa and the plains. I was hoping I could rest in Jicarillo for the night. Plan to make my way to White Oaks in the morning, if that'd please you."

"That gun's troublin' to me, stranger. You runnin' from somethin'?" he asked. His suspicions were clear.

"The gun's no trouble to you or anyone in Jicarillo, Sheriff. As for running, I can't say I come from anywhere that's looking for my neck to hang. I'm just drifting through, looking to pay for a bed and perhaps a barkeep for a libation. That's all."

Without a sound, the sheriff begrudgingly waved him on. The cowboy felt worse than when he'd entered. He tipped his hat toward the sheriff and proceeded to locate a dilapidated inn at the centre of town.

+   +   +

YOU IDIOT.

I paced through the apartment while Elvis Costello's "(The Angels Wanna Wear My) Red Shoes" played on the stereo. I needed the comfort of music but found myself skipping over almost every track, unable to find anything that wasn't too fast, too dippy or too dark.

For the second time, I was living a moment that was soundtrack-proof. I was treading back and forth from the kitchen to the living room absent-mindedly, finding only second thoughts.

Despite the extravagant lunacy of the time traveller–host proposition, what happened earlier in the night gripped me. I'd been looking out the north window of the apartment, onto the traffic below, creaking in anticipation of a green light. I saw an ad covering the side of a passing transport container: three attractive young women coiled on a rug, staring at me seductively. The phone rang, catching me by surprise. I picked up and heard a click on the line, as if the other party had hung up. Rather than the signal dying, a soft wash of static surfaced on the other end.

The stern voice of a woman clearly pronounced: "This is a pre-recorded message. Please write down the following information. We will pause, to allow you to get a writing utensil and paper."

The way she spoke seemed practiced; the way she accentuated "writing utensil," as if I were standing in candlelight, holding a quill. There was a notepad and pencil by the phone already. I stood, blinking numbly, listening to the white noise on the other end of the line. My blood seemed to stop flowing. The air seemed to stop moving.

"Derrick van der Lem," she continued, "you are to collect your guest this evening at nine-thirty p.m., or twenty-one thirty hours."

With the same formality she described the pick-up location as if it were the itinerary of a grocery run. It was on the outskirts of my 'hood, in a residential alley in Little Italy.

"Please note: you must be alone. Do not attract automobile or pedestrian traffic. After you make contact, assist the projected sheath immediately back to safe quarters. If there is any risk of discovery, you may use a limousine or taxi. Just remember —"

A thud against my front door jolted my attention away from the receiver. It took a panicked moment to realize it was the upstairs neighbour hauling her bike through the stairwell again. When I shifted my attention back to the phone I realized the woman was still talking in her careful, assured tone. She had been talking the entire time.

"...three zero four," she said.

The blood drained from my face.

"Please respond with either a yes...or...no...in the subsequent pause, to confirm that you understand the instructions we have provided."

Awkward pause.

"Um, I didn't hear the number you just read..." I said, focusing carefully on what I was going to say next.

"Thank you."

click

I stood listening, in a dawning panic, not wanting to hang up, hoping desperately that I'd get a second chance. But with each passing second the chances that a second operator would intervene eroded. There would be a fail-safe, for sure, I thought.

Abruptly, I was returned to the cold organ chime of dial tone.

"No. No!" I beat my fist against the wall.

Dr. Wallace Turner had all but disappeared; I called his number five times without an answer.

It was 20:46, which both the living room and kitchen clocks verified mercilessly as I paced around the apartment.

My last call to Wallace went as follows: "Wallace. It's Derrick....Um, just checking. Thanks. Bye."

I had to leave, but into what kind of disaster I couldn't imagine.

I tore off the notepad page, complete with incomplete information, and stuffed it in my pocket...

You moron....

and on a new page penned a bullet point Last Will and Testament with startlingly few revisions. I stashed the pages in a discarded toilet paper cylinder behind the kitchen stove, unable to improvise a better spot to hide them.

You're going to get killed out there.

+ + +

[Journal entry | Seneca Lewis | May 29, 2055]

They just gave me the date and told me to come to the lab that night for seven-thirty. I know it'll take at least an hour to slip on the suit (which seems like a piece of fetish gear, to be honest) and test it, but they mentioned I'd have a relaxant to drink this time. Yum. I hope it's scotch.

The morbid part, completing my will (!), went uneventfully. You don't know how both complex and simple this sort of thing can be until you're obligated to do it. Of course, Cathy kept downplaying it — it being my fear. If she hadn't I'd probably be writing this in another country, hiding in Labrador or something. Nervous.

The good thing is that she assured me that they would call the host ahead of time — I still have no clue who the host is — just to make sure that everything goes smoothly. I have no choice but to trust her on this. Secretly, I hate that.

Wish me luck, whoever reads this (and by the way, who are you and why are you reading this?). Contact info for the Society follows below, in case this goes, well, badly. I'm slipping this in a chip under my mattress. It's the kind of spot only detectives in movies would consider checking.

Love (certainly to most of you),

Seneca

+ + +

NINE-BLOODY-THIRTY.

In an alley.

Black seemed an appropriate colour. I caught myself in the hallway mirror on the way out, wearing a black turtleneck and leather jacket, with black jeans: I looked like a French cat burglar.

My gut ached from stress and I couldn't clear my head. Laundry hadn't been done. The hydro bill was overdue. I still needed to sand and refinish that vintage dresser I bought on Roncesvalles last year.

"Hey! Do you know where the liquor store is?"

A kid with oversized athletic clothing was standing on the opposite sidewalk, staring at me. It was nine-fifteen. I looked ahead of me then back at the kid, until a few seconds ago convinced of my invisibility.

"Uhh…"

"Look, you know if there's one around here?"

"There's…uhh…"

"Bro, I just wanna know where the fucking liquor store is. You speak English? The liquor store. *Onde fica a loja de bebidas?*" the kid shouted, a cigarette bouncing out the side of his lips.

I shrugged stupidly and continued up toward College Street, humiliated and rattled.

An old card table.

An orange.

An accident guest starring me as an unwitting accomplice who can't take directions.

Son, could you tell the officer here about the strange man you saw on the night of the sixth of June?

Yeah, he was, like, this guy. And shit. And, like, I kept asking him where the liquor store is. And, like, he just stood there. Like he was stupid, or lost, or something.

This is where I disappeared, where all of my afternoon alley walks came into play. I cut across the playground in Fred Hamilton Park and continued through a service lane behind the Dominion grocery store at Crawford, then doubled back south. I accessed the alley system at Montrose, which kept me parallel with the bustle of College without the foot traffic and witnesses, taking me across to Grace. From there I slipped south to Henderson to avoid patio crowds, crossing Clinton to Manning. I took a breath and looked behind to make sure no one was following.

BZZZZZZ

I shoved my hand into my jacket and pulled out my phone. The display read: KAREN.

BZZZZZZ

Um, no, Karen.

BZZZZZZ

I turned into the appointed alley, sheltered by a five-storey commercial building on the north side, hydro cables like black tentacles. I'd been here before, taking photos during late summer. With her camera. The alley traversed several blocks. Ten metres ahead it intersected with a residential laneway lined with garages. While the alley was strewn with gravel and pockmarked with mudholes, the laneway was concavely paved to allow rainwater and melting ice to drain through large sewer grates.

I couldn't hear anything suspicious above the dull thrum off College. Street lights on hydro posts took the shadows to task. I checked my watch as I approached the intersection — nine-thirty p.m., she said — then lifted my eyes to spot a dark object lying on the pavement, halfway down the lane. I couldn't remember checking my watch. I couldn't remember what time I'd just read. I stood frozen, fixated by the shape on the ground, willing myself to be truly invisible. Better still, willing myself to be at home. Safe. Getting drunk.

I wasn't sure what I was looking at. Mercury vapour lamps overhead, bright and cold, made the object harder to discern.

That's not an orange, I thought.

I couldn't deny what I saw. Even from this distance, no matter how much I wanted to believe it was a black garbage bag. I crept on the toes of my old army boots to get a closer look, the matter becoming less real and more movie-like.

It moved. A leg. Twitch.

I stopped mid-step. It was human. It was someone in a dark bodysuit sprawled on the side of the lane. I wanted to say something, but was interrupted by the sound of soft footsteps on the alley gravel behind me. I leapt as quietly as possible, prancing bluntly toward the deep shadow of a garage overhang. The person-shaped thing was lying across from me. I couldn't say what temperature it was outside, because I was sweating as if I'd ran here in August.

"Steven, why are you being such an asshole?" sobbed a young woman's voice from the alley.

Standing still, I stared into the blackness for the source of the racket. The crunch and slew of loose gravel underneath footfalls, isolated in space as if pre-recorded.

Answer her, Steven...

"Answer me!" she pleaded.

I looked again and confirmed that there was a person — a woman — lying across from me on the pavement.

"Look, why the fuck don't you talk to me?" a young male voice responded.

I crept forward, exposing myself in the light. I knew that if they walked further down the alley, they'd see me standing here like a...guy picking up a body in the alley. I squatted by her, my knees shaking. I had to remember to breathe as my brain dealt with the events, my eyes filling with shooting stars of anxiety.

"Because you're being an asshole!" she yelled.

The bodysuit was like something a scuba diver would wear, complete with hood and black goggles.

"If I'm being an asshole," Steven shout-whispered, "it's because everybody keeps talkin' about you. And I haven't fucking heard shit from you in a week. A week."

"Well, 'cause I don't wanna talk, that's all."

In the split second I had to consider the weight of their arguments, I felt hers didn't sound convincing.

I reached over and found what I hoped was the right spot on the stranger's neck. Pulsing. Warm. There was a sector of my mind yelling that this was no projection or sheath. A bunch of reflective particles? This wasn't blurry and it sure as hell wasn't virtual. It was a real person and she was unconscious, possibly dying.

"Just tell me! What's the problem?" Steven pleaded.

I knelt down to pick her up, changing my footing to support her weight. Her body was in a state between stiff and pliant. I was able to lift her torso up and, wrapping my arm under her legs, I tried to lift her body, but a hot lightning bolt shot up my left arm: nerves healing, now on fire. It was her legs. I couldn't support her legs with my arm. Not for ten blocks. Not for ten yards.

"Just tell me!"

Somewhere a sports car with a custom muffler was blaring Portuguese hip hop.

In lieu of waiting for what happened next, I lifted her off the pavement, turning her so that her torso was bent over my shoulder. She exhaled as I steadied her, my arm throbbing from the stress. She was heavier in parts and lighter in others. As a package, she made no sense. I raised myself as best I could — lift with your legs, I could hear a legion of manual labourers in my head cry out — my body half hunched over, staggering with her on my back south to Dundas West, away from where the young couple stood their ground. It fed into another alley system. If anyone saw me now, I was a dead man.

"Fine, Steven! I'm pregnant, okay? I'm pregnant!"

I stopped and cocked my ear around, the body draped over my shoulder, as I took deep, stuttering breaths.

"What the fuck?" Steven said.

Indeed.

Her leg twitched. I abandoned the conversation and struggled to carry the stranger hunchbacked down the lane.

+ + +

I HELD MY ARM tenderly, catching my breath, watching her on the mattress unfold like a specimen thawing. She was of medium height, though her suit was so constrictive it seemed she could have been any size, any height.

I sat in a chair I'd brought in from the kitchen, facing her on the mattress, not quite knowing what to do.

"Hello," I said. "What's your name?"

It was the fifth time I'd asked since I'd carried, then dragged and eventually taxied her to my apartment, a distance easily walkable alone, but much too far with a body over my back. I'd convinced the cab driver I was just helping a drunk friend. Despite the pathetic transparency of my story, her glimmering black skin-suit and goggles, the driver didn't ask any questions, perhaps for fear of being implicated in the absurdity of our situation.

"Remember: you must be alone. Do not attract car or pedestrian traffic."

I held the remnants of a harsh whisky in a teacup, bracing my nerves and my dizzied head with every sip.

"I have no goddamned clue who or what you are," I slurred, looking at the twitching shadow on the bed.

No response.

I set the glass on the floor. I wanted to undress her, worried that it may be unhealthy for someone to recuperate...

Can you believe this is happening?...wearing a skin-tight suit. For the sake of keeping things professional, I decided not to. After some searching online, it seemed she had a healthy pulse: 65 beats per minute. I couldn't help but also find that it was the same bpm as "Misty" by Johnny Mathis.

I took off my clothes in the washroom, changing into a sweatshirt and flannel bottoms. At first I figured I'd sleep on the couch but, not knowing if she would need medical attention, I decided it would be best to stay close to her. I switched off the light on the bedside table, then rounded the mattress and pulled my side of the duvet over, slipping in beside her. She was breathing steadily.

Keep it up, Space Girl.

I named her Space Girl.

Wallace hadn't called. No one had called. Or texted. I'd even gone down to check the mailbox. Nothing. Just the two of us and an incomplete set of instructions.

"What's your name?" I whispered, my head feeling so heavy against the pillow. I stared at her silhouette. Kate Bush was playing downstairs. I glanced at the sweaty strands of blonde hair, poking out of her elastic headcap, pressed like wet petals against her cheek.

"And while we're at it, where the hell do you come from?"

I drifted to sleep, exhaustion overtaking me, and noted that she turned her head toward me before I disappeared.

+ + +

IT WAS LIKE a dream.

I woke to the smell of coffee. Dexter Gordon was playing from the kitchen radio down the hall. I was lying in the centre of the mattress, realizing that last night's events were not imaginary by virtue of the fact that I couldn't possibly be here and in the kitchen at the same time. I sat up slightly, propping myself on my elbows, and looked around the room to make sure no one else was there with me.

The faucet in the kitchen turned on then off. Nothing.

I called, "Hello?"

I looked out to the hallway without knowing who or what to expect.

Nothing. A silence I couldn't recognize. The silence of two people rather than one.

"Hel-lo." A woman's voice: bright but deep.

I sat up and crossed my legs, not knowing how best to break the stalemate. The hellos weren't greetings so much as

Marco Polo confirmations that something indeed happened last night.

More two-person silence.

"Are you who I think you are?" I asked, careful not raise my voice too much, shaking my head at how strange it sounded. This is what they say in movies.

The sound of feet padding on the floorboards toward my room, and then I saw a long shadow in the morning light approach the doorway. She poked her head in, a tangled bob of curly blonde hair with an overwhelmed smile.

"Hi," she said.

I sat in my flannels staring as she crept completely into view. She looked nothing like I'd expected — first, the black suit was off. She wore an ill-fitting assemblage of my clothes: a pair of jeans with the pant legs rolled up into cuffs, a black T-shirt that hung below her waist. Her hair was tied back with an elastic.

"Hi," I said.

"What's your name?"

I was surprised by the question. I'd presumed, somewhat foolishly, that she would have known the answer already. It occurred to me: her diary. The pages were in my office desk drawer, thankfully not sitting out on display. The question dawned whether she'd been encouraged to read anything I had written...

"Derrick," I said, clearing my throat. I waved.

"I'm Seneca."

"Seneca. Nice to meet you."

"Yeah, you too," she smiled calmly. "I was looking around, you know, trying to find your name — no luck. Don't you subscribe to a letter-mail service?"

"I don't get much mail," I said, then, "Sorry, did you say *Seneca*?"

"Yup. Do you want coffee?"

It was too much to handle, given how little time I'd been awake. She didn't seem to know me, or she was a good enough liar not to set off suspicion.

I tried to do the same.

"How long have you been up?"

"Don't ask," she grinned. It was mischievous, and her face was blushing. "I'm ... let's just say I'm making coffee because if I don't I'm gonna freak out." She chuckled, looking around the room incredulously.

"Understood," I smiled.

"Coffee: is that a yes?"

"Yes, please — thanks." I got up slowly, undecidedly, while she turned back toward the kitchen. The first thing that occurred to me was not the possibility of tangible proof of time travel's practical existence via quantum mechanics, but that I rarely allowed guests to make coffee: it usually ended up being weak.

"It's a bit strong," Seneca/Space Girl called out from the kitchen. "I hope that's okay. It took me a while to figure out the gas ignition."

"Perfect!"

I grabbed a pair of jeans and a dress shirt and started wondering about who she was, this stranger.

"So, how are you feeling?" I asked while getting changed.

"Oh boy ... where to start. Tired, mainly. Mind and body. A little disoriented. A little confused."

"I know what you mean."

"I'm just flying by the seat of my pants. I don't know if I should be standing or sleeping."

I buttoned my shirt and made my way to the kitchen with the swagger of fake courage.

"So, where's your suit?" I asked, watching her stand at the sink counter with disbelief, like a barefoot puppet come to life, stirring a cup of coffee.

"How do you take it?"

"Black, one sugar."

"You've got organic sugar. Neat," she said, adding a tea-spoon to my coffee. I paid attention to her voice. It was upbeat, nearly singsong, which was disarming because it was clearly scared as well. Perhaps this is what she was like when she was nervous. Thing is, she didn't look nervous. She looked relieved.

I sat down at the table, in the chair I didn't normally sit in, so that I could stare at her standing at the counter.

"Hope you don't mind if I borrow your jeans and stuff," she said, turning around to face me, "the suit's too tight to walk around in, let alone make coffee." She smiled, nodding back to the bedroom as she brought our cups to the table. "Would you like me to put it back on?"

"That's ok. We aim for comfort at this hotel," I said.

She sat across from me and was just about to take a sip from her cup when she set it down. She stretched her hand out. I put my cup down, smiling, and gently shook her hand. It was warm and dry. I looked up at her.

"Nice to meet you," she said.

"Yeah, same here. Glad it...uh...worked."

"Me too," she said. Her unease was tangible.

+ + +

SENECA WAS IMPRESSED with the size of my apartment, per-haps the only person who's seen it to have that opinion. Like the sugar, she took interest in the small things — she looked bemusedly at my coins on the living-room coffee table as if they were precious metals, and when she asked me how I connected to the Internet she began snorting the moment I used the words *cable modem*. Of all things, however, she was taken with the windows: she kept asking whether they needed to be coated, and when she saw that I kept the bathroom window ajar she asked whether I was concerned about air quality. In both instances I asked her, why? Nothing. She either walked away or shook her head dismissively. Lovely.

I found her interest in everything invigorating. I found a part of myself wanting to impress her, if not with my own virtues than with antiquated knick-knacks kicking around the apartment, like my poster for Hitchcock's *Vertigo*. She was the first person in Toronto I've met in years who wasn't trying to pretend that she'd seen everything. Above all was this quiet, nearly atonal song she hummed when she was walking between rooms, tidying up things distractedly. She didn't hum it when we were together. I figured it was something she used to comfort herself.

I gave her a tour of the apartment. It lasted five minutes. I didn't know what she knew and when I asked what she knew she couldn't tell me — she just smiled and lightly shook her head. I redundantly explained how the gas stove worked. In spite of the fact that she was using it earlier, a part of me was left me wondering if she was going to blow up my apartment.

"I don't suppose you have…you know, an agenda?"

She was doing stretches on the carpet. She looked at me strangely, not sure how to respond. The magic dust about her darkening a bit. There was an all-news station on the TV, which she found fascinating. I was sitting on the couch, wondering how to make myself useful to her, aside from being a tour guide of mundanity. She took turns bending down to reach her toes.

"I was going to ask you the same thing," she said, sitting up straight. Her breath was deep and smooth. "It was actually one of those questions I meant to ask them."

"The Society?"

She waited a couple of beats. I wasn't sure whether she was monitoring something inside of her or figuring out how to avoid the question.

"Yeah."

There was a pause. I interpreted it as the point where we considered each other's complicity. I was at least grateful we worked for the same people. I think.

"They're great on the pitch," I said, supportively. "But a little shaky on the follow-through."

I could see how attentive she became, how something in her body stiffened in response to both the question and my comment. I leaned forward.

"Sorry," I said. "They — you-know-who — were really upfront about everything...except you and what would happen after you arrived. I was expecting you'd have an itinerary of some sort. You know, all I have is a code. Well, sort of. And a set of hosting rules. But..."

She turned to the television screen, waiting for me to finish my sentence. I didn't, because I couldn't. Because I felt like I was digging a grave for myself by just opening my mouth.

"They called you, right?" she asked. I couldn't look at her. A chill broke out over me, borne of guilt at not having been able to retrieve all the necessary information during the phone call last night. The two of us sitting there, the TV as intermediary, proof beyond doubt that it was June and this was indeed the real world continuing in its mostly fucked-up advertising-subsidized way. Yet I knew she shouldn't be here. Not a physical person doing stretches on my carpet. I couldn't shake the cold in her voice. I shifted in my chair. If nothing was as it seemed before, it was now worse.

"They did," I said.

"You used your telephone service. You spoke with Cathy..."

She reached over her opposite shoulder, locking it with the hand of her other arm coming up behind her back from below.

"Cathy? I guess? I was nervous." The news anchor kept talking and the sound of his voice was annoying. I couldn't shut it out. "She didn't give her name. It was a woman, yes — older, I think."

"Cathy. That was Cathy."

"Sure. Your Wallace, I guess."

"What does that mean? Who's Wallace?"

"My Cathy."

"Okay, whatever," she said, the edge of her voice showing. "What did she say?"

"It was like some pre-recorded message... from Cathy... with a space in it where I was to say yes and no."

She switched arms. The lower one now above and reaching over her shoulder, locking with the other underneath.

"And yooouuu...?"

"I tried to respond, but there was an interruption — my stupid neighbour and her precious bike and so... And, so my... my yeses and nos... I think I may have missed a part. There was a part with a series of numbers. It could have been a phone number." I laid my head back against the couch as if I'd thrown a Hail Mary, hoping she would continue where I left off and complete the rest of the puzzle where I couldn't.

There was nothing for a long time. I still couldn't look at her.

"I guess you wouldn't happen to know...?"

"I have no clue, Derrick," she said. "I mean, I'm the one who's been transported. You're the host."

"Yeah, I know," I said, sounding neither sufficiently apologetic nor sorrowful enough to soothe the tension. My cheeks began to burn: it was one thing to let myself down, but the realization that I'd let down Seneca, let down the Society. I thought about it and the extent of my error grew beyond the scale of what I thought I knew before.

There was a news update about a local fire. She sat forward. I wondered what exactly she was looking for. I wasn't sure if it was the story, the cable station or the TV itself. I couldn't tell if she was watching anything specific: she seemed engrossed in something personal, something that seemed both everything and nothing to her in the moment.

"What's weird is that..." She turned toward me. "I didn't really expect it to be this way. I was under...I was kinda... Figured this wasn't going to be...a physical sort of thing. You know, not with me physically here," she said, ending in a whisper. "You know, in person."

Finally.

"I wasn't going to say anything...But, yeah. I was expecting a..."

"...a virtual sort of thing," she nodded, looking at me, her eyes hoping I would agree with her.

"Yes," I said, staring at the ceiling in relief. For a moment there I didn't think I would ever use the word *yes* again. "Yes, you were supposed to be projected. Some sort of particle suit that reflects blaggity-blah and gets fuzzy sometimes. You were supposed to be this virtual thing that was fuzzy sometimes. Not..."

"Yeah. It was supposed to go different from this." She gestured her hands accusingly at my living room, the television screen. I suppose I should have assumed she was expecting to see something other than a suicidal bachelor's apartment.

I told her about Wallace — my Cathy — and that I'd called him several times for more info without so much as a text message back. At this point it seemed her trip had taken a toll: she was in the process of neck rotations, but she slowed down, almost drunken; her eyes, when I could catch them, didn't seem to focus on anything in particular. It was possible that, like me, she was running on caffeine, an empty stomach and a justified suspicion that something had become undone in the sequence of our understanding of our mission. Whatever that was.

Whee!

"I'm sorta in the dark here, too," I said, feeling guilty that I'd missed such a vital piece of information. My habit of noting the fine details of my periphery was to blame for pretty much everything so far. I asked if there was any sort of communication device in the suit, a transmitter perhaps.

"That's the thing — it's just a tight suit. I could barely fit my hair into it. But I checked it out this morning, and I couldn't find anything. It's like they just gave me a Catwoman outfit — like that was the height of technology or something."

She looked back toward the television.

"I'm trying not to freak out, Derrick," she said. "And I'm sorry if I'm shitting over everything. I...I..."

"It's ok," I nodded.

At that moment I wished I'd cleaned the place more thoroughly. There was a thick layer of dust on the television and stereo. I noticed her again staring at the TV screen and I realized I was doing the same thing. I suspected, for some reason, we both expected to see ourselves in the news.

+ + +

[Notebook excerpt | Derrick van der Lem | June 7, 2008]

When dealing with secret societies, one has to assume that — in the event of a serious altercation, where the inner workings of the society collide with the life of an outsider — their need to conceal the organization from public scrutiny will make any investigation of the situation all the more difficult.

Let's say the Society of Experience has truly been around for decades, and, as Wallace says, includes someone from every sector, from every industry. He said it clearly: "Our strength is in our depth." One has to wonder how many levels of society have they integrated themselves into? The police? The government? The media? They already screened universities. Remember Vijay Abapathy, whoever he is? In the end, if there's an altercation, what possible advantage would an outsider have in resolving it? What if said society can simply flex their hive muscle and void even the possibility of arbitration? Make everything disappear? Everyone? Including me.

+ + +

BEFORE I GOT the call, it felt as if the oxygen was being removed from the apartment. We'd spent most of the day isolated from each other. She was sleepy and admitted it was most likely an after-effect of the projection. Neither of us dared to voice our skepticism about the experiment, which seemed in a state of suspended incompleteness. It also began a period of Seneca camping out in my bedroom with the door closed. Whether a show of exhaustion or unease, it only propelled me to explore the subtleties of my guilt. I took turns staring out the living room window, standing in the kitchen and pretending to watch muted television in the living room.

Any insecurity I had about her being something other than what I had led myself to believe she would be — virtual projection, robot assassin — dissolved in the fact that she seemed to be turning anti-social. I started thinking of gosh-golly "antiquated" technological things to present to her for her amusement — making me wish I had a fax machine — but I fell back on my default stress reliever: chores.

I thought she was out cold on my bed. I was washing the dishes when, reaching for a tea towel, I looked through the kitchen doorway and caught her staring out the living-room window. I held my breath.

"I can't see the CN Tower," she said, noticing me.

She stood to the side, her face nearly pressed against the glass, straining to see it in the wrong direction.

"It's there," I said. "But you can't see it from here — there's a bend in the street. And you should be looking east. They put lights on it recently. It's still a concrete antenna, but now it does Laser Zeppelin."

Oh yeah, Derrick, she'll totally get the Laser Zeppelin reference.

"I always wanted to see it."

I assumed she meant the tower. "Why's that?"

The CN Tower was another grey attraction in Dad's grey amusement park. It never resonated with me. She looked away. I saw that no answer would be coming, despite her obvious curiosity.

"Did you…do you live in Toronto?" I asked.

She tried to say something, twice, but nothing seemed to satisfy her. I could only imagine how hard it might be for her. Finally, "Yes."

I nodded and flipped a tea towel over my shoulder while I sponged around the sink.

"I went to the Princes' Gates last summer," I said. "I've lived here most of my life and I've passed it a hundred times. But one day I just wanted to walk down to the Lakeshore and see it. Not during the Exhibition or anything, but on a regular day without the crowd and candy floss and stuff. I had this memory stuck in my head from when I was a kid. The Princes' Gates were like…this portal. It led into something that, I dunno, just made everything within it magical."

She faced the street below, listening with her eyes closed, her forehead pressed against the glass.

"All the old buildings were gone. The Automotive Building looked like it had been condemned, and the gates were still beautiful…but they just seemed like markers. It didn't seem to open up to anything, just a parking lot with a convention centre. It made me sad. It's like everything that had magic when I was a kid just disappeared or was left to decay while they built condos and nightclubs around them."

She looked at me.

"I need to be outside. Especially now."

The place downstairs started pumping music: "Some Kinda Love" by The Velvet Underground.

"What's that?" she asked.

I smiled.

"That's music."

"I know that," she said, chuckling, "but is…is that your neighbour downstairs?"

"There's a jukebox downstairs. It's actually a bar. They're open now."

That's when I felt the buzz in my back pocket. Before I could grab the call, it had already gone to voice mail.

It was Wallace.

I was beginning to wonder whether they were intentionally trying to frustrate us, to make us freaked out at the lack of communication. It didn't matter. It sounded like a pre-recorded message; another robo-call like the one last night, only this time there were no pauses for me to fill in.

"Hi there, champ. If you're getting this message then it means that you've gotten this far without making any mistakes. This is good." There was a frankness hanging in his voice, the mist of ill temper, as if he had a hangover. "There is something we would like you and our guest to do for us. Consider it a matter of checking in.

"Today is an anniversary. Thirty-five years ago, we were first contacted by our fellow members, forty-three years from now. Rather than issue commemorative T-shirts, we would like something retrieved instead."

Awesome.

"A key was just left in your apartment mailbox. It unlocks an access door at one of the west entrances of the Eaton Centre. There are instructions enclosed with the key to help you identify what it is that we require. After all, I hate leaving long messages.

"If you have any problems do not call me. Contact Cathy at the number she left. Best of luck."

The number she left...

Hey, Spacey, we've got an assignment from HQ.

"What's that?" she asked, calling out from the living room.

"Wallace left me a message. My Cathy. A voice message on my telephone service," I said, frustration simmering, standing at the front door. "I have to go and grab something downstairs. From my local postal service mailbox. You need anything?"

"Like what?"

"I don't know. Cow milk? I'm just asking."

I was nervous. When I was nervous I got twitchy, asked stupid questions, noticed the hallway activity of neighbours rather than listen to the information being transported from the future.

"Ok. I'll be back soon," I said, feeling that everything I was saying was totally redundant. She still didn't say anything. I opened the door, shaking my head, and went downstairs. Sure enough, even though I checked it earlier, inside my mail slot was now a folded piece of paper with a key wrapped in an elastic band. I could hear the music from the bar: "Say It Isn't So" by Hall & Oates. It followed me as I went back upstairs. I didn't want to ask myself how the Society managed to access mailboxes.

"Got it," I said.

"What?"

"Nothing," I said. "No, actually, no. No — I have something, alright? Does that work? I have something."

I couldn't stop feeling like I was being a jerk. I realized it was because I probably was a jerk and just hadn't been explicitly aware of it until now. I walked into the kitchen and Seneca followed, staring at me as if she'd been prepared for whatever followed. I tossed the key and note onto the table, like evidence from a crime scene.

"What's that?"

"It's a door key, wrapped..."

"I know what a key is. We have that. We have paper. What's going on, Derrick?"

She had her hands in her hair. In that moment I thought I would make a joke, like Paul – and in a fraction of that same moment I realized that that was the last thing she needed. She was scared and she was a stranger.

"They've given us something to do. They want us to go to the Eaton Centre and grab something."

"The what?"

"The Eaton Centre."

She looked at me as if I were talking about something in another city and the longer she held that expression – failing to register what it was I was saying – the more I began to dread what I didn't know.

"Oh, okay. Yeah?" she said, unconvincingly.

I paused long enough to mark my suspicion.

I nodded to the table. "That key is for a service entrance. The note explains the rest, I guess. We have to retrieve something. An anniversary present. Know anything about that?"

She reached down and proceeded to disentangle the key from the elastic band. She tossed it onto the table casually and fixed her attention to unfolding the note. She was all business. Her expression opened up; her eyebrows widening as if adjusting to take in more information. I could have picked a couple of mugs from the dish rack and started juggling them, and she would not have prioritized anything but the contents of the note.

"What does it say?"

She didn't answer. She stood over the kitchen table, going over its contents. If it had been more than a single page I would have grabbed whatever she discarded.

"Look," I said, clearing my throat, "I'm kinda the host here and..."

"Do you have a lighter?" she asked, her eyes still on the page.

"Yeah, sure."

I walked out into the hallway, unhappy with her lack of disclosure, and grabbed the lighter from my jacket. It was a little embarrassing. I didn't smoke cigarettes anymore so the only purpose of having a lighter was for lighting joints. I didn't know if it was as evident to others as it was to me. I heard the electric *snap-snap-snap* of my gas stove's igniter in the kitchen. I walked back with the lighter in my hand and saw her standing above the stove. The note was on fire.

"What the hell are you doing?"

"Sorry," she said, staring down at it. I moved to reach for it but she turned her back and shielded it from me, making sure it was consumed by flame. She was going to make sure every inch was incinerated. I saw how she would probably sacrifice burning herself to do so. Her clenched jaw, her stance, the way her elbow jutted out to keep me away.

I let her "sorry" smoulder between us. I had no choice. She held what was left of the note above the sink I'd bloodied weeks before, frowning. She knew I was angry. It seemed as if she had a valve inside her, capable of judiciously feeling and not feeling. She dropped the last ember into the sink and kept staring down at it.

And what else was she trained to do?

"You done?" I asked.

Nothing.

+ + +

[Journal entry | Seneca Lewis | June 6, 2055]

I spent two hours in the washroom, sitting on the tile between the bath and the sink. It was the quietest spot in the apartment. I didn't have to hear the construction outside. I didn't want to be part of the Great Renovation. I wasn't part of it. A bunch of people died — I get it. For a time, the world shut down and it was scary and now we have to march forward for freedom, etc. — I get it. I just don't need any of it right now. I wish I could give up my civic rights, just cash them in and let other people make decisions for me. I suppose that's how we got here, isn't it?

What are my needs? At every point in my life I've always asked myself: what are my needs? And here I am agreeing to so much of what the Society is asking, and here I am, about to go downstairs in three hours and get in a car and take part in something I'm still not sure I completely understand. And whenever I hint to them that this is how I'm feeling they're all like *hey it's fine, girl.* But this isn't fine.

I'm scared to see that I could feel so bad, and have so little belief in myself, that I'd volunteer for something that was so completely dangerous.

Why am I doing this?

+ + +

"ARE YOU GOING to tell me what it said?" That's what I ended up saying. What I wanted to say was: "Shove it up your ass."

We were circling each other. Neither of us would break the tension.

"We have to go out tonight," she said.

"What? That soon?"

I'd dragged her out of an alley less than twenty-four hours ago.

"The Society is taking care of the security and cleaning staff at the Eaton Centre tonight. We have to do it tonight."

I didn't like hearing her speak on behalf of people I did not trust, especially when our relationship — if it could be called that — was so tentative. Aside from arousing suspicion, the one-sidedness made me feel very alone in this deal. What did she mean by "taking care" of the staff? What did that involve?

"Awesome."

"I don't expect you to understand, Derrick."

I laughed.

"No, you shouldn't expect me to understand. Not when you burn the instructions."

"That's the way it goes. That's how I'm trained, Derrick, I'm sorry. I don't know what you've been told."

"Well, you'd think we would be collaborating. You'd think we would have been trained to share information rather than act like spies for different camps."

I stood leaning against the counter, the black soot of the note behind me in the sink's drain.

"So what's going on?"

"Don't get angry."

"What should I be then, Seneca? You burnt the..."

"You forgot the number!" she yelled.

"I didn't forget it, I missed it. Because I'm fucking human. This isn't a lab. These aren't controlled circumstances."

"That's not what I was told."

I came so close to throwing up my hands like my sitcom character alter ego.

"Well, I'd ask what you were told by the Society, but I'm afraid we'd be shot by snipers if you said anything."

Neither of us looked at each other. I wanted to throw something.

"So what's the plan?" I asked, staring at the floor.

"We have to be there by twenty-three hundred hours," she said. "We'll need tools."

"Tools..."

The insistence, the lack of room for debate.

"We're going to need..."

"Wait, so they realize that you aren't virtual? All we're getting are pre-recorded messages, notes and things like that. I'd like to talk to a real person, live – to find out what's going on. I mean...jeez."

I looked up and saw her sitting at the table, staring at me as if trying to block my concerns from hers, the mode she had switched to and then broke the switch to spite me.

"We're going to need fifteen to twenty feet of rope," she continued. "We'll need to tie a weight securely to one end of it. They suggested using a cue ball? Something that has weight but is still light enough to swing over our heads. What's a cue ball?"

"It's for playing pool," I said.

"That's a game, right?"

"It's a game. Not unlike this."

"Are you able to get these things for tonight?"

I looked at my watch. It was three o'clock, or fifteen hundred hours.

"Sure. Are we both going tonight?"

"Yes, why?"

"I'm not supposed to expose you. At least not the virtual you. I'm assuming the rules still apply to the real you."

"This is why it's happening at night. This place is closed at night, right?"

"Yes."

"What is it?"

"It's a mall. A shopping centre. People purchase things there. Sometimes with coins."

She got up and walked out of the kitchen.

"Not much longer," she said under her breath.

+ + +

I HAD LITTLE leverage, seeing as her memory was the sole retainer of our instructions. I found some satisfaction in giving Space Girl my list of demands. Insignificant as it seemed — I being the non-future-based or skilled person in this pairing — I insisted that, since I was the host, I was entrusted to making sure as few people as possible saw us. I demanded she wear sunglasses (even in the dark), a baseball cap and that she didn't talk to anyone. In other words, I would do all the talking, all the social signalling between the apartment and the Eaton Centre. And what an odd location: smack dab in the middle of downtown, in a mall surrounded by windows that bystanders could peer into if they wanted. I gave her the black turtleneck from last night — I didn't want to wear the same getup in case people were looking for me. We found some other dark clothes she could wear with unisex dignity and I picked up a pair of cheap black sneakers for her at a second-hand store down the street.

I found the rope at a local hardware shop. I couldn't remember what I told the owner. I decided on a coffee mug instead of a cue ball; the only place with a pool table nearby was an old-timer Portuguese place, and I would've got stares just by walking inside, let alone slipping out with a cue ball in my jacket. A coffee mug weighed about the same but had a handle so it could stay tied to the rope without slipping out. The overarching question – what the deal was with all this in the first place – I kept suspended from inquiry in the back of my mind. For all I knew we were going to steal watches from Birks, or something.

I stood above the kitchen table, looking down at the contents of my knapsack.

"Anything else?" I called out.

Her comment about the Eaton Centre – "Not much longer" – seemed to have spooked both of us: me to have heard it, her to have said it. We were playing human chess, standing strategically within range of each other, to be able to hear yet not necessarily see the other.

There was no answer.

She walked into the kitchen.

"Do you have the key?" I asked.

She blushed and walked out of the room.

After a moment, solemnly: "Got it."

"I don't suppose, seeing as it's nearly time to leave, that you're going to share what exactly we have to do? Or, like, where in the mall we're going? It's a very big place. It's also quite open in there. Someone at one end would technically be able to see us at the other."

She walked back into the kitchen.

"Security is taken care of. We went over that. I can't tell you anything more until we get there."

"Sure," I said, zipping up the knapsack and throwing it over my shoulder. I moved to the front door and she followed.

I turned to her: "Which entrance?"

She stopped.

"The key opens a service entrance, right? Which one? I need to tell the cab driver where we're going. Do we get off

at Queen? Bay Street? Dundas...?" I could tell she was hold-
ing back. Her telltale eyes. "Look, let's work together, ok? I'm
trying to anticipate problems before they happen — I don't
want you to have to talk to anyone out there, or have them
hear your voice."

"They said it's by the courthouse," she said, looking up at
me, blushing. "I have no clue where that is."

"That's fine — I do."

"Derrick?"

"What?"

"I'm just as scared as you. I want you to know this. But I
am also under orders. And the people giving me those orders
are the only people who can get me back home."

I took a breath.

Fine, I thought, be vulnerable.

+ + +

"IT'S TIED TO a goose."

We were staring at geese. Fake ones. Hanging from the
glass roof by wire, like marionettes. It was incredible to be
standing there, the two of us alone. At least I thought we
were alone. It was as if we were standing in an airplane
hangar or some old European train station like what Dad
wrote about. The arched, glass-panelled ceiling revealed the
night sky. I could hear his voice narrating this scene, like one
of the monologues he recorded for the BBC.

A part of me had taken some delight in spoiling her author-
ity. I'd called for a cab to pick us up from my building and I'd
stood at the bottom of the stairwell waiting for it to arrive
before I clapped my hands twice to signal that it was safe for
her to follow. She had my leather jacket on and she'd pulled

the collar up, which obscured her face but ironically drew more attention as a result of looking so secretive. I wore a simple hoodie, which only made her stand out beside me. I'd opened the back door of the cab then come back and escorted her, bent forward so that people across the street wouldn't be able to see her. When we got in, I'd insisted that she slouch down in her seat so that her head wasn't visible to people outside. I felt sorry for her, being transported to a time before hers only to be smuggled around like luggage, unable to interact.

We'd gotten off at James Street, just west of the Queen entrance to the Eaton Centre. It was dark and empty enough on the street that we jogged up in our disguises without attracting attention. She had noted the freshness of the early June air, the way it cooled and freshened. Her sensitivity to it was noticeable: deep breaths, rubbing her face as if it were something purifying. I'm sure she could have stood outside taking it in forever. For her, it seemed tinged with adrenaline.

We had found the right door and the key worked. I was still thinking this would all unravel into a terrible joke, but perhaps that's just how I came to expect things. The service entrance had led us through a spartan corridor, which eventually took us through a pair of swinging doors into the tiled public washrooms hallway that fed back into the concourse. From there we were able to enter the mall proper. We exchanged glances the entire way: fear, relief, fear, relief. We'd passed an abandoned custodian trolley in the hallway, like a yellow droid, complete with toilet paper and spray bottles filled with surface cleaner. I wondered again just how the security and cleaning staff had been "taken care of."

We stared at them, an immense art installation incorporating dozens of life-sized fibreglass Canadian geese in mid-flight. In my hyper-stimulated state I counted over fifty of them suspended above us. I realized what was missing, other than the sound of people: muzak.

"Don't suppose they told you which one?"

Pause. I didn't have to look at her. I could anticipate the answer.

"No."

"This is awesome."

At any moment I expected someone to walk out and spot us. An angry voice to break the silence.

"They said the first one, okay? The first one, whatever that means."

I looked at the flock, stepping from side to side, switching perspectives to understand the pattern. They were all in various poses: wings up, wings down, webbed feet tucked under, stretched out for landing. But it eventually made sense.

"See," I said, pointing up. "The whole flock narrows from there..." I said, pointing to the back where there were too many to declare a prominent one, "...to here." The flock funnelled toward a leader at the front. Approaching, I realized the problem. There was no way to reach out and grab it. It was unreachable from any corner of our platform, suspended ten feet above and nearly the same distance away from the railing where we stood. Even if I had a baseball bat it would be too far away to smack like a piñata.

I removed my knapsack. The chaos was dissipating.

"Time for my cowboy routine."

"What's that?" she asked.

I realized then she was so completely out of her element. The information from the note was the only item she could cling to for authority. Outside of that, she was lost.

"This one," I said, nodding to the leader goose, "should be the one we take down. But we can't reach it. This is why they asked for those supplies, right?"

I didn't wait for her response. I don't think she had one — she probably knew just enough to get us here and the rest was pinned on me to figure out. I knew I had mistakes to make up for. I pulled out the rope and tied one end around the handle of the coffee mug. I looked over and saw her staring at my knot tying. At the point I'd released enough slack rope in order to swing it over the railing, over my head, I turned to her.

"This is ridiculous."

"I know," she said, smiling, somewhat relieved.

At least we were in agreement this once.

I'd never done anything like this before; less the trespassing onto privately owned property than wielding makeshift bolas. The Injured Cowboy would be pleased. I started by keeping the slack short, deciding to lengthen it as I got some torque behind the swing. I had it going for three rotations, then I heard something break and the rope crumpled to the ground.

The mug had smashed against the frame of an illuminated visitor map behind me.

I looked at her. We both erupted into laughter.

She raised her hands to her face: "What are we going to…"

I pulled out a second mug from the knapsack.

"Smart," she said, relieved.

"Damn straight, lady."

I kept my eye around me as I swung the new weight over my head. I moved closer to the railing and slackened the rope so as to reach further with it. Seneca held her hands up as if prepared to cradle her head if it didn't work. I simultaneously slackened the lead and extended my reach — to my amazement, the mug twirled around the goose's wires completely.

I stood there for a few seconds admiring what I'd done.

"What do I do now?" I asked.

"Pull?"

I snapped the rope back sharply and saw the goose plunge down sixty feet to the food court below. By the time I could believe I'd done it, it was shattered on the tile floor at the bottom.

I glanced over and she was looking at me, as if she'd been discreetly looking at me for a while. What was she thinking? Her curls tucked under her ball cap, her wild eyes surveying me. I wanted to put my hands around her arms. I wanted to know whether she would like that, how she would feel.

I broke off and walked toward the escalator. I caught a glimpse of a plaque at the railing where I'd downed the goose. Installed in 1979, two years after I'd been born.

"Shit, this is a Michael Snow sculpture," I said.

She didn't say anything.

+ + +

I LET HER go first. Brushing off the dust and fibreglass debris, I was surprised to a see her lift a small red box from the ground.

She held it up, as if a trophy. It looked like a jewellery box. Something you'd put a necklace or broach in. The black Society insignia was inscribed on the top.

Open it up.

Open it up.

"Open it up," I said.

She did but turned her back to me, similar to when she burned the note in my kitchen. I saw her pause and pull something out of it — a card perhaps. She spent some time looking at it. All I could see was the rise and fall of her shoulders, her breath. Before I could ask the obvious question, she put whatever it was back in the red box and closed the lid.

"I can't show this to you," she said, putting it awkwardly into the pocket of her jacket.

I stood holding my knapsack out, expecting I would be allowed to hold onto it.

"Why?"

She looked as if she'd been anticipating the question.

"I can't show it to you until you're ready."

"What?" I could feel a red mist sweep over my eyes. "What the hell does that mean, until I'm ready?"

"It was in the note, Derrick. It's not my decision."

"Not your decision, but you'll gladly take the authority of holding this information over my head until I need it. I'll make sure I explain that to Cadillac Fairview when they look at the security footage and ask me what was in the goose I destroyed."

I realized how little sense my outburst made. She was here on a mission and I had to be honest with myself at that moment: I was there for kicks. My adrenaline was racing. I didn't personally care if I was on national TV right now. I wanted to see what was in the box. I wanted to take off her baseball cap. I wanted to taste her sweat on my tongue.

+ + +

"I'M SORRY."

We sat on the top of my picnic table in Trinity Bellwoods Park, sheltered by a maple canopy now in bloom. Stars peeked through the blue-black galaxy above. There were crickets. Her sunglasses dangled uselessly from the neck of her shirt, her dark mess of clothing made her look like a mannequin someone had given up on.

We'd traced our guilty steps backward, leaving the mall along the same path as we had come. The custodian trolley still abandoned, questions of its user still unanswered. We should have gone straight home. She'd insisted as much before we got into a cab, but I broke with protocol and led her here, asking the driver to drop us off just short of the park. From there I had steered her discreetly through private alleys and public sidewalks.

In light of the fact that we had survived this sortie, I felt bad about my earlier snark and resistance. I felt bad about missing Cathy's information on the phone. It was an eerily familiar feeling that, somehow, everything I touched broke, even when — in the case of the Michael Snow goose — it was part of the plan.

"I'm just a part of someone's experiment, I think," I said. "My sense of space — everything seems like it's being messed with."

She was quiet for a moment. I wasn't sure if she was breathing; staring outward, looking further into the void than I felt I was able to.

"That's fine. But it's also a little one-sided," she said, curtly. "I mean, I empathize, but I think I'm the one more affected. I'm out of my time. Out of my life. Regardless what happens, you still have your apartment to go home to. I don't even know if mine still exists. Or a job." She nodded, as if it was a cue for me to agree with her. "Assuming you have one of those too."

I nodded uncomfortably. She was the last person in the world I wanted to translate the details of my work to.

We were sitting on what seemed like the opposite ends of the tabletop, yet still the tips of our shoulders touched. Cars buzzed above from Dundas West like faraway hornets. I looked up into the night sky through the branches: the ghost clouds, the patches of stars. Depth. A different complexity than ours.

"I realize, you know, that this is hard — in ways I probably can't imagine," I said. "But as your host, your unhappiness lands back on me. Like I said earlier, I think we're part of someone's experiment. This is someone else's plan. I keep asking myself, what am I supposed to learn here? Look at you — you're stranded here with me. That can't be an accident — the whole physical-you being here and not a virtual-you. And what next, they want me to rise to some unarticulated occasion? It was never intended for us to construct it or figure it out. Meanwhile a part of me...just wants you to tell me baseball scores from the future so I can get rich."

She huffed, the shoulder of her jacket pressing against mine. The ambient park light cast a cool glow on her face. She glanced at her feet resting on the seat of the picnic table.

"That's very illuminating."

"I'm sorry. It sounds like I'm self-centred. And normally I am, but in a good way, I think. I'm normally not a jerk. Maybe I am. Maybe I'm a sociopath. I've had...you know, I've had some problems lately. So, yeah, by virtue of that I've had to be a little more me-conscious. I just wish you didn't have to see me like this. Like, at this point in my life."

"As opposed to? Could you not be so vague?"

I caught her staring at me.

"Not spending every second thinking about death. About my role in things. Or lack thereof."

Her face softened.

"Is something wrong?" she asked.

"No, no," I said. I was blushing. I brushed my forearm. "No, I uh...My dad passed away and I — well, it's been pretty bad since then."

I couldn't tell her everything. Who could? Someone less acquainted with shame. I really wanted to but I didn't want to freak her out any more than she was. Any more than I had.

"I'm sorry to hear that."

"It was a while ago." I waved away the concern. "I'm fine, for the most part."

She ran her hand through her hair. She took off her baseball cap and put it on her knee. "I didn't expect..."

"I know. It's fine. I'd thought that maybe..." then I trailed off, thinking about her journal excerpts in my desk — my *samizdat* cheat sheets. I wondered again if they had done the same for her.

"I figured they — Cathy and them — would've mentioned stuff about me. I guess not."

Secretly I hoped they had. Now I had to contend with the fact that I may have just weirded her out and permanently muddied what relationship we had.

She laid her hand on my back. It was unexpected, though I tried not to show much surprise. This was not what I expected from someone who was upset with me. Karen would've been halfway through the park, flagging a taxi by now.

"They didn't tell me, Derrick. That's too bad."

I waited. I didn't want her hand to move.

"Anyways...This is me right now. Feeling crappy, sitting in the park with Space Girl."

She burst out laughing.

"Space Girl? Oh my god, that's hilarious!"

I turned to her, blushing, happy to be there with her. Smiling. Happy to be there. To show her this place. Happy to be with her and to hear her voice and her laughter as we sat alone together.

+ + +

AFTER EXTENSIVE PERSUASION I took her to a bar. If we were to have only one thing in common, it would be a proper Canadian outing: alcohol on an outdoor patio in late spring. I didn't know why, but the fact that she came from the future seemed to obscure the fact that she lived in the same city I did, yet I acted as if I were hosting a foreign exchange student.

I drank Bushmills and she drank red wine. She was intensely interested in their selection.

"So what happens now?" she whispered.

The question was written on both our faces.

"We go play the ponies, then I take you down to Mexico."

She snorted, nearly coughing wine out her nose.

"Sorry," I said, smirking. I wasn't.

"That's okay." She was flushed, dabbing her mouth while taking a deep breath.

I had to convince the waiter to give us a patio table, it being only twelve degrees outside. It meant we would be guaranteed to be alone. She remarked again on how fresh the air was, how it was giving her a high. Was it this that allowed her to be exposed, despite our violation of the Society's rules? I'd chosen the place specifically because the patio was surrounded by junipers, which obscured us from the outside world.

"I think I've been a little hard on you," she said. "It runs in my family."

"No, no apologies. I took this too lightly."

"Well, no," she rested her glass. "This — me — it's probably just as crazy for you. So, I apologize."

I peered through a narrow opening in the shrubbery for something to engage us with. All I saw were dark storefronts.

"What's it like?"

"What?" she asked.

I gestured abstractly with my hands. "The future."

"I can't..."

"I know you can't give me explicit details: just paint a picture for me. Watercolours. You can be expressionist if you want."

She smiled.

"I dunno. It's faster, I think. It's certainly dirtier."

I smiled and raised my glass to her, as if remembering my part of the script.

"To fast and dirty."

After taking a sip, she set the glass down and looked at me.

"Just so you know — and I know you know this — but I really can't give you any specifics about anything."

I knew this, I knew she knew I knew this, but something gave me pause. No specifics. But I wasn't interested in stuff. I wanted to know about her. "I understand. No baseball scores."

"No scores; no stock prices; no commercial, cultural or technological information. Nothing that can..."

We looked at each other intently.

"...affect the outcome," she finished, sounding like a lawyer.

The sound of a transport truck's engine brakes shuddering in the background marked the existence of the world beyond our conversation. Loud spirits at night.

I took a lingering sip from my glass, exchanging looks with her. She sat uncomfortably, looking exhausted. Being with her emboldened me with a sense of calm, of rescue, even if I had to be paranoid about her exposure. Even if the question of what we retrieved tonight went unanswered. She nodded, though what she was signalling was unclear.

The whisky coating my throat began to burn.

"This was supposed to be virtual," I said. "It was actually the only assurance I asked for. I'm no scientist, but it was the only thing I'd explicitly asked about. Not affecting things." And yet I wondered whether I was saying this to fool myself as much as to placate her. Had I really been that concerned? Why was I so desperate to keep her happy?

"Rippling the chain of cause and effect," she said, nodding. It was the first thing on her mind. The words came as if pushed out by a weight, like an admission of guilt. And what I'd dared not take seriously before began to settle: that everything she touched and potentially every person who saw us could conceivably threaten her existence and the configuration of everything that was to be the future she belonged to. Assuming she got the opportunity to go back. All this time I'd expected to take part in a bold, new experiment, possibly something that would give some meaning to my life, and instead I was handed a thoroughly confused woman who had to wear my clothes.

I felt more and more like a contributor to her darkness.

"Do you think the answer may have something to do with the numbers she gave me on the phone?"

Silence.

"I heard 'three zero four.' Assuming that's a phone number, do you recall what the other digits could be?"

She stared at the table.

I whispered, "There's only one other person who can help me figure this out, and that's you. If I knew you were going to be real, I would have actually given a shit from the start. Honestly, Seneca. Honestly. I'm sorry this is so complex. I expected this to be some sort of joke."

"I can't finish this," she said, frowning at her glass.

"I'll pay up and we'll head back."

I wanted to put my arm around her, to comfort her in some way. The best I could do was to give Space Girl space, albeit within the confines of my apartment.

+ + +

WHEN MY CELLPHONE rang the next morning, the two of us sprang from our respective sleeping spots: Seneca from my bed, me from the living-room couch. I got to it first, holding the display up to see who it was. For a second I caught myself gazing at her, having rushed into the hall looking tired and anxious. Unguarded. Pretty.

PAUL, it read.

"It's not..." I looked at her and shook my head. Her shoulders hunched with the news. She was wearing one of my T-shirts and a pair of my flannel pyjama bottoms.

I answered it, if only to disengage from wanting to address the frustration I saw in her face.

"Hey, Paul," I said, shrugging apologetically to her, as if there was nothing I could do.

"Oh...hey, Derrick. Sorry if I'm waking you — I was actually just going to leave a message."

"That's alright. What's up?"

Seneca turned and padded to the kitchen. I stared at her as she passed me, absorbing everything about her: her stride, her hips, her feet. I could feel heat in my chest staring at her.

Paul continued speaking in my ear.

"Sorry, what?"

"I was saying that one of my spies from CSIS told me you were with someone last night."

I couldn't feel my heartbeat. I felt myself breathing, but I couldn't tell whether it was oxygen or poison. A wall fell between myself and Paul, myself and Seneca. And the Society. Four such walls, a prison.

From Paul's quadrant: "So...? Huh?"

"Me? Uh, no. Nope."

"Really? Huh. Interesting. Because Kimberly, Doug's friend — the one Lisa left Eric to live with — said she thought she saw you with some blonde girl. Said she was cute. Sporty."

"Uh, no. No. I wish." I chuckled unconvincingly to sell the point, too tired to think of anything more effective.

"Huh. Interesting. Maybe you have a doppelgänger."

"A doppelgänger. Sure. I'll accept that as a possibility."

"Oh, and I got that gig."

"The...?"

"The role — the acting gig. I'm playing the Italian guy. Do you believe it?"

"Wow. Wow! That's great, man!" I was thankful to focus on a distraction. "When do you start?"

"Tomorrow. It's like...amazing. I feel like a real actor. Not an unemployed guy who tells people he acts."

The coffee grinder blared from the kitchen for an unmistakably loud few seconds. I whipped my head around, but it was pointless since Seneca wasn't within sight.

"What's that? Someone drilling?"

I crossed my eyes and clenched my fist.

"Oh, no — it's just the...uh..."

"Or you got someone there? Huh? Eh, tiger? Eh?"

"No. No. It's the neighbour. Cheap walls. Anyhow, I gotta go get the newspaper before someone steals it. I'll give you a call later, okay? It's great about the part. I wanna hear about it, alright?"

"Oh...Okay. Sure thing. You have fun," he said suspiciously.

I swore after hanging up.

"What?" Seneca called from the kitchen.

"Nothing. A nosy friend." I tried to keep my anxiety in check. I approached the doorway to the kitchen, leering at the coffee grinder.

"Did he hear that? She?"

"He."

"I'm sorry."

"That's okay," I shrugged. "At least we're trying our best."

She chuckled.

"You've got a pretty good sense of humour, mister. I like that."

I glowed. "Well, between me losing important pieces of information and you making yourself at home..."

"Hey, what's that?" She looked at my arm. I was wearing a T-shirt and the scar on my forearm was evident. I'd been too busy racing for the phone to realize it was visible. I stared at it. It was too obvious for me to comfortably explain in the moment. I thought of lies, truths, ultimately knowing that the pause provided its own answers.

"No specifics," I said, turning to the bedroom to get dressed.

+ + +

[Notebook excerpt | Derrick van der Lem | June 8, 2008]

What is love?

I might be exaggerating, but it seems that in every movie with an extraterrestrial traveller, he or she or it comes face to face with a human earthling protagonist, whom the alien inevitably asks this question.

The answer is unmemorable. I've never been able to remember exactly what they say. Taken aback by this otherworldly naïveté, the human ends up explaining love in the way we would explain it to our children. Love is round and soft. Warm, and often coloured with red. Kisses. Hugs. Etc.

Meanwhile, any sober adult hearing this would ask, how do you explain to the alien how love can be a complicated whore? How do you explain how people are equipped not only to generate love, but also pervert it? That Love is the less evil of a binary universe, where the other choice is Nothing.

Love inspires religion. Love is an illusion. Love is a cult waiting for its Jonestown.

+ + +

136 SHE TOOK A shower while I got ready, dressing as if I were stepping out for the day, going to work. When she came out wearing my terry-cloth robe, a towel wrapped around her hair, I was waiting at the kitchen table. The kettle was steaming on the stove.

She couldn't have missed my stare, having positioned myself so that I was looking out the doorway.

"I'd like to talk to you."

Pause.

"Can I get changed?"

"Sure."

She came back in a few minutes wearing my black dress shirt and a pair of faded jeans. Her damp hair curled, straw-brown. She stood barefoot to the side of the fridge, smiling politely. Expectantly.

"We're not going to get very far if we can't open up," I said. There were two cups of coffee on the table.

She gazed at the cabinetry, as if stuck for a response.

"You should know me," I continued. "Not because I'm the host but because I can't have you or anyone else here without...I don't know. Context? It drives me nuts: you know nothing about me, and I know less about you because you're trying to be a good Space Girl and protect me from the future. So, let me tell you a little about me," I said, sensing her anxiousness.

If I could just keep talking, somehow I felt I could convince her of...

"My name is Derrick van der Lem. I'm the son of Peter van der Lem. He was a writer. Well-known."

"I saw some his books on the shelf in your bedroom. You have a lot of them. I didn't make the connection until I remembered your last name. I didn't want to bring it up. I don't know what you've been instructed not to tell me."

It surprised me. His books were on my bedroom bookshelf, and yet most of the time they existed in a quantum state where they were invisible to others and ignored by me. Everyone else saw a regular bookshelf, filled with antique dictionaries and disjointed encyclopedias I'd picked up at yard sales. I caught her staring at me. She diverted her eyes to the floor.

"I never got along with him very well. When he died it messed me up. And one night...I tried to kill myself. And thus...." I nodded down to my arm where she'd seen the scar earlier.

There was a damp pause before she spoke. Her face flushed.

"Why would you do that?" Her voice was stern. There was disappointment. And if there wasn't disappointment, a part of me was more than capable of inserting it.

"I don't have a pat answer to that. It's a bit soon for me to –"

"I don't believe that. Come on, Derrick. People don't just... there's always a reason. Do you suffer from illness?"

"No, not really. Maybe? I can't tell because I'm too good at tricking myself. Look, I went my whole life hiding something." I tried to hold her attention. "I can't explain why I hid it, but my Dad was part of it. He's somewhat responsible for this."

She sat still.

"I'm a writer."

She blew out a breath and rolled her eyes.

"I thought you were going to tell me he raped you or something."

"No! No."

"You were sooo serious. I thought..."

"No, let me explain: he was a great writer. When I was a kid, I wrote too and one day, when I had a weekend with him, I gave him something of mine to read. He didn't like it. He wouldn't stop pulling mistakes out of it, and I realized that it was useless to have that dialogue with him. After that wore off, I just stopped telling him. I didn't make it known, to him or anyone else that I wrote. He was prolific and respected, and I didn't want his pressure and I didn't want people comparing me to him. So, when they asked me if I wrote, I said no."

"He died before you told him...?"

"Yes."

I was blushing, overcome with embarrassment. Embarrassment. Was it all about that? No. Yes. More.

"I really thought he was a good writer. And more than anything I wanted to show him my work. It wasn't about whether or not he liked it..." I trailed off, my voice choked by mucus building at the back of my throat.

"Derrick..." she whispered, standing with her arms crossed, seemingly unable to move toward me. I saw a mix of concern and fear in her expression; I managed to control the swelling in my chest.

"Seneca, look: I'm not saying this to be pathetic. I just want you to understand who I am, because I think there's a meaning behind us being together."

She lifted her head, looking at me solemnly.

"There's a key in this." I pointed between us. "Why would they randomly choose someone who just tried to kill himself, whose father just died — and I know they know all this — why would they pick me? This has been going through my mind ever since I first met Wallace. Unfortunately, part of it comes down to the fact that I didn't give a shit at the time. Time travel?" I spread my arms out. "Sure. Hell, I was happy to still be fucking alive."

"So... I don't get what you're saying." She looked as if she were labouring to follow, weighted by a competing thought. Nonetheless, she was focused on what I was saying.

"The key to understanding the problem is to understand what they see in us or our relationship. That's the nature of their business, right? Experiences. And if it wasn't for them being so meticulous about everything... But we can't understand the key to this problem without spilling all the pieces on the table and looking at it from their perspective like a jigsaw puzzle. That's why I'm telling you about me now, and that's why I need you to tell me about you."

Her blue eyes dug into me. "There are rules I have to follow. It's one thing to hide in public — I don't mind that. I love the air and the company. I love seeing the way things are in the world right now. You have no clue how they've changed. But the rules about disclosure... Derrick, you wouldn't believe how many times they lectured me on this."

"Yes, and those rules conveniently keep us from knowing more — those rules are only serving the Society's need for confidentiality. Not ours. Think about it."

She looked off into space.

"There's gotta be a way you can tell me your story without revealing things."

"I'm sorry, Derrick. I'm just freaked." Her face had a feverish complexion. "I don't like this any more than you do — really. I know that when I'm in a strange space I can come across as cold. If only you knew. I mean, I'm scared, Derrick. I feel like laying under the covers, afraid that if I go out there I'll screw up the future. I mean, what if that drink we had on the patio last night was it? What if by that alone I've irrevocably changed what happens? Will I exist when I get back?"

"Not to mention how are you getting back?" I added reflexively, regretting it as it hung in the air between us.

"Yes," she said. "That, too."

It was my turn to look down.

She cleared her throat.

A buzzing came from my pocket. I got out of my chair and pulled out my cell. Anybody now but...

WALLACE.

I glared at her darkly. She could see from my expression. She mouthed Cathy's name and her expression of anxious hope in that instant made me furious, thinking that her top priority all this time was to run away from me. I took the call rather than answer her.

"Hello?"

"Hello, Derrick." His voice sounded tired, almost a whisper. It seemed like weeks since we'd last spoken.

"I can only assume you lost the number you were supposed to call after twenty-four hours."

"No. No, I left messages for you…"

"I know you did, Derrick. Let's just say I wasn't expecting them. In any case, please tell me our guest is safe."

I turned to her.

"Yes…Yes, she is safe," I said. I gave Seneca a vague nod and a wink.

Less is more, I told myself, preparing to speak to him in a tone that wouldn't betray anything he didn't need to know. Less is more. He doesn't need to know…

"Good. That's a relief to hear. After all, I'd hate to think that you'd do something stupid. Like take her out for a god-damned drink on a patio."

I swept my hair back nervously. The colour drained from my face. The only thing I felt capable of controlling was my eyes. I could not look at her. I did not want to worry her or look even more incompetent than I appeared.

"I'm assuming you're still there, Derrick, and that the instructions that follow won't be discarded as quickly as Cathy's."

"Y-yes. Yes, I'm listening."

"Good. At least this much is going well. Listen closely: tomorrow morning at eleven a.m. you will be meeting a representative from the Society who will take your guest off your hands. Do you know the Distillery District?"

It was such an odd question. The only things I equated with the Distillery District were microbreweries and posh art galleries.

"A bit, yeah."

"On Cherry Street, south of Mill, you'll find the old Powter Building. It has not yet been developed into an overpriced destination for tourists. The employee entrance on the south side will be unlocked. Just you and your guest. Eleven a.m., tomorrow morning. Do you require our courtesy wake-up service?"

I was determined to commit the information to memory. Seneca glared at me suspiciously, resting her head against the side of the cabinet, unsure what responsibility I was being tasked to handle. The tone of his voice unnerved me, the questioning of whether or not they could trust me to do the simplest thing without destroying the planet.

I cleared my throat and, pretending that I was dealing with a film producer, proceeded to respond without actually responding to the things that terrified me.

"Loud and clear. Absolutely. I've got the address. Done."

"And you will keep our guest's exposure to an absolute minimum, as per the agreement you signed."

"Yup. Yes. Of course."

"That's great to hear, Derrick. Please keep up the good work."

He hung up.

She asked who called after I lowered the phone, looking defeated. I noted her emphasis on who it was rather than what had been discussed.

"Wallace…" I turned and looked at her, having avoided her eyes for what seemed like too long. "He wants me to take you to some place, some location tomorrow where you'll be 'taken off my hands.'"

I made quotation marks with my fingers.

"Where?"

I took a deep breath, thinking about her burning the instructions over my sink, thinking about how she hid what was in the red box from me. That I wasn't worth trusting.

"I asked where, Derrick."

"I can't tell you that."

I didn't avert my gaze, despite the fact she stood facing me. I fought the temptation to look at the floor. Then I found myself staring at the floor. Her feet, the floor, her feet, the floor. I couldn't hear a thing, save for the cadence of my breath and my heart flexing with blood.

"Why?" Her impatience was crystalline. I hoped she would hear me out.

From downstairs I could pick out the song "Edie (Ciao Baby)" by The Cult. Of all the appropriately inappropriate moments, of all the misaligned singles in the jukebox of circumstance. I'd had a girlfriend named Edie in my late-twenties. I'd fallen madly, stupidly in love with her, but I was too enthusiastic (read: needy). I was too fast and soon for her and my thirst for her to commit was too zealous. She cut it short, mercifully in retrospect, and I fought the unfairness of her decision alone. It was the first time I'd heard this song in years, and it sounded terrible. Nothing like I remembered it: instead of longing for Edie, for that possible us, all I could think of was being in my twenties and hanging out in dance clubs, chain-smoking. I found myself once again regretting my formative music years.

"I'm sorry, I blanked out there."

I looked up and she locked eyes with me, nodding for me to continue.

"I won't tell you," I said. "I'm afraid you're going to run away if I tell you."

"Why would you think that?"

"You've been in a state of shock most of your time here. And half of it feels like some sort of reaction to me."

She blushed.

I don't trust you. There you go, girl. I said it. Something about you is fucking weird. This was one of the few times in my life when I felt like I was speaking the truth: the truth as I felt it to be and not what the jealous, evil part of me would have. The part that didn't care for philosophic grace or complexity, but wished nothing more than to cave in and devote myself to writing an evil little manifesto.

"You're making a mistake, Derrick."

She withdrew to the bedroom, her face a cool sculpture of frustration. I had no regret. I kept waiting for the regret, but it didn't come. It didn't feel natural to regret, at least when I was speaking the truth. Even if I'm wrong, my argument would have to be settled later. I spent the next eternal half-hour at my office desk, looking over her journal entries with the door locked. I was convinced there were clues contained within them. My gut ached.

I heard her come out of the bedroom, heard her pad toward the kitchen only to slow to a stop, then turn around, less sure, and pad toward the office.

"Derrick?" she asked from behind the door.

"Yes."

I folded the sheets and quietly slid them back into the top drawer.

"Look, I don't...I don't give a shit about the Society right now. I don't want to make this about rules, okay?"

It was clear to me that, whatever kind of place she lived in in the future, she was not used to being told no. I had to use a sort of judgment different from what I was used to. Light things were heavy, heavy things were light. The more I accepted my responsibility, the stronger my refusal to budge on telling her the pickup location. Someone is being taught an elaborate lesson, I thought.

"You're supposed to help, Derrick," she said through the door. "What did Wallace say? Is there something else I should know?"

Before she could try the doorknob, I got up and opened the door. She was almost right up against me, staring at me. We were the same height. Her expression was intense. I stepped back to my chair, allowing her in.

"You have nothing to gain from having the address," I said, sitting down. I looked at her squarely, trying not to cross my arms. "What are you hiding?"

"Excuse me?"

"Well, okay, I'm the host, right? If that's my job, and you're my guest and passing you back to the Society is part of the protocol — and if it's all about the protocols — then why do you need to know the address?"

I saw the fight in her face.

"I trust them about as much as you do," she said. "I mean, come on, Derrick, I'm supposed to be in a laboratory, decades from now, in some fucking warehouse on the east end. I'm not supposed to be here, in person. Real. I'm supposed to be a fuzzy contraption. You're supposed to be talking to a virtual person, not a real person. Can you please see this from my perspective? I shouldn't have to keep explaining this."

"But why do you need to know then? It's happening, and you're leaving, and that's that."

"Derrick, I never said that I wanted to leave."

It felt like she'd made an error. As if she'd said something she didn't mean to say, when in fact...

"I don't understand. What are you saying?"

"Who said I wanted to leave, Derrick? I didn't. I just got here. I'm still trying to figure things out."

"But why...I don't understand. For the past thirty-six hours you've been so guarded, but you don't want to leave? Is it this place? Is it me that's the problem?"

"No. I like you, Derrick. What you've told me...about your father and..." she trailed off. "Some people would be freaked out, but trust me, I have respect for what you're going through. It takes me a long time to come around to people. I grew up in West Forest Hill, and before that I was living in...I don't know what it's like now, but I just don't trust people very easily. I've been lied to so many times by people I've loved or was told to respect that it's become a reflex. I thought you were some stooge set up by the Society, but after hearing your story I get what you're trying to say: this doesn't look like an accident, the two of us being put together. You're not just some guy."

"So what am I, then?"

"I don't know, someone I want to get to know? It's just the rules, Derrick. You probably think I'm cold, but I'm not. I want to tell you everything about me, but I can't. Do you know how hard that is? Getting along with someone – connecting and stuff, and wanting to connect more – but you can't tell them anything for fear of messing up the world?"

I heard the plaintive voice of her journal in these words; someone trying to find their direction. Any direction. I began to see the straitjacket she'd agreed to wear, in order to be transported away from her world and now standing in my office. I was free to come to any conclusion, but the one thing that fascinated me most stood manacled before me. The feeling was that we were both condemned.

"And what if you did tell me something about yourself? What if you left out the details — your last name, for example. What if you just talked to me like a colleague and not a hall monitor? I refuse to believe they just threw us together to be cruel. There's a point to it, Seneca. I'm sure of it, and I want to know what that point is. As a writer, there's nothing more important than knowing what the fucking point is."

"I don't want to hurt you. There could be things I say that I can't unsay once you hear them."

"But what would you be hurting? I don't know you, and after tomorrow morning I won't be able to know much more."

"You want to hear something about me, Derrick? Fine. My dad was a loser. My real mother died when I was a kid. The only people who loved me left me. The person I call my mother represents everything I hate about society. I have no one, Derrick. Everyone I ever began to love is gone."

Her eyes were welling up.

"I can't," she said, holding up her arm. "I don't know what's worse, going through the horse race with the Society, not knowing what their plans for me are, or you trying to force me to do something I swore I wouldn't allow. Unless, of course, you're one of them. Are you going to give me a blood test with a slice of sugar cake after?"

My phone rang in the kitchen.

"For fuck's sake!" I rose from the chair, past Seneca to the kitchen, leaving her hanging onto her words in the doorway. I grabbed it after the second ring. I didn't recognize the number. I looked back, seeing her with her arms crossed. She shrugged. I wasn't sure what it meant.

I answered. "Hello?"

"Derrick."

Karen.

I pounded my fist into the door jamb, raising my eyes to the ceiling.

"Hey."

"Hey, yeah — I hope this is a good time. Look, I'm calling from my new phone. I'm standing on the streetcar."

"Oh yeah?"

"Yeah, just got it last week. It had the better video camera. We're doing a show on it, so there you go."

I turned to Seneca, unable to communicate anything beyond a perplexed head shake.

"Cool. So, what's up?"

"Well, I kinda felt weird, or I'm still feeling weird, about how we left things. You know, the other day and stuff. Even though it's really been a month."

Seneca reading my face for clues.

"So, you know, I just wanted to see if you wanted to get together some time. Maybe this afternoon."

"Ah, Karen...I'm not sure I'm interested in where that's going. I'm also kinda busy and...I've actually got someone here, to be honest. So..."

There was a pause on the other end while I stood staring at Seneca, sweating ice cubes. She turned away.

"Okay. Look, that's fine. You take care and I'll talk to you later. Okay?"

"Yup. Alright."

"Bye." She ended the connection.

I pursed my lips and muted the ringer. I wanted to vomit.

"That was just some personal shit. Sorry. I'm so sorry, Seneca..."

"I want to go to the top of the CN Tower."

"What?"

"That's what I want. Do that for me and I'll talk. About me."

"The CN Tower," I said, pointing at a wall. "That's not exactly keeping a low profile. I just had Wallace tear into me about us going for a drink last night. And they're powerful and stuff."

"I don't care. I mean...I do, but this isn't living," she said, motioning around the apartment with her hand. For a moment I was hurt that she didn't like my place. A part of me conjured images of hustling her around town with a blanket over her head, wearing face paint, perhaps a beret. She was waiting for me to respond. I also realized that, intentionally or not, she was encouraging us to break the rules.

"Okay," I said. "Let's do it."

+ + +

I HELD A disposable camera, staring at her.

It was well past noon. Tourists, visible in a way only tourists can unguardedly allow themselves to be, were already staking their interest, standing in small groups outside the ticket kiosk at the base of the tower. Seneca stood off to the side, wearing my laundered black Toronto sweatshirt and sunglasses. Again, the sunglasses were non-negotiable. For myself, I'd picked a plain-looking short-sleeved dress shirt from the back of the closet and wore an old pair of khaki slacks. I looked as if I'd just finished a shift at Winners. Security through obscurity:

the logic behind our disguise was born out of a coined phrase
I'd heard a computer hacker use in a made-for-TV movie I'd
worked on. We were protected from recognition by dressing
without aspiration, blending casually.

"Smile."

"I don't want anyone seeing this," she said through her
teeth. "I can't have this be the only recorded statement of
my fashion sense." She smiled obediently nonetheless.

On the way over in the cab — no blanket, just a variation
on what she wore to the Eaton Centre — I caught her quietly
marvelling at what she saw out the windshield from below.
It was daytime after all. I wanted to ask her what she saw, all
the things she was comparing to the future.

"Don't worry, it's just a prop. I'm sure it will be confiscated
later," I said, holding the disposable camera like a child's toy.
After hauling Karen's camera around, it was like switching
from snooker to eight ball.

We got our tickets and waited in line for one of the two
elevators. As was our habit, I did all the talking when it came
to purchases. I noticed how she paid attention to the people
I dealt with, studying them with fascination. She seemed to
become less burdened with responsibility the more easy-
going these last hours were.

"So, have you been up there before?" she asked in a hushed
tone.

"When I was a kid, yeah."

"Wow," she smiled, becoming more and more excited as
we neared the end of our cordoned queue. "I can't imagine
what it would've been like as a kid."

"It was pretty cool, I remember," I said, feeling myself light-
ening up. "I actually had a little bit of an issue with heights at
the time, so it was like scaling Everest. But, yeah, it was fun."

When our time came to board the elevator with three other couples, she took my hand. It was odd to feel her fingers. I wasn't sure if she was attempting to play a role — my partner — but she held my hand warmly, giving small contractions. Each contraction fed my mind with a confusing blend of sexuality and complicity as our glass capsule ascended above the skyline of my father's cathedral at 22 km/hr. The higher we climbed the more she gasped excitedly, and my heart swelled. She squeezed my hand more. The expanding landscape, our tourist compatriots oohing and aahing around us, everything seemed supplemental to this moment with her. With every glance of her face I tried to absorb her subtly. It was part of a communion that I didn't really know I wanted until then: that, against all calculations of fate, I could find someone I could fall for without hesitation or guilt.

"My god..." she whispered, but the acoustics of the elevator were such that she could've been whispering into my ear.

The city became both remarkably smaller and wider as we were lifted from concern. Our view was snuffed when the capsule entered the base of the observation deck.

+ + +

"DO YOU WANT some candy floss?" I asked jokingly, helpless against her enthusiasm. She reached out and tried tweaking my ribs, grinning, blushing — I backed away, blocking her jabs weakly. We stood outside on the observation deck, looking at the city and the lake with no one in the world as tall as us for that moment. The city appeared as a city and not what I thought it would be: the carcass of a starved animal. I could clearly see its massive scale, and I could form objective, non-critical impressions. I had found perspective. Toronto shared a horizon with the rest of the world and seemed navigable now, particularly with Seneca beside me. Since boarding the elevator I'd wished I'd done this sooner.

She has to go back.

She was looking at me. Her sunglasses were off. I hadn't realized it until now.

"You okay?"

"Yeah. Wished we'd done this sooner, you know."

"I know."

She stared across the lake, her smile fading as if honing in on the cause of my silence.

"I say that," I said, "because I'm seeing more of you now — the inner part. I mean, that's what really interests me about you. About people generally, that is."

"You like me and I like you."

She didn't say it to me directly, but spoke matter-of-factly. I followed her gaze along the lake to the horizon, not knowing how to respond.

"Is that Hamilton over there?" she asked.

"Uh, yes. Or Rochester. I can never remember."

"They're kinda the same, I guess."

I chuckled.

"If Hamilton sold beer in variety stores, it would be Rochester."

"My parents had friends in Rochester," she said. "Before they divorced, I remember my dad took me to the George Eastman House when I was really young, before they repurposed it — the one with the theatre. We watched screenings of old films, from archives of prints. I always wanted to go and find where they moved the films to, but the older I got..."

152

"No time."

"Yeah. No time. I don't even know if they show those anymore."

I thought about what I'd said earlier about the Princes' Gate, about other landmarks like the CN Tower, which I inevitably seemed to resent, maybe because of their inability to change without somehow also losing their soul. I also wondered what her definition of "old films" was.

"That's the problem with living in a big city," I said. "Even if you come from smaller cities or towns, everything around you only exists as some sort of memory from when you were a kid. You end up driving through a town like Brantford one day and you can't recognize the place anymore."

"Bradford?"

"No, Brantford. Brantford."

"Not Burford, but Brantford."

"Brantford, yes."

I looked over and she was grinning, looking at me sideways.

"You did that on purpose."

"I had a friend from Brantford once. It used to drive her nuts."

"I'd agree." I leaned in. "Did you know that it's near Paris, London and Scotland, Ontario?"

"No, I didn't."

"Very strange," I said. "They obviously couldn't come up with anything better than other place's names."

"Yeah, but it's kinda cute. I mean, if they were given original names they'd all be called stupid colonial things like Burlingshire or Elgin Lake."

"Nelsonbridge."

"Milton," she said. "Is Milton still there...?"

"The town?" I looked at her puzzled. "Why? Why would it not?"

"Nothing."

I shook my head.

"What? Meteors? They vote NDP?"

"Nothing," she insisted, ending the discussion with a curt shake of her head.

I looked down at Billy Bishop Airport, its runways a series of sandy polygons from our altitude, as if landscaped by ancient UFOs.

"I'd ask for your phone number, but I guess it wouldn't work from here, would it?"

I thought about what I'd said and blushed. She smiled diplomatically, her guardedness returning if only by half.

"A little long distance, don't you think?"

"Yeah. And I'm sure my wireless provider doesn't cover it."

We became silent. I could hear her breaths building up to say things and retreating like waves.

"It'll be sad to leave."

"Yeah. Agreed," I said. A part of me wanted to probe further, seeing an invitation in her words.

"Do you have any clue what the Society will do once I'm gone?"

"No clue," I said, wishing I could look into her eyes and not melt. "I'm not sure what the lesson is yet."

"That's what they're all about, isn't it?"

"You? Any lessons?" I asked.

She appeared to make the same sort of expression I might have, as if she were contending with the same thoughts and hesitancies.

"I don't know. It's too early to say — and to be honest, I don't want to spoil the present thinking about it."

"My present, your past. Your present, my future."

"Sorry, yeah."

She reached over, lightly touching my arm and, rising slightly on her toes, kissed me on the cheek. I was unable to breathe. It felt as if my heart had stopped.

"Thanks for taking care of me. I don't think I've been a grateful guest."

"I'm not interested in gratitude, Seneca," I said, marvelling at my ability in the moment to speak proper sentences, proper names. "This has been pretty amazing."

I could barely focus on what I was saying, but it felt good to say it because the closer she was to me the happier I felt.

+ + +

WE TOOK A cab back to the apartment. Seneca wore her sunglasses, which seemed satirical in light of our blatant exposure minutes earlier on the observation deck. Evening drew its curtain and I tried to comfort myself with distractions in the apartment.

"Is there anything you wanted to see on TV?"

I stood in the middle of the living room, remote control in hand, pointing it at the television, as if giving a demonstration of how televisions work.

"No — I'm fine," she called out from the bedroom where she was changing.

I nodded.

"You okay for food?"

"I'm not that hungry right now."

"Cool," I said, standing with the remote still pointed at the television.

I heard her leave the bedroom, padded steps into the bathroom. She was humming to herself, the same atonal song I heard our first morning together.

"I'm going to brush my teeth," she called out. "Is it okay if I use your toothbrush? I used it last night but I didn't ask first. I figured I'd ask in case it wasn't too late. Or, you know, if you have rabies or something."

"Sure, yeah. You know where the toothpaste is?"

You mean right on the counter by the sink, you moron.

"Yup, I see it. Thanks."

I heard the door close and the exhaust fan turn on. She turned it on whenever she was in the washroom and I assumed it was for the privacy of white noise. I felt like my feet were glued to the floor. I couldn't move. I knew if I asked her another question I'd be giving myself away, even though I wasn't exactly sure what that meant. I couldn't move and I didn't want her walking out and seeing me standing in the middle of the living room pointing the remote at the television. I tossed it onto the couch, withdrawing from my daze into the kitchen where I proceeded to lean against the counter by the sink, the spot where I'd stood the night I tried to kill myself. I thought of the knife and shuddered — what happened to it? — the memory of everything that night rendered in foggy smears. My back muscles were numb.

I heard the bathroom door open, the drone of the exhaust fan whirring.

Her voice emerged from the hallway: "Do you need to use the bathroom for something?" she asked. "Brush your teeth?"

I'd been dating long enough to know that a girl never asks if you want to brush your teeth unless she wanted to taste it on you. I swallowed. Still dizzy.

"Uh, yeah. Sure. There in a second," I said in as natural a voice as I could muster. I waited a moment, hoping the dizziness would dissipate, like a drug wearing off. It didn't. I turned to follow her voice and couldn't help but picture myself lying on the kitchen floor, surrounded by small splashes of my blood. I'd been unable to figure out just what it was that had driven me to stay alive that night, aside from fear and a ninth-inning realization of what I'd done. Planning to die had been pretty meticulous. What, then, was the plan for living? I was just beginning to see how haunted I had been, and was still.

I heard her step into the bedroom. I ran my fingers through my hair, staring once more at the spot where I could have been found dead by the landlord, and walked down the hallway numbly as if through someone else's apartment, touching the walls for security, to make sure they didn't close in on me. I shut the bathroom door and spent a moment hunched over the sink, holding myself up as if drunk, staring silently into the mirror as if at a close-up of a stranger's face. Small bulbs lined the top of the medicine cabinet as if I were backstage in a theatre dressing room. I turned on the tap. Then I splashed my face with cold water, my pulsing neck, dabbed them with a towel afterwards — a towel it turned out she had used for her shower. Damp. I could smell her. Proceeded to brush my teeth with quiet ceremony, the whirring of the exhaust fan above.

Time.

I opened the bathroom door and switched off the light, the exhaust fan. The silence was eerie. Like the first morning I woke up with her, the silence of not one but two.

"Hey," her voice came from the bedroom. She wasn't calling out. Her voice was clear and intimate. She was next door, expecting me. My heart pounded.

I turned the corner and saw her sitting cross-legged on the bed. She had changed into one of my white dress shirts and a pair of loose-fitting jeans I wore for apartment renovations.

"Hey," I said, smiling warmly, but feeling like a stranger. I approached and sat beside her on a corner of the mattress. She looked at me squarely. It was all her.

"How's it going?" she whispered.

A moment's hesitation, mine, between us; it made me blush and laid bare our silence as a hoax. For a second I wondered if someone would tell me my lines.

I reached out slowly and touched her leg. I stared at my fingers, my hand drawing down to her ankle. I felt her fingers stroking my temple, around my ear. I looked up, my dress shirt on her buttoned down; saw her reaching toward me, staring into my eyes. I closed them and allowed her to draw her curious fingers along my face. I wrapped my arms around her frame and felt awash with blood, the surreal warmth of fantasy, opening my eyes slowly, pulling her closer. One kiss. A heated pause to stare into each other's eyes. I caressed her cheek. We came to each other again, magnetically, each successive kiss more willing, fingers gliding over each body as if seeing through touch. She drew her hands to my face then gently pushed it away from hers. Peeling my left arm off of her shoulder, she rolled up the sleeve. I had to keep from pulling it away, to keep from grabbing her by the wrist. My breaths were short and scared. She looked at me for a moment — her lips blushed and heated — then bent over and gently kissed my palm, my wrist, all the time stealing glances at me. Those blue stones. She touched the skin around the scar and kissed it, the touch of her lips like wet leaves. Too

158

much: my heart overflowing, skin flushed, awkward pride humiliated, my cock swollen to capacity.

I ran my fingers through her hair, gently drawing the back of my fingers down the side of her neck. She raised her head and stared into my eyes again.

We stretched out on the mattress and undressed each other tenderly, as if undressing wounds.

+ + +

WE LAY BESIDE each other, the sheets strewn at our feet, my arm around her as she rested her head on my chest. I'd been trying to summarize the Injured Cowboy stories for her.

"I thought I would approach fiction as a means to express philosophy. To write approachable storylines, but with an allegorical subtext. Like *The Prophet* by Kahlil Gibran. You've read that? They still print that?"

"I read a little of it?"

"If somebody described me as the Canadian Gibran I could go for that. I could accept that."

"I don't think anyone would know what that means. It's like someone saying they wanted to be the Danish Hemingway. Can't you just be yourself?"

"I guess. It's a bit of a lofty goal, maybe. Maybe not the best wish to make. But it helps me to keep focus."

"Are they prescriptive?" she asked. There was caution in her voice.

I adjusted myself a little and looked down at her.

"The stories? They're not sermons, no. Their semantics are kind of ambiguous. It turns out my philosophy tends to be clichéd and ambiguous."

159

"That might actually be fun to read," she said, propping her head up to look at me. "I suppose if you were vague enough you could convince people that what you were writing meant exactly whatever it was they wanted to hear."

Her voice and words hung in the air for a while, like cigarette smoke.

"So...what did you do previously?" I asked, realizing I knew so little about her.

"Oh, you know. Here and there. Bartending. Theatre."

"Theatre."

"Yeah, I did theatre tech for friends. Sometimes a little acting. I'm really good at things that don't make money."

"Maybe you should take up a trade or something, see what happens? That might help you focus what is and isn't a priority in your life."

"I can't do straight jobs. They're too straight. I'm destined to work in cultural industries."

She looked up and caught me looking at her, wanting to hear more.

"My mom, the rich one...hijacks me with job openings at her friend's mega-companies. And because I don't follow up — or when I do it's a fucking disaster, and I end up hearing about it from her or my stepsister — she hates me as a result. It sucks."

"You're like me," I said, unsure whether I'd ever uttered that phrase before. "Every year a part of me wants to move to Vancouver or Portland and get the fuck out of here. But then I realize it would be a city full of people like me, running away from responsibility until they hit the Pacific."

"I'd do Montreal. I'd do it in a second."

"Yeah, I thought of Montreal, but it's an even smaller fishbowl over there. Colder, smaller...I can't stand the insulation.

It's like a prison here. Stuck in a city ruled by a prescribed cultural elite. We put them on a pedestal and give them grant money, which they turn around and waste on self-indulgent bullshit with impunity, and nothing ever happens because there's only so much room at the top. They start as DJs, then become film directors. Suddenly you're seeing them being used to sell condos and you just know you're looking at someone who's going to be the next Governor General."

She nodded slowly, smiling. "Some people would say, there's a person who won't be happy anywhere, no matter how good or bad things are. Who maybe is...ohhh, pro-jecting his own personal frustrations on things. Be honest: there are worse places in the world to be stuck."

"I know. I just don't want to be settled. Here, I mean. I don't want to settle in a place I have major philosophical problems with." I pulled her toward me. "It's not even got anything to do with Dad's generation: the colonial attitudes, the provincialism. I don't know — I'm still figuring it out. Sometimes I'm haunted by the sense that there's a disease here, a spiritual disease, and I'd be lying if I didn't think there wasn't a mark on anyone who tries to make it different."

She sighed and slid her hand across my chest.

"You're not going to solve it tonight. You may not solve it, period."

I realized how morose I sounded. Our last night together, telling her that I couldn't be settled.

"But other than that it's great," I added.

She broke out laughing, turning to look up at me quiz-zically. I caught her glance and blushed, her gaze the most significant thing in the world.

+ + +

[Excerpt from "Bruxelles-Nord," from *Benelux* |
Peter van der Lem | December 12, 1995]

Inevitably, travelling through the Benelux countries, you
will find yourself here. Usually waiting. You will probably
get here in the middle of the night and have to wait until the
ticket stations open in the morning.

Bruxelles-Nord.

It is not Antwerp. This is not Brussel-Centraal. There is
no rapture in the decorum and your camera will feel most
comfortable in the safety of its case. You will not hear angelic
choruses in your head, no rich European inspiration to spin
around in awe of the architecture. This is no cathedral.

You walk down the stairs from the platform, wondering
what awaits in the basement below, only to follow an echoing
subterranean hallway that leads to the main foyer. The ceilings
are tall and arched. Grey and disenchanting. It docks into a
more modern-looking indoor promenade, which serves as the
base of a commercial tower: rows of empty black seats greet
you as you enter from the station.

Your only memories of Bruxelles-Nord are in the twilight
hours; indeed, if you want to travel inexpensively, you will

find yourself waiting for connecting trains at this time. I tell you a secret: it is the best way to see a city. Asleep. Vulnerable. Silent. However, I wish it were not here.

The promenade is barely warmer than the station, which is barely warmer than the brisk night outside. Bruxelles-Nord is a lesson in thoughts: controlling warmth, controlling interest, controlling fear and time.

There are stores lining the sides of the promenade, meant for the daytime business-folk on their way to and from work. They are closed while you are waiting, and you are left longing for their services: orange juice, coffee, croissants, magazines. The rations of the late-night traveller. It's like another empty airport gate, complete with large windows facing out upon the sleeping city's outskirts. It is empty, evocative and silent: a dark, blank canvas.

Everyone stops here at least once, forced to wait, forced to pace, luggage in-hand through the station in the early hours. No one is comfortable enough to sit for very long. You make your own amusement and your own bed here; travelling Europe by train is not for those who lack imagination. The benches are not made for comfort; the plastic-moulded chairs are not for sleeping in. They were made for sitting. But you can't sit still: you're tired, you're impatient. You are a captive.

A Russian who speaks more French than you asks for a cigarette. There are smiles and empathetic smirks at the awkward use of an unprofessed tongue, the knowledge that you are both just waiting for a connecting train and, with that, escape. That is all you want here. The ticket staff within the bulletproof booths do not profess to be helpful.

This is not Brussels.

It is Bruxelles-Nord station. It is a world that we all must pass through.

+ + +

I WAS TORN away from her by the sound of my cellphone ringing. Blurry-eyed and naked, the previous night's sex and chatter swirling in my head like a dream I didn't want to forget, remembering how seconds ago her arm had been wrapped around my chest. Her long fingers pressed against my skin. Her heat, her scent.

WALLACE, it said.

I managed to grab it in the kitchen before it went to voice mail. My heart sank as if I'd made the wrong choice. I thought to play silent, say nothing. I wondered if he would think it was a bad connection then, and hang up.

"Rise and shine, snowflake."

"Hi, Wallace."

Please leave us alone.

I looked at the clock on the stove: just after nine a.m.

"I thought I'd take it upon myself to make sure that your appointment was met. Are you clear on the time and place, or do I need to...?"

"Yeah. The Powter Building. Eleven a.m."

"Good. That's great. This is the kind of redundancy I like, Derrick: I barely need to remind you because you already know."

"Happy to please."

"Mr. Cremaschi, an associate with the Society, will be there to guide you and our guest."

"Understood. I'll make a note of that."

"Remember, and this is crucial: no souvenirs. You understand what I mean by that?" Silence from both of us. "The turnover must be quick and clean."

My head was already prepared to let her go. It was part of what made me so dizzy the night before.

"Anything else?"

I heard him breathing into the receiver on the other end.

"No. You and I will have a little post-mortem in a few days. Wait for my call."

"Great. Thanks."

I hung up and walked back down the hallway to the bathroom, quickly washed my face and found myself looking in the mirror afterward, unable to wipe the expression of incredulity from my face.

I stopped short of the bedroom, hanging at the doorway, staring at Seneca sleeping, like a replay of our first night: asleep while I marvelled at her beguiling otherness.

+ + +

"WHAT'S THIS?"

I had woken her up with a kiss. From that point forward throughout the morning we would pause at intervals to touch each other, clasp hands, embrace.

She was smiling but it was a serious smile. She took me to the entrance of my office. Out of habit, I'd left the door open. I thought she was going to pull out her journal entries from my desk, my heart beating anxiously.

She pointed to the bookshelf under the windowsill.

"Those," she said. "Those are old film canisters, am I right?"

I looked at the green Fujifilm and yellow Kodak rolls, lined up on the shelf like pop art bullets.

"Uh, yeah. Yes, they are."

"You'd put those into a 35mm still camera, right? An old one."

"Yeah."

Please stop saying old.

"So..." she demonstrated with her hands, a clever smile on her face, her fingers outstretched as if holding onto a pair of radio dials, "you'd load the film canister into the back of the camera...and as you took the pictures it would wind the exposed film onto a take-up spindle."

"Yes," I said, taken aback at how foreign and antiquated she made the process seem.

"So, where's your camera?"

I broke out into a sweat. I smiled politely and looked around the room for an answer.

"I'm asking because I work with photos, too. Sort of. I mean, it's all different and stuff, and I can't say anything about it, but I saw the...uh," she paused, losing her train of thought.

"Canisters," I said. It sounded instantly old-fashioned. As old-fashioned as the word *instant*.

"The canisters, sorry — and the names looked familiar to me."

"My camera's in the shop," I said, blushing.

"Do you buy so many canisters, individually like that, because you take a lot of photographs?"

I raised one hand to my head and the other to my waist, appearing both impatient and secretive. Either that, or I was about to sing, "I'm a Little Teapot."

"No. No, I don't buy much. Many. Those are actually... They're...I've already shot them," I said. I looked at her squarely. "They're exposed already."

169

Her smile was still serious. She looked at the rolls on the shelf and then back at me, working to understand what I was saying.

"So…what: they need to go somewhere next? To get processed?"

"Uh, you know. I would, normally…I would take them to a lab. One of the labs in town."

"Okay," she said, sounding less comfortable. I didn't know whether it was the ancient technology and a less than savvy understanding, or whether my inability to be straight with her was the cause. She looked around my office. There were no lights on, save for the cool spill of light coming through the window. Pale walls. Abandoned electronics parts. Sticky notes stuck to the walls like small islets of unmoored ideas.

"Is that something you plan to do sometime?"

At first I thought it was a voice in my head replaying something she had said, but I turned and saw her saying it.

"No," I said.

"Why?"

She had her poker face on. All business.

"I don't need to see them, Seneca. It's not important that I see them."

"So…Okay. Okay," she said, nodding, processing. More, please.

"I don't know why. It looks odd and I don't expect you to understand. I mean, you could, but I get it if you don't. I just… I needed to have the camera. I needed to get outside and get out of my head. The pictures don't matter. I'm sure I captured a lot of cool images, but I don't want to work on the pictures…I want to work on…"

"You," she said.

I looked at her. "What?"

"You needed to work on you."

A chill drove downward through me. I was looking at the rolls of film, lined up on the shelf like pop art bullets.

"Yes."

+ + +

A SILENT BREAKFAST. The silence of two. Just the news on the radio in the background like the sound of traffic. It was enough.

I kept expecting despair to unfold, black drapes of pessimism to block the warmth. It never came. So long as I was near her, so long as I was able to intermittently re-establish contact — a look down the hallway at each other, a caress when she reached for her cup — everything outside the two of us seemed non-essential.

"His name is Mr. Cremaschi," I gestured with a glass of orange juice. "That's the guy you'll be meeting with."

She sighed, tilting her head to the side slightly and closing her eyes.

"I'm trying not to think about it," she semi-whispered.

"Me too."

Rules, I thought. Stage directions.

People came in and out of the café, their footfalls amplified by the empty basement beneath; every crossing on the floor sounded as if on a theatre stage.

We found ourselves avoiding each other's gaze until, after arranging the half-eaten hard-boiled egg and sliced tomato on her plate, she looked squarely at me.

"What are your plans? For the future."

I looked at her and smiled. I loved how a question so banal at any other juncture had such a different meaning when it was shared between us.

"Get my shit together. Make something of it: writing, living. If only for myself."

Stay alive long enough to see you again...?

"That's good. I guess when I get settled I'll look around and see if you've been published."

I smiled sweetly. There was a burst of confidence within me, as if my veins were cleansed of fear, but I had no idea where it came from. So much had happened in so little time in which to process it. There were certainly no evil little manifestos on the horizon.

"That would be nice. I've always wanted an admirer from afar."

"Well, you've got one."

I could sense we were both on the verge: happy tears, sad tears. Hearts plumbed by exquisite absurdity. She reached over, as if reading my thoughts. We rose from our chairs and held each other tightly. She planted a lingering kiss on my cheek, as if to leave a mark. I could hear her breath stutter. I ran my fingers through her hair and kissed her forehead.

I looked at the clock, reluctantly: 10:25 a.m.

"I should get changed," she said in a low whisper.

"Yeah, I guess. Yeah. Look, wear what you want — I mean, take what you need," nodding to the bedroom. "I'd rather you be comfortable."

She sniffed quietly, staring into my eyes, smiling.

"Thanks."

Experience.

+ + +

WE FOUND OURSELVES cruising in a taxi; a sombre replay of the previous day. I could barely recall giving the driver the address: Cherry Street, just south of Mill. I could only remember asking him to stay off his cellphone and keep the two-way radio silent. She was in my Toronto sweatshirt and we were both wearing sunglasses. In a strange, unheralded way we were celebrities: it was only now that I was able — and barely so — to comprehend the gravity of what we had experienced. It took my breath away to think about it. We were like new astronauts: the first of the time travellers. From this point forward, man and woman would have total control. It began to dawn on me just how fantastic and horrific the idea was.

"I'm nervous." It was all I could say. Anything more would've caused me to tell the cab driver to pull over so I could vomit.

She nodded.

"I don't want to think about it until I have to," she said.

I saw her staring at me from below, tucked down on the bench seat as before, her head and shoulder resting against my chest. I nodded, drawing in a stiff breath to keep my feelings from possessing me.

"This could hurt," she said.

"It will." I looked out the window. "I don't think either of us doubted that."

"Leaving you a note..." she paused to gain her voice. "Leaving you a note is against the rules, Derrick." She reached up and rubbed my arm. It was then that I recalled Wallace's comment about souvenirs. "I just wanted you to know that, because I know you're the type of person who's going to rip open all of his furniture when he gets home to see if I left you a note."

I looked at her and chuckled.

"I just wanted you to know that," she repeated. "I wish I could've, but I made a commitment to them. I've spent a very long time trying to live up to my word, not to be stupid. Taking responsibility for once."

"Understood," I nodded. "But the rules don't stop me from thinking about you."

She looked up cautiously.

"Just don't obsess."

Her gaze darkened. She diverted her eyes when I gestured inquisitively.

"I was conditioned," she said. "They trained me to contain everything emotional in a soft box that I can open when I feel protected. They warned me about carrying emotional impressions around and trained me to contain them. It's not the safest approach, but it was practical considering the task. I just wish...I wish I hadn't been so harsh in the beginning. To you. I...This is just going by too quickly, and I have regrets."

"You were as scared as I was. I was being an idiot. I don't hold it against you."

We closed our eyes and held each other, knowing that within minutes we would be unable to do this. The ambient ocean lulled us into a state of dreaming: the percussive breaths of passing cars, the rhythm of the taxi tires on the asphalt.

I'll protect your memory. I may never speak a word of you, but you will be everything to me.

"Is this the address, sir?" the driver asked.

I sat up, opened my eyes reluctantly and saw an abandoned distillery reminding me of the old warehouse I'd stared at weeks earlier, after I'd heard Dad had died.

He's in there.

"Sir?"

"Yes, thanks," I said, spotting the Powter name chiselled on the facade.

The driver pulled a U-turn and parked in the front lot. I handed him a twenty-dollar bill and held Seneca as I opened my door. I looked in both directions as I stepped out: no traffic, no Society spooks to be seen.

"Okay, sweetie," I said, as she shifted her legs to get out of the cab.

The driver opened his window and stuck his head out: "I'll be waiting out here for you, Mr. van der Lem."

I caught his glance: I'd never given my name over the phone. A chill crept up my back as I began to doubt whether I'd ever given the driver the address in the first place. I wondered how often this had happened in the past few days, the last few...

"The entrance is on the side. Mr. Cremaschi is expecting you."

I couldn't bring myself to nod. The further I walked away from the car with her, the happier I was to be free from the Society's paternal watch.

"If this were a movie, you'd have a gun," she said.

"Yeah. I'd be a professional bounty hunter," I said, breathing nervously, "and you'd be the mixed-up mistress of a mafia boss. Sound about right?"

"Yup."

She stopped and we put our arms around each other. I lifted her off the toes of her cheap sneakers. I kissed her, our faces pressing together one last time, pulling away as our task presented itself.

"A soft box," she sighed, touching my chest with her fingers, looking at me. "A place for you to keep for later. When no one else is around. Just remember that."

I nodded.

We approached the employee entrance, hands held. It was unlocked, as promised. The interior was bare and abandoned; an industrial foyer with a concrete floor, divided by a wall with two doorways that accessed the rest of the building. I noticed how clean the space was: there were no cobwebs, no garbage from squatters, no dust drifting in the sunbeams.

I pricked up my ears. I caught the telltale hum of a speaker activated somewhere above us.

"Good morning," spoke a male voice over an intercom. "If the host is here, could you please state that you are present."

It wasn't Wallace. It certainly wasn't Cathy.

I squeezed her reassuringly.

"Yeah, I'm here."

"If the guest is here, may she also speak?"

Seneca cleared her throat and called out, "Yes, I'm here."

A pause.

"Has anyone followed you?"

I turned around and looked behind my back.

"Just the cab driver. Are you Mr. Cremaschi?"

Another pause.

"That is correct. Please address your guest and ask her to enter through one of the two doors in the foyer. You will not follow her. After allowing our guest to leave through one of the doors, you will leave the way you came."

I felt her clutch my hand before I turned to look at her. For a split second I thought about us in the CN Tower elevator.

"Safe trip," I said, holding my gut firm.

"I'll miss you, Derrick."

I leaned forward and kissed her. She cupped my face. I swept my hands over her figure one last time and then we found ourselves separated, staring at each other as she moved toward the doors almost as if this had never happened.

"Take care," I whispered, my voice breaking up.

She smiled back, her face blushing, a portrait of wishful thinking. She approached one of the old wooden doors. It had a large pane of smoked glass in the centre. She twisted the handle and pulled it open. I could see just a little further inside – dimly lit, but by the look on her face she didn't seem intimidated. Perhaps Wallace was waiting there for her. I hoped he was; someone I trusted more than a stranger. I watched her turn around briefly and raise her hand. I did the same and saw her slip away, the door closing behind her. The inevitability of my beginning to forget her face.

"Thank you for your participation," the voice echoed from above. "Please leave the building the same way you came. Your taxi is waiting outside. A representative will contact you in the near future."

I stood trying to see through the glass of the door, to see if I could make out any movement or shadows. Nothing. She was gone. A part of me wanted to stay in case she came back through the door, in case she broke the rules. I couldn't help but imagine the doorknob turning, Seneca racing into my arms, the two of us bursting out of this joint, forging an uncertain future on our own. On the lam.

"Please leave the building," the voice repeated.

I turned and exited through the door we'd just come through. Sure enough, the cab driver was idling in the driveway. He was working on a crossword. When he heard the door shut behind me he tossed his paper into the passenger seat.

I climbed into the back seat and closed the door, my stomach filled with cement. The driver switched gears and steered us back onto Cherry Street. I tracked the south entrance of the building through each window of the taxi as we turned around. Nothing. No one was coming out. It was over. I saw the twenty-dollar bill I'd handed the driver laying beside me on the seat.

"Back home, sir?"

I looked into the rear-view mirror. I hoped to see the driver's eyes, to see an anonymous friend behind the wheel and not an enemy, or, worse, yet another unknown side of the dice I'd thrown when I'd agreed to the experiment. But I realized it was all rehearsed: the driver wasn't looking, would probably take me back home by default whether I said yes, no or nothing. So I said nothing, choosing instead to keep my eyes on the fading distillery in growing disbelief.

+ + +

THE NEXT DAY I couldn't clean anything. I wouldn't. I wanted evidence of her around me. The cup she'd drank from on our last morning rested on the table. I sat on the couch with the white dress shirt she'd worn held up to my nose.

The disposable camera was split open on the floor, the film canister removed. I'd stuffed it in the dresser, tucked under some shirts. But at least the cab was free. A part of me thought it would be an interesting test in the future, not telling the next cab driver anything to see if it worked again.

I didn't want to turn on the television. I didn't want to touch the Internet. Like the sounds of traffic milling beneath the apartment window, I knew that time was moving forward, perpetually un-paused. Inevitably, there would be a small plane crash in the countryside. A crowded ferry in Bangladesh would inevitably sink and take hundreds of lives with her. An inevitable election, or three. The continuity of tragedy, signifying that my time on Earth was to be referred to more and more in the past tense. That is, less and less time alive.

For the first time since the night I'd found her in the alley our tenses of experience were now realigned: she would no longer be experiencing a present in the past, and I would no longer be glimpsing the future, or what little I was able to glean.

I got up and grabbed my Moleskine from the computer desk. I flipped it open to my last entry, remarking about her upset reaction to my refusal to tell her the location of the drop-off. It seemed so immature now, but I was happy that I'd managed to capture it. I tucked the book into my jacket and made for the door. I thought about museums and art galleries, the Powter warehouse; I thought about the entropy of memory and the need to record experience, even if the results were inexact, even if what was ultimately called "the record" was half-amusement.

+ + +

SITTING UNDER MY tree in the dog bowl, I spent the next two hours writing: sketching characters, noting story arcs, drawing incidents. I had seven, twelve, fifty stories, poems, novels, screenplays auditioning themselves in my head, spinning like fruit on a slot machine.

I couldn't be bothered to look around, to see little dogs chasing each other, couples in love, the sound of children in the playground above. Every time I felt distracted, I saw Seneca's face, I thought about Dad, I remembered the hospital where I'd found myself alive, the nurse who left me alone. I felt indebted to these experiences, somehow, as if conscripted to wring out and examine each feeling and thought.

Page after page, my pen, my hand weren't fast enough to capture the clogged volume of material spilling out of my head: paragraphs, proclamations in all caps, point-form annotations, words circled enthusiastically. I spent the whole afternoon this way, pausing only to come back to the apartment when the sun slipped away. I continued at my computer unabated until I could no longer keep my eyes focused.

When I slipped into bed, beside the spot where she preferred to lay, I slid my hand over, imagining she was there. I was falling asleep when I slipped my hand beneath her pillow and clipped a hard object.

I sat up, switched on the light and pulled the pillow away. There.

A box.

Red leaves.

The red jewellery box from the broken goose in the mall, the black Society insignia on the lid. I picked it up and turned it over, holding it under the lamp, incredulous.

You crazy, crazy lady.

It took me a moment to build up the courage to open it. I lifted the lid and saw, in a bed of downy cotton, a small photograph sitting in the centre. It was a photo of my father, much younger, unshaven, with the sort of glasses that people only wore ironically now.

I knew this photo. I could barely remember it.

It was a photo of my dad holding me. I was laughing. I was a child with cherry red cheeks — five? Seven? Laughing. He was smiling. Where were we?

Where were we?

+ + +

"YOU GET SOME SUN?"

They were Paul's first words as I walked into The Paddock on Bathurst, taking a stool beside him at the bar. I'd panicked on the way over, not sure what I was allowed to say about the last several days, tempted to explode with description. I hadn't heard from Wallace, no matter that I'd left another message, and so the unresolved question of what I was and was not free to disclose felt like a cruel restraint. The photograph drifted in my mind like a ghost. I couldn't shake my frustration at its incomplete meaning.

"What do you mean?" I asked.

My eyes were still adjusting to the tungsten light and dark panelling.

"I dunno — did you get away or something?" He still had his eyes on me, warily.

"No. No. I didn't."

"Hmmn. You just look rested."

He was right. I finally felt I'd shaken the existential cloud that had possessed me. My sleep since Seneca's departure had been deep and long, and my mind had been able to focus better on the outside world than before. I knew it was due in part to my effort to keep the fire in my gut after she'd left. Lest anything in waking life displace my memories, I was determined to never tire in preserving my memory of our time together and what shook loose from within me as a result.

"Well, I got away from things, I guess," I said, hoping it didn't come across too vaguely. The last thing I wanted was another discussion like the one at city hall, where I was forced to dress things up in ways that satisfied neither of our needs.

"That's good!" he said. "That's great. You're...I'll tell you, it's been a long stretch. You're the first person I've seen in ages who isn't either angry with me or a major source of confusion."

"I'm happy to oblige."

Paul smiled tiredly.

"We've been renovating the kitchen."

"Aha. And?"

"I'd rather deal with having casting directors tell me I'm useless."

"Ouch. Double ouch."

"Never tile a floor, Derrick," he said, running his hands through his hair.

I ordered a drink, and then, struck by something, turned to him.

"The gig! Oh my god, I forgot all about it, I'm sorry. How was it?"

Paul smiled bitterly.

"Oh, that. Christ," he rolled his eyes.

"Or I could ask you more questions about the kitchen."

"No, no — that's ok. I went. It went." He threw his hands up. "I'm not sure. I mean, I don't honestly know. All I know is that I was away from the house, away from cutting drywall, working with solvents. Didn't exactly win Boyfriend of the Year on that one. And it turned out to be just a bunch of bullshit. It was a one-time thing. I thought it was going to be a recurring role. I'm serious," he said, shaking his head. "I have no clue what I did."

"Well, isn't that just…being an actor? Walking into a weird situation, saying your lines the best you can and then leaving?"

He raised his hands with exasperation then dropped them. Then raised them again.

"I guess? I don't know." He crossed his arms. "You know, I'm at this stage in my non-career where I don't know what I should be expecting. And so, I never know what's normal. I don't have a template of normal to work with."

"Did you get paid?"

"Yes. Paid well, actually." He took a sip from his glass. "At the very least, I got paid."

The bartender set down my drink.

"Did you do a good job?"

"Here's the thing: I met them, these two...whatever, corporate types. They sat me down, and then I just read my lines into a mic while they watched and gave me cues. It was odd because I thought it was going to be on-camera, but I didn't see one. I just did what they asked and that was it. I was too nervous to ask questions. And they seemed to like what I did."

I raised my tumbler and we clinked glasses.

"There you go: you did your job and got paid."

"Yeah. At least I had lines. Hard to call yourself an actor when all you're doing is standing in the background, smiling and pretending to talk."

"You had lines," I said encouragingly, not unlike the way Paul spoke to me at times. I raised my glass again. "Voice work can be lucrative. Your future as a drywaller may be in doubt."

Paul nodded belatedly in agreement, swallowing his drink.

"'Thank you for your participation,'" he mimicked, raising his glass.

"What's that?"

"I had, like, all of six lines or something. Did it all in one take, too. I was like Richard Burton."

He was full of pride. I nodded.

"'Please leave the building the same way you came. Your taxi is waiting outside.'"

I was about to say something. I closed my mouth and set my hands on the bar. I sat for an immeasurable space of time, motionless.

"Paul. What did you just say?"

"It's one of the lines fr –"

"I know that," I said, staring at my hands. "What did... Where did they record this?"

Paul stirred his ice cubes.

"Some hole in the distillery," he said, blushing. "Not sexy."

I froze on my seat.

"The good news is that I didn't have to walk far for a drink somewhere afterwards."

I felt as if I'd been poisoned, as if the tumbler in front of me held bleach. My stomach curled into itself and my skin felt cold. I heard Paul's voice beside me.

"So... what's going on with you?" he asked as innocently as possible. "How were the Masons?"

+ + +

THE CAB IDLED in the parking lot of the Powter Building. We sat in the back seat, staring at the south entrance. Paul looked confused, our time at the bar cut short. My anger turned on him as if in a bad dream. I had turned it on our cab driver earlier, quizzing him before I would tell him our destination. I didn't give a shit about either of them. I was prepared to break every precious thing in the world to understand what was happening.

"What's going on, buddy?" Paul asked in a hushed tone. I refused to tell him, demanding we go to the "shoot location" first. I wanted to corroborate that it was the same place, and it was.

I got out of the cab and walked over to the employee entrance. It was locked. I looked up and walked around the perimeter of the building, stepping over weeds, stumbling over loose concrete, trying every door and checking every window. There was no sign of any activity inside. Another dead warehouse.

When I came back to the cab, I looked at Paul exasperatedly and pointed to the side door.

"You went in through there?"

"Yeah? Derrick, what's going on? Should I get out?"

"No," I said, climbing back in and shutting the door. "Who did you meet here? What did they look like?"

"You know, a couple of guys. Producer types. They wore suits. They had a script — said it was for some project."

"Names?"

"I... Yeah, I mean, they had names, but I don't remember. Jim? Was there a Jim?"

"Was there a girl?"

"Who's called Jim anymore? A girl...? No. I don't know. They were shuffling some shit around in another area while I read my lines into the mic. I think I heard someone — a woman — humming something, near the end, walking in the background. Look, I was just there to work." He looked forward as if mimicking what he'd done that day. "I'd sit there... I'd read a line, then they'd give me a cue — point at me to read the next one. It wasn't like there was dialogue where, like, there's someone else I'm talking to. It went like that, and it was fast and pretty easy and then I just got the hell out of there after they paid me."

I covered my face with my hands.

"Derrick, you're starting to freak me out. What's going on?"

"How did they pay you?"

"Well, it was weird, because they paid in cash. I thought it was going to be something, like... You're scaring me, man. You're scaring me. I'm sorry... b-but I don't know what I'm apologizing for."

"It was a ruse. The whole fucking thing…" I curled over and clutched my legs in the back seat. My gut ached as if all this time I'd been carrying a sliver of glass there, digging its way further into my abdomen. I took deep breaths to combat the oncoming pain.

+ + +

THE CN TOWER loomed southeast, poking up behind the maples, beyond the ridge of the dog bowl. Another totem, making Seneca impossible not to imagine, here and away from me. I gazed at it, and wondered whether I would ever again look over my life as I had standing over the city that final afternoon.

I inserted the tip of my pen between the slats of the picnic table, staring blankly at dogs playing like children. Halfway inserted, I wrenched it down, breaking off the head and splintering the casing. It spurted black ink like blood, marking the wood, my pant leg, my fingers.

I had not yet called Wallace. Refused. Despite a ferocity boiling within me, I would wait. I would stay still in the cold. Die if necessary. It was their game, rules unpublished and beyond my understanding. I would let them finish it. On their terms, to the pain of waiting for such a time as they deemed appropriate.

I did not suspend judgment: I despised them. Every morning, assuming I slept the previous night, I woke up feeling violated. I woke up wanting to call the police. I whipped rocks against garage doors in my alleyway walks, damning everyone: the Society, Seneca, Paul, myself. I threw out the rolls of film in my office. I didn't need them anymore.

Every attempt to describe the events to Paul laid bare the extent to which I had been childishly gullible. I had to assume his role was most likely as an unwitting chess piece. He didn't have anything more to contribute to my barrage of questions aside from a perspective more perplexed than mine. Why they decided to use him was another question: surely a demonstration of power and not cruelty? Perhaps a part in a larger game.

It was difficult to think straight. I looked at the ink on my hands, glistening black on my fingers, reminded of the night I stood in the kitchen, drugged.

Hot water, by God.

I let the shattered pen fall onto the grass. I smeared the ink on the pages of my notebook. Passages written intermittently over the last few months: words, ideas. Beginnings. Stained them with anger. Redacted indiscriminately.

When I was done I slapped it shut, pressing the covers together so tightly my biceps shuddered, so that the ink would congeal and paste the pages together like glue.

+ + +

WALLACE'S NUMBER WAS out of service.

Dr. Brenda McAlistair, one-time sweetheart of Wallace and possible Society stooge, despite her request at our last appointment to schedule a follow-up, had inexplicably left the clinic on a sabbatical. According to the receptionist at the clinic, she left the country to focus on international medical efforts with Brazilian street orphans.

The *favelas*, she said to me. The favelas were needful.

The Society had withdrawn from sight just as subtly as they had appeared, leaving only Paul and myself. I had no choice

but to trust him. It was either that or surrender to the impli-
cation that absolutely everyone around me was complicit, if
not under surveillance: the hardware store where I bought
the rope, the place I got her sneakers, the waiter who served
us on the chilly patio. Then I thought about the nurse. The
box. The photograph.

The Portuguese sports bar on College Street was exactly as
it was before, when I first sat down with Wallace, complete
with the same posters of Cristiano Ronaldo and Luís Figo; it
had only been him and I then, and the waitress. Now, a bunch
of overweight men in their fifties, staring at me.

It predictably didn't make sense.

I had gone a week avoiding contact with anyone or any
place associated with the Society of Experience, disgusted
with myself. It was a scam. Not the prank-for-kicks I first
thought it might turn out to be, but a scam of the cruellest
sort. And yet, even here there were doubts. A part of me was
convinced that, as a scam, it wasn't logical. No money had
been involved: I checked my bank account every day and
what little was left was untouched. Nothing had actually
transpired to result in either a financial gain or loss. Add
that Wallace had gone so far as to compensate me during
"training" and it became all the more absurd. Everything in
the world was still in it's proper if uninspiring place.

It did not stop me from feeling like the walking injured. I
told Paul everything, hoping that – between the two of us
hashing it all out – we could piece something together. I told
him about the nurse and the card, the contact I'd made
through McAlistair's clinic and the proposition Wallace made
to me: the nature of the experiment, all of the contextual
things I wished I'd been able to say when we'd met at city hall.
I told him about Seneca, feeling as freshly fooled now as

before. Paul took advantage of friends he'd made in law school, particularly one who worked closely with a city councillor. A thorough search of municipal records revealed nothing about a Society of Experience and nothing about Doctor Wallace Turner. As a practitioner he wasn't registered with any of the non-Society societies. This was not to say that there were no secret societies out there, just that — as Paul put plainly — they were secret by name only: in order to avoid a tax audit they had to be registered one way or another.

681

+ + +

I WAS STARING at a copy of *Toronto Life* on the magazine rack when someone sat down across from me, wearing mirrored aviator sunglasses pushed up over his hairline. We were in a public library on the outskirts of downtown, overlooking impatient traffic through a large window.

I needed answers. I worked the social media angle, which I hated because social media represented people who either hated or loved life. I was too distracted by a memory fragment. I needed answers. Something Wallace said. After everything went bad, I began to collect my thoughts about our conversations, collecting as much detail as I could recall in the hope that something might have been said — an intentional clue, an inadvertent admission. I bought a new notebook just for this purpose.

"Hey," he said under his breath, laying an unfolded newspaper on top of the table. At one time we actually knew each other, casually. He pretended to look at one of the articles in the commentary section; he might as well have been staring at the bare tabletop. I hadn't pegged him for the Le Carré–type, but when I'd arranged for our rendezvous he'd seemed to really want to have things be like in the movies. Considering he was the one with access to the goods, I humoured him. He reached down, pulling out a folder from the canvas grocery bag by his feet, then slipped it under the section of newspaper he was reading, showing no semblance of interruption, as if those arms were someone else's arms and he was perfectly content to stare at his *Globe and Mail* while an object was inserted underneath. After a few moments passed, he checked his watch, cleared his throat and got up from his chair to leave. I felt like yelling, "Thanks, Scott!," but that would've been cruel. We instead gave each other a knowing glance.

I waited a few minutes and then reached over and slid the newspaper toward me, not particularly caring if someone was paying attention to our choreography. In reverse order of my acquaintance, I pondered the same page of the editorial section then slid his envelope underneath toward me, into my courier bag.

When I got home, I poured myself a rye and sat on the couch with the envelope, eager to read about Vijay Abapathy.

+ + +

I DIDN'T KNOW anything about cricket, but I didn't expect to see what looked to be a miniature steamroller to the side of the field. Everything I knew about sports had to do with iconic symbols: batting cages, basketball hoops, badminton netting. The grounds here were wide and flat, pine trees dotting the wide outer boundary. It took me a while to note the flattened rectangle in the middle of the pitch.

Using baseball as the closest comparison — a sport I know only marginally better than cricket — the "pitcher" (guy throwing the ball) wound up and whipped the ball like he wanted to break the other guy's legs. The other guy, with the "bat," swung it, kind of like a cross between a golf swing and a bunt.

I took three sets of transit to get here, which was okay because I was stoned and listening to The Jesus and Mary Chain. The players' equipment and uniforms looked almost new, better than the mismatched gear my friends played baseball with — tattered gloves they'd kept since high school and such.

As strange as this sport may have initially seemed to me, what was undoubtedly absurd was my being here, standing alone under a tree, just outside the parking lot of a cricket field in Etobicoke, with no one to meet. Maybe that, or my fool hunch that someone Wallace mentioned in passing was real and not another contrivance for my benefit. Maybe it was all true. Why the photo? I'd studied it on and off since Seneca's stage exit. So long since those childhood days, which seemed so alien to me now.

The guy with the bat, seeing that he'd hit the ball the way he wanted, ran. He ran in a particular direction while the players on the other team scrambled, ostensibly to disqualify him.

Was that even me in the photo? Of course it was. I knew that smiling face — it made me cringe when I saw pictures of myself above Mom's fireplace. I simply couldn't convince myself that it was just a prop. Like Seneca herself.

I might as well have had a sign over my head, seeing as there was nowhere to sit near the round cricket "diamond," outside of some aluminum stands for friends and family. There is nothing more suspicious than the sight of someone who doesn't understand or like a sport at the sporting match where you are playing. I might as well have been staring at them through binoculars wearing black leather gloves, with a moustache. I had a newspaper. That was my prop. I never opened it. I'm not sure how it was supposed to camouflage me.

Awkward White Guy.

Possibly a Mountie.

But why at all? Why bother? Why would they go through such an elaborate set of procedures only to leave me with a souvenir from a photo album? What was it supposed to mean? How much could it all have cost them to do this? Most importantly, what good had it done them, to have concealed a photograph in a piece of public art for thirty-five years?

I'd gone back to the Eaton Centre on a Saturday when it was bustling with tourists and shoppers — in other words when it was least likely I would be recognized. Just being there compounded the idea of being duped, but as I had made my way through the Queen Street entrance (certainly not the service entrance this time), I discovered that the goose — the one I'd taken down — was again hanging from the glass roof. I remember walking forward in a daze, brushing past strangers, walking toward the railing, people staring at the illuminated map where I had smashed the coffee mug with my cowboy routine. It was all there. Intact. Or replaced.

The batter managed to evade disqualification through means I could not figure out. His team rejoiced, sort of. I felt like a jerk. Twenty minutes later, I bummed a cigarette from someone on the way home.

+ + +

"IT WAS STUPID, I know."

"You went to a cricket match in Etobicoke? Looking to find a guy whose name was Vijay?"

I bowed my head in shame, my hands shoved into my pockets. We were walking down Huron Street from Bloor, having met at G's Fine Foods. An overcast afternoon in late June, sidewalks soaked in rain.

"Sorry," I said.

"Sorry isn't really necessary. I don't know. Maybe it is. What were you expecting to see? I mean, you were expecting to go there..."

"Yeah. Shut up."

"...to find someone named Vijay..."

"Shut up."

"Where to start...like, did you expect them to wear name tags?"

"Fuck off."

I could see his eyes contemplating the scale of my plan's half-bakedness. Then he looked at me, shaking his head. "You must have been disappointed. You couldn't have walked away from that feeling good."

"No. No, I did not."

"How did you get the package, if you don't mind me asking?"

He hadn't told his girlfriend about the incident with the Society, partially at my insistence, partially because it would not make his decision to become an actor any more wisely considered in her eyes. He'd told her he'd used the money from his gig to join a professional training program, focused on improvisation techniques. It was meant to complement his skills and look good on his resumé. Our meetings began in my apartment and quickly moved beyond, becoming part of an ongoing series of "classes," half of which were alcoholic brainstorm sessions. When speaking over the phone or by text, our code phrase became "improv class."

"When I first met Wallace, a thousand years ago, he did this whole song and dance, telling me how they'd plucked somebody out of university. He was supposed to be this genius that they were saving from having his talents wasted. His name was Vijay Abapathy. I got the idea to do some digging with my own contacts and I remembered that I knew someone who's now an assistant prof at U of T."

Rainwater dripped on my head from the tree canopy.

"He knew someone in registrations who could drill through the alumni database, do some digging."

"Nice work. Sort of illegal, too, I think. Maybe we should start our own society."

"It doesn't hurt to fight fire with fire," I said under my breath.

He shook his head lightly. "Are you writing these days?"

"What?"

"Are you writing?"

I threw up my hands. "I don't know. Not really. Not for now?"

"That's interesting, because I've noticed that you speak in clichés when you're writing. What did it say?"

"Wh...?"

"The package you got."

"Right. Right. So..." I couldn't focus my eyes anywhere without being distracted in another direction. "Surprisingly, Vijay was exactly what Wallace said: boy genius science guy. Blew everyone's mind at the university and ended up getting noticed. He's one of those one-in-a-million types, where you just know you're going to read about them some day in the newspaper. Except he sort of came and went without anyone hearing anything from him afterwards."

"So," Paul said, "does he love his alma mater?"

"He hasn't kept in touch with anyone at the university. The address they had on file is stale — it was from back when he attended school. Belongs to a student bunker in Kensington Market. I even called his folks' place to see if he lived there. Assuming she's not an actor too, his mother said he's not there. Wouldn't give me a current address without knowing who I was. You know what I said?"

He shook his head.

"I'm his friend, Wallace."

"And?"

"Nada. Didn't mean anything to her. So I hung up. The only unfollowed piece I had left from the package I'd been given was that Vijay played with the engineering facility's cricket club. Member of the EDCL."

"What does that stand for?"

I shook my head. "Something-something-Cricket-thing."

Paul stopped. A devilish grin was on his face. He stared up toward Robarts Library, across the street from us like a brutalist crown.

"Continue. So how did you find him?"

I didn't have the nerve to look at him. I was embarrassed.

"It took awhile."

"I know it took awhile — come on, Derrick, this is our sixth fucking meeting. Should I tell Julie I'm getting my master's degree?"

"The phone book."

"The . . . ?"

"Phone book. Yes. The phone book."

I could hear a streetcar chime from over on Spadina. A part of me wanted to run toward it, to throw myself under it.

"So, you were about to hire a private detective."

"Yes."

"And you went to a ..."

"Yeah."

"You went to a cricket match in Etobicoke, looking — randomly — for someone you've never seen in your life. Didn't know what he looked like."

"Yup."

It took a while. Watching Paul's eyes dart around incredulously. I waited. I knew it was purely at my expense — I didn't mind waiting while he stared up at the sky, slowly shaking his head. It was like an encore for my ineptitude.

"All done now?" I asked.

"Sure."

We reached Harbord Street and turned west, walking toward the sun.

"On my way back from the, uh, cricket game, I was cutting through the Royal York hotel on my way from Union Station and I walked past a pay-phone booth and there was an honest-to-God phone book attached to the booth. Barely dog-eared. Maybe the staff takes the phone books at night and irons them."

"I can't remember the last time I saw a phone book," Paul said.

"I figured what the hell, walked over ..."

"I used to throw them out and they kept delivering them. I don't see them anywhere now."

"Vijay Abapathy lives in the east end."

He and I exchanged glances silently. We noticed the light at Spadina was counting down so we both sprinted across while we could make it.

"You're going to track him down?" he asked, catching his breath.

"Yes."

"Brave man."

"We'll see. I can chicken out of this anytime."

"So you say. What are you going to do? I mean...really? What can you really do?"

I found myself staring through the window displays of the bookstores on Harbord, staring at my reflection. Remembering staring at myself in the mirror the last night Seneca and I were together. Wondering how it came to be that my face felt alien to me.

"Find the truth, I guess. Get some context on this."

"But why? I mean, remember that these people are connected, Derrick. They have the power to screw with things on a massive level. And I'm sure they have the power to silence things, too."

"Maybe a little bit of vengeance," I said.

"What did you say?" Paul was chuckling.

"A little bit of vengeance."

He shook his head, his lips pursed.

"I hope for your sake they don't play cricket in Etobicoke or you'll never find them."

I turned to him. "Paul, I want them to know that I know. That I can touch them. I want them to know that I won't give up and that I want an answer."

"I think this is bigger than you, dude. Way bigger. I'd walk away."

Whose side are you on, I thought. I began to dread that he was a mole. That I had just surrendered the complete strategy behind my last remaining option, and the person I'd shared so much with for so long was not really himself. That he was doing someone else's bidding, trying to steer me toward surrender.

"I'm going there tonight. To Vijay's. And I'm telling you this because of that. If you don't hear from me by noon tomorrow, call the cops."

"And tell them what, exactly?"

It was too late. I had no choice but to trust him. I could stand here and get angry at how few friends I had or trust that this person was not about to stab me in the back or abandon me.

"I've written down everything and put it into the folder on Vijay Abapathy. I stuffed it all into a PVC pipe behind my stove. It's bound with the journal entries from Seneca. Everything. Even if none of what I'm telling you today makes sense, just remember that it's all behind the stove."

A few seconds passed. I wanted him to say something. I wanted him to do something to give away his collusion.

"Her journal entries are faked, obviously," I added. "Every layer is just another layer of deception on top of another layer of deception."

I wished I could stay angry; that being angry all the time could take me somewhere.

"Well, I know the actors' union will certainly want to have a word with them," Paul said.

He gave his remark as much oxygen as possible. We reached a pedestrian crossing at Borden Street, which was where we typically parted ways. He looked at me and saw that my face was flushed. My eyes were welling.

I had no one left in the world to say this to.

"I fell for her, Paul."

+ + +

I STOOD IN the foyer of a low-rise, off a side street six blocks east of the Don River, staring at a directory of names behind a thin plate of glass, specifically at apartment #407: V. Abapathy.

It was around nine in the evening and I was dressed in my French cat burglar outfit. I'd spent the hours after our last improv class thinking about what I was going to say. Or do. I cleared my throat, raising a finger to the intercom panel. At first, I thought the honest approach was best. Put all the cards on the table at once. Give peace a chance. Canadian Gibran and all that.

4

But I realized that any mention of the Society would probably scare him off — Vijay was just as capable of not letting me into the building, after all. Short of my wit's limit, I didn't want to have to smash open the door.

So, I reasoned, how does one encapsulate the situation to a stranger, in a way that's neither bluntly off-putting nor long-winded and desperate-sounding? He could just step away from his intercom and that's it. No entry.

o

Of course, this could all be more elegantly achieved, I reasoned, if I could just send my argument to him on paper. Perhaps email.

Sadly, apart from appreciating the strength of my argument, there would still be no enticement for him to respond.

7

In other words...

I cleared my throat. My heart pounded as I waited.

"Hello?" came a voice from the speaker. Male. Younger.... lie, like the clever bastard you are.

"It's Wallace," I said, twisting the tone of my voice as accurately as he could. "I need to come up."

A pause. Too long. I was sweating, my head hanging ever lower as...

The lock on the door buzzed. I stared at it. I pushed it open, feeling as if I'd just bullshitted my way into Fort Knox, then walked to the elevator, pressed the 4 button and leaned back against the wall. It was as if I hadn't breathed in five minutes. I was still exhaling when the doors opened on Vijay's floor. I stepped out and walked down a narrow, carpeted hallway. I scanned the doors and eventually saw that #407 was left slightly ajar. I approached quietly, listening, but couldn't pick out any sounds coming from inside. My heart racing.

I hadn't actually planned anything beyond getting past the lobby. I curled my fingers into fists, readying myself for the worst, wondering how I would be leaving: on foot, in a police cruiser or in an ambulance. Whether it would even be reported...

Play it cool, I told myself. Be Wallace until you're not.

I cleared my throat, pushing open the door, indulging myself with a mental conjuring of Al Pacino from *Scarface*, my booted footfalls audible on the slate tile of Vijay's small foyer like a theatre stage. I heard a faucet running. It stopped. There was a hint of cooked onions in the air, mixed with the smell of latex paint.

"Hey, Wallace," a young man's voice called from somewhere inside.

I cleared my throat.

"Hello," I said, as Wallace-like as possible. I didn't intend to keep the ruse going – I couldn't. I'd hoped he would answer the door so that the element of surprise would work in my favour and I could rush him. Instead I found myself standing in the living-room foyer of a decorative yet spartan apartment, waiting for a puzzle piece to show his face.

Please.

"Just in the washroom — be there in a sec."

Reminded me of Seneca.

Take your time.

It was a small flat, maybe six hundred fifty square feet, and the more I looked about, my heart beating harder, the more I noticed odd things. The stereo receiver and wide-screen television were bleeding-edge new, worth thousands of dollars. I couldn't even recognize the brand name on the speakers, but they dwarfed anything I owned. There were a few oil paintings hanging. One depicted a baby doll in the mouth of a greyhound. Maybe it wasn't a doll. The apartment was so clean, so thoughtfully decorated that it was as if I were standing in a condo showroom, but without the genericism. Everything looked real, lived-in. I could smell cologne.

"Wallace, I –" Vijay walked into the living room. He stood taller than me, taller than I had hoped. He looked about five years younger. Thin, but not lacking muscle. He wore glasses with dark, rectangular rims.

"I'm not Wallace," I said.

It was evident.

My hands were still in fists, as if my fingers were glued together. I was completely out of my depth.

"No shit," he said, standing still, confused.

"I'm not a thief. I'm here for some answers."

I was relieved to catch the same unease in his expression as I felt. I'd half-expected Wallace to walk in, that this would be yet another Society dollhouse. I was relieved to have the upper hand, if fleetingly.

"I'm not stupid or violent, but if you are not one hundred percent straightforward with me, I'll blow this all away," I said, pointing to the furnishings, hoping something in the gesture — cobbled from the countless vengeance movies I'd grown up watching — made an impression. "I'll blow this open for everyone to see."

I had no way of knowing whether anything I said made any impact. What was I going to do if he politely asked me to leave or threatened to call the police?

His face softened, almost frowning.

"I need to sit down," he said, as if he were suddenly weighted with something.

+ + +

WHILE VIJAY SAT uneasily on his showroom sofa, I fixed us straight whiskies in red and blue crystal tumblers, surprised at how my presence seemed to throw him off-balance.

"The good news is this shouldn't take long," I said, sitting down across from him in an Eames chair, placing our tumblers on an oblong coffee table.

"If you're honest, that is," I added.

I wasn't sure when to let up on the Lee Marvin routine. He couldn't look in any one direction for more than a few seconds. He lifted his glass and took a disinterested sip and then winced at what he tasted, staring down as if the answer were written on the ice cubes.

Has he drunk alcohol before, I wondered. Is that his bar even? Is this his apartment?

"Here's my problem: I was told that you helped the Society of Experience develop a way to transport people through time. A projection transport system."

For the first time since seeing me in his foyer, he looked me straight in the eye. Perhaps all this time he'd been working on a line of bullshit to tell me. Perhaps he truly was their one weak link. If he was half as smooth as Wallace, he'd have found a story to tell me by now. Vijay wasn't smooth at all. His expression softened as if realizing that anything he said would be scrutinized.

Keep the pressure steady, van der Lem.

"I was supposed to pick up a virtual projection of a person from the future – a woman who was to physically remain in the future while a virtualized probe travelled back in her place – and what I got was a real person – flesh and blood."

I took a sip and set my glass on the table with a percussive tap beside some sheets of algorithmic jottings. I traded glances with my detainee.

"She's nothing like what I was told to expect. She's real and not some blurry it, she's difficult, and I get my instructions fed to me through a broken answering machine from this lady from the future, Cathy. Long story short: when I take her back, after I return her to one of your spooks, I realize she may not even have been a time traveller at all. She may actually, in fact, be an actor. That this may all be one big fucking joke."

I paused to linger on his reactions, but I couldn't register anything beyond that of someone who didn't know how to respond when a question wasn't clearly asked.

"But what's odd," I continued, "is that when I pulled a thread out of Wallace's story – you – it turned out to be legitimate. You are what he said you were and, by the looks of things, they've rewarded you for something."

I nodded around the apartment.

"So, tell me, Vijay Abapathy, what's the truth? Or are you an actor, too?"

Something strange happened: he widened his eyes ever so slightly, then leaned forward demonstratively. I wasn't sure what to expect until I saw him slowly reach for a drafting pencil on the coffee table, then for one of the sheets. I saw him turn the page over and he began to write something on the back, small enough that I couldn't make it out from where I was sitting. When he was done he swivelled the page around and nodded down to it.

"I read one of your stories once," he said with an unexpected gentleness.

I had barely uncrossed my leg to look over the note. I looked up at him.

"What?"

"You published it under another name, right?"

I stared at him, dumbfounded; the business with his scribbled note abandoned for the time being.

"I liked it," he said. "It was good. I wrote a story once that got published, too."

He pushed the note closer, keeping a suggestive gaze on me.

"It's about a scientist who discovers an inner layer of nervous sensitivity in the circuits of everyday electronic equipment, as a result of the collaborative electromagnetic properties of various precious metals."

I looked down at the note. At first I was suspicious: it consisted entirely of numbers.

"But the more he measures what he theorizes are primal emotions in these electronic objects, the more he realizes that they also truly feel things. Pain, among other things. It all sort of comes to a climax when he happens across a solar-powered calculator that has been discarded, spending its life inadvertently left on a windowsill in his office."

Noticing my confusion, he continued telling me the story while he reached over and circled the numbers with his pencil, so that they were separated into two sets.

"It lives without an off button, right? He realizes that the calculator had been driven to madness because it spent so much time exposed to sunlight, unable to shut off. Ever. And he eventually discovers, in the end, that this emotional machine has been screaming in agony all these years."

I stared at the circles, realizing that one set was a local telephone number. It didn't seem to have any context until I stared at the last three digits of the second set. I looked up at Vijay and he nodded affirmatively.

"It's such a relief to have something published, you know?" he said. "It's nice to know that someone...somewhere, anyways...had a chance to read something you worked on."

This was the whole set of the fragmented code I'd received on the pre-recorded phone call the night I gathered Seneca from the alley. I wasn't sure what the phone number was, but I suspected the second set was an extension.

"I...I have to agree with you," I said, folding the page and putting it in my pocket. "I miss people reading my work. And it is a rush getting published."

+ + +

HE COULDN'T SPEAK openly. About the Society, about anything that would implicate him — or so I was left to assume. I continued with our publishing discussion, presuming the note in my pocket would lead me closer to an answer. I left his building thinking that I was either a terrible interrogator, or perhaps the greatest that humanity has ever known.

Another day ends, wired by circumstance with no one but myself to confer with. I sat against the front window of the skinny bar at Dundas and Ossington, a dram of rye sitting like a little brother next to a pint of ale. I didn't want to see or talk to Paul. Not yet. It was best he remain confused, or at least more confused than normal. Away from my madness, of eternally being one step away from another step.

A year ago, I'd impulsively disassembled the 50mm lens of Karen's Leica. Piece by piece. Taking it apart had gone surprisingly well. But it was while attempting to piece it back together, toiling with miniature screws and jeweller's tools, that I experienced a madness similar to what I felt now: the urgency to solve a problem I couldn't afford to leave undone despite that I was out of my depth and had zero hands-on experience to draw from. Knowing that anything but success would justify her outrage. By the end my hands were shaking, my breaths shallow. Worst of all, I couldn't think of the reason why I felt compelled to take the lens apart in the first place.

A song came on the jukebox at the end of the bar: "These Days" by Nico. I took a look at the bar, at the younger men sitting along it. It struck me how odd it was to see people in their twenties, drinking beer and listening to Nico, their faces unshaven yet clean, their passions hard-cocked. The Teutonic, motherly simplicity of her voice, at that moment a requiem and a lullaby to youth.

I was bothered by how good Vijay's story was. He'd offered me a copy of the chapbook it was published in as I left our odd charade. I politely declined. I knew it was good. It was probably near-effortless for him to have written. Some people had an air of clarity about them, so that no matter what they said you just assumed everything you heard was coming from a source of assured expertise. Even if, as in Vijay's case, it was introverted. Two, maybe three revisions?

It felt as if I'd hung out with a celebrity.

When I was done with my pair of drinks, I settled up with the bartender and made my way out, then back into the same building through an adjoining entrance, the jukebox echoing through the walls of the staircase, all the way to my apartment on the second floor.

+ + +

"YOU HAVE REACHED the voice mail of Perimeter One International. If you know the four-digit extension of your party, please enter it now."

It was the sort of patient, well-enunciated voice one expects when reaching voice mail.

I pressed 6 3 0 4.

Pause. The tone of the line changed, becoming scratchy and pitted with signal drop outs. Like the night I'd received the call.

"You have reached the mailbox of Cathy Matapang. Please leave a message after the tone and I will return your call promptly."

I stood with my head against the wall, staring at the floor.

Say something.

Anything will do.

"This is Derrick van der Lem. I'm looking for Cathy." I paused. "I'm looking for Seneca."

All this time, I had no clue what I was going to say. Probably because I never knew the format that I was going to express it in. And when it came, the rough truth came out of me unfiltered: her. Her face lodged in my mind. Something about her provided the impulse that allowed me to get this far, to believe however stupidly that she was not simply an imposter.

I barely remembered to leave my cellphone number. I wondered if Cathy would be any different than Wallace.

+ + +

[Excerpt from "The Injured Cowboy and the Curse of the Mad Coureur de Bois" | Derrick van der Lem | December 14, 2007]

"Why did your wife run away, mister?" Sally asked him. For a youngster, her stare was as piercing as a rattler.

The cowboy kept looking at the birch canoe trailing away along the bank of the Athabasca, with Trapper Ivan's body, the two Mountie constables paddling with resignation.

"If I knew that I wouldn't be here," he replied.

It was the truth, but it became apparent to him that it wasn't what Sally wanted to hear. He knelt down in front of her, looking over to the hulk of the dead grizzly bear to remind him of the scare she'd been through. She deserved something more.

"Sally, this here's a question a lot of grown-ups have trouble with. Fact is, I was only beginning to know her — it happened that fast. As quickly as we took to each other, not long after we booked the chapel, she disappeared."

He turned downstream to glance at the canoe's progress.

"That's the speed of love: fast. And when she left me, everything slowed. Some days I wonder whether the world moves at all."

He coughed into his glove and touched his vest where he kept her parting letter, folded in the inside pocket. He sat down at the bank of the river, took a few breaths for his health and looked at Sally.

"I suppose that's why I'm always moving. A part of me reckons that...trying to move the world means moving yourself first."

+ + +

THE NEXT IMPROV class was at the Dance Cave.

"I don't know how to dress for this shit anymore," Paul yelled over the shoegazy din of My Bloody Valentine. It was a retro-'90s night. Posters around the club advertised a retro-'80s night too, suggesting that contemporary taste was just an ever-changing cycle of nostalgia. There was nothing odd about Paul's clothing, just perhaps, like me, he wasn't looking for nostalgia. We stood at a black countertop that stretched across the length of the dance floor, as if the club were staging a science fiction courtroom scene. I nodded in sympathy, numbly. I would've nodded at almost anything he said at that moment. Why were we here? Why keep him tethered to this mess? He was a witness, yes. But a witness who had also been used too. Not as cruelly as I, but still. I saw the uselessness of him being there.

"Here's the scoop," I said, raising my voice and leaning into his ear. I was going to tell him about my meeting with Vijay, my solving of the phone number that I should've written down. But I stopped when I felt my cellphone vibrating against my waist. I looked at the display.

UNKNOWN ID.

I looked at Paul, raised my finger, then turned and slipped through clots of club goers haunting the bar, racing into the stairwell where the entrance to the men's room was. I answered just as I'd secured the stall furthest away from the door.

"Hello?" I was out of breath. The noise from outside made it hard to judge the quality of the phone connection.

"Hey there, trooper."

It wasn't Cathy.

"Hello, Wallace," I said, my back stiffening, a familiar anger filling my head.

"What are you up to right now?"

"I'm standing in a dance club toilet stall. You?"

I heard him chuckle on the other end. His voice seemed warmer somehow. There wasn't the tension I'd heard before. Not that this meant anything. He wasn't disadvantaged.

"Glad to hear. Look, I just happen to be sitting in a car parked on the street in front of your dance club."

I blinked.

"Quite a coincidence, don't you think? Aside from that, I was wondering if you'd like to talk. The good kind of talk. You know?"

I readjusted myself in order to avoid a surge of music as someone came inside the bathroom. I stared at the painted bulkhead inches away from my face, the rusted fissures and dents. Drywall damage and sloppy patchwork. Vertical hearts crossed out, replaced with horizontal hate lines. Swastikas.

"That's fine," I said. "Will I be coming home tonight?"

Pause.

"That's up to you. In the end, that's your call, Derrick. You also have to realize that this isn't a discussion that can be delayed. It's kinda time sensitive, if you get my drift."

Clenching my jaw.

"I'm quite serious, Derrick."

"I'll see you down there in a sec," I said, hanging up. I felt like whipping the phone against the floor. I wanted to see it split open into pieces. I wished I didn't sound so fucking polite when I was angry. I wanted to kick the door to my stall open like a badass, but it opened from the inside.

I came back to the dance floor and saw Paul at our counter. He turned around and nodded affirmatively. He was on his phone.

I kept my expression blank as I approached.

Are they calling him? How far does this go?

A surge of adrenaline. In a world with fewer consequences my hand reaches out and slaps the phone out of Paul's hand, traitor bastard. Slaps him across the face, twice.

"...but it's, you know, fun. The music is good," he said, smiling apologetically to the person on the other end, a finger plugging his other ear. He caught my attention and nodded. "And...Anyways, I should go. We're doing great and I'll see you soon. Okay, sweetie? Bye."

He didn't know what to make of my stare, looking helpless.

"Who was that?" I asked.

"Julie," he said. "Look, I don't think she's buying the whole improv class thing," he said, yelling above Sonic Youth.

I nodded. Whether he was guilty of anything was a question for another day. As far as I was concerned, the improv class was just another deception in a long line of deceptions. As far as I was concerned, everyone in the world was equally innocent and complicit.

I put my hand on his shoulder to punctuate the thought, gave him an understanding nod and made my way back through the growing crowd to the exit.

+ + +

THERE WAS NO point in glancing through the Prius' windows: they were opaque. The front door was locked. The rear passenger window lowered itself.

"Back here, Derrick."

The window closed and the door opened. I climbed into the back seat. Wallace sat beside me, waiting.

"It's not a limo, I know. But it's ubiquitous and sexy," he said with relish, as if relieved I was within reach. A bulky driver kept still in the front, awaiting further instruction.

"Buckle up."

I didn't say a word, neither a smile nor a scowl. Wallace glanced at me, waiting for me to get settled, patiently expecting my response. I nodded to show I understood even though there was no question.

The Prius pulled away from the curb, onto Bloor Street traffic. I tried to pretend I was in a cab. I looked out the window, glancing at the neon, the drunken students.

"First, you're probably wondering the basics: what's going on, where are we going. That sort of thing."

"Sure."

I thought about what he would do if I punched him in the ribs.

"We're taking a ride a little east of here," he said, his voice souring. "Head office."

I noted how well dressed he was, as if coming from a formal gathering. Or going to one. I rubbed my palms against my jeans.

"Head office..." he shook his head with an odd smile. "You know, we made a deal with them — our chapter of the Society, others... there are a number of camps, Derrick, and I won't waste your time getting into politics. We basically said to them, you can keep head office where it is, on condition that you agree not to ask us to visit so often," he said, chuckling. It bugged me how he found amusement in what he was saying. Everything around him was on the edge of becoming a delightful joke.

"Where is it?" I asked.

He didn't say anything.

For a while, neither of us spoke — certainly not the driver, whose presence was nonetheless felt. He manoeuvred us northbound through main roads and residential streets as if having knowledge of every obstacle and traffic pattern in our path. Each finger of his right hand had a ring on it. We turned north onto Avenue Road and Wallace broke the silence, his attention switching less jovially from us to the play of street lights outside his window.

"We needed to know whether you were going to call the police, you know. If you did, it meant that you believed it was all a charade. And, you know what? It probably would have ended there."

He looked at me plainly. Then shrugged, turning back to his window as if the rest was implied.

"Instead, you sucked it in and you gave it some thought. You cooled off and remembered Vijay Abapathy. We didn't have to throw you a bunch of clues. Not that many. The phone book at the Royal York . . . don't get me started." He shook his head. "You asked yourself the right questions and made your way to him. You figured that if he existed then there was a possibility that it all actually happened. Right?"

I sat still, not wanting to take his bait.

"If he was real, you figured, then she could be real. Couldn't she? And not an actress — actor, sorry. My wife keeps telling me I should call them actors."

He turned around in his seat, as if realizing his approach wasn't absorbing very well, giving me his full attention. For a second I thought he was going to grab me — that my door would swing open, and I'd be pushed out into traffic.

"I'm happy you didn't call the police." He extended his hand and smiled.

I had to contend with the idea of shaking Wallace's hand, as if playing out some quaint gentleman's game. I also wondered whether or not I stood a chance in a fist fight in a Prius. I shook his hand while looking the other way, wishing immediately I'd squeezed it harder.

"You could say the last while has been a test. If you hadn't passed, we wouldn't be speaking now. You'd probably still be doing paperwork at 14 Division. Consider this a success. Though I can imagine you want to hit me right now."

I smiled politely, averting my gaze.

"And put an end to our enduring relationship?"

"Fair enough. Fair enough," he chuckled, nodding. He looked out his window as we took a corner. In his reflection I saw a smirk. "In any case, I'm not wearing a taser or anything. We know your temper threshold. I've prepared myself for some foul language."

I looked at him for a moment, sizing him up.

I couldn't hold back: "What do I know about her that's true? The diaries. The...What she told me? You have to understand: if I never see her again the significance of her memory stands second only to knowing if it had all been a trick in the first place."

He looked at me and, nodding affirmatively, leaned toward the driver.

"Hurry it up, please, Cal."

We sped past several police cruisers, clearly exceeding the limit, yet I noted how calm Wallace was. He was waiting. All too patiently waiting, and it drove me nuts not knowing what was going to happen.

"Living in a city as diverse and neurotic as Toronto allows us a fertile theatre," he said. "It has been the perfect formula for our successes in the past. The people who live here aren't very curious and the real estate's cheaper than Geneva."

Cal threaded us through traffic, from Avenue to Lawrence to Bayview. A couple of right turns and we were on a dark residential road. Everything was landscaped and wealthy-looking. Before long we had slowed in front of the wrought-iron gates of a grand estate. The driver didn't need to lower his window. After a few seconds' pause, the gates lazily unlatched and floated open. Wallace leaned forward, looking through the windshield, alert to a small group of people in formal wear staring at us through one of the ground-floor bay windows. The Prius passed over the paved half-moon driveway toward a deep two-car garage. One of its rolling doors was left open.

"Crap."

I turned and saw Wallace holding his hand to his mouth. Our car was engulfed by the darkness of the garage bay. Only the moonlight behind us provided any illumination.

"Cal?" he asked.

I expected to hear an answer, but saw and heard nothing.

"Cal, do you have an extra pair of sunglasses?"

I could barely see Wallace's face. I needed to see it.

I saw the shadow of Cal's thick hand reaching back.

"Take those, will you?" Wallace said.

"Me?"

He didn't answer. I reached out and took them from Cal's hand. Wallace pulled his cellphone out and began to text someone. In the light of his screen I saw he was wearing sunglasses.

"Put them on, please."

"What?"

"What... The sunglasses. Now!"

I heard something surge within the garage. At once high-pitched but roaring like a furnace, cycling faster, but instead of levelling out, the sound grew louder.

"Hold on, Derrick."

I fumbled the sunglasses on, and as my eyes tried to make sense of the blacker blackness, the noise began to swell and a very fine light began to flicker around us. I began to see that the garage was completely dotted with these small, white, cross-shaped –

+ + +

[Journal entry | Seneca Lewis | June 12, 2055]

They talked a load about fulfilling people's experiences, but they never told me what particular experience I was to participate in, let alone fulfill. Perhaps I should have asked.

I went into this feeling like a failure and I feel like I'm walking out of it a fool. Every time I think about what's happened it ends with a question mark, as if I was never really sure what it was I was supposed to be doing, despite the training and coaching. No one's told me whether I made a difference or asked about how things have impacted me.

What's worse is that I'm writing this in a café with live folk music. Another power outage in my building and this is the only place nearby. Some people have even brought their children here. I can feel the thump of their enthusiastic foot-tapping through the floorboards (but whether their footfalls on the floorboards were amplified by the empty basement beneath I could not say). It's come to this.

I'm left hoping that the answers to all of my questions lie in what's coming next. It's occurred to me that maybe it's the very questions I'm raising that are the intended result.

In the event that someone is reading this, I will accept a written explanation from Cathy. Or Wallace, or anyone from the Society, any time. Without fuss.

[...]

I waited for you.

217

I stood at my window on more than one occasion, waiting to catch a glimpse of you outside (which makes no sense – God knows how your lungs would hold up out there). Or hear your voice behind me. That warm, boyish voice. Those warm, caring hands, giving me shivers of longing.

[...]

I waited for you. And some days this stupid act of faith has all but destroyed me. No one ever told me that you would come back. I just wanted it to happen. I want it to happen, and now I feel abandoned, even though I guess from your perspective it looks like I was the one who was doing the abandoning. And it seems like we have to live with that.

I don't know who I am anymore. Nobody recognizes me. I think it's because I don't recognize them. Since coming back (Did I ever leave? Who knows: I woke up in the lab and then they put me to sleep, and then I woke up a second time and I was in my apartment) I feel as if I'm still wearing those sunglasses. I feel as if I still have that anonymity you insisted on. But now I'm a stranger everywhere. I feel like a shadow lurking about the walls.

They want to talk to me. They poked and prodded me, put needles in and drew blood from me, did a genetic recount, had strangers staring through windows at me when I was naked. But have yet to talk, to tell me what the next step is, besides waiting for them. Waiting for you.

+ + +

"I DON'T MEAN to whisk you, but...well, I'm whisking you," Wallace said, smiling, his hand on my back. I was coming to. I couldn't understand how I could be walking yet only now awake. The first thing I saw clearly was the beads of sweat spotting Wallace's forehead. I opened my eyes wider and I could see we were passing a set of large arched windows. We were walking through a massive stone-brick foyer. I could see a large body of water outside, far below. Dark blue. Beyond that, the silhouette of a mountain range in the morning light.

"Where are we?"

"Why Geneva, of course," he said.

He hurriedly escorted me through a grand lobby, past a group of bemused older strangers in crisp clothing. We passed a long row of framed oil portraits. Trying to keep pace with Wallace, my legs lazy, I caught a glimpse of a few, managing to spot Andy Warhol, Eleanor Roosevelt and Rabindranath Tagore. I thought I also passed an iceberg painting by Lawren Harris.

I was navigated toward a set of dark oak double doors.

"Right. Here we are," he said breathlessly, shielding me from looking back toward the lobby, the paintings and the strangers catching glimpses of us. "I'm going to let you in," he motioned to the doors, "and after that, you're on your own."

Imposing on me like before. But he was nervous, the beads of sweat betraying something not even he could disguise.

"What is this?" It was all I could think to ask. My head couldn't get past the portraits.

"Well, remember on the phone, earlier? Remember when you asked whether you were coming home tonight?"

I couldn't respond.

"It will be decided right here. Now. In this room," he said, nodding impatiently toward the doors. I couldn't figure out which it was: whether he was late for something, or that my entrance into the chamber was more pressing. I heard a grandfather clock chime in the background. Out of nowhere, I wondered if his wife was expecting him for dinner that moment.

His semi-fictitious wife, I thought. Who may just be an actress — oh, actor...har-dee-har.

"Either go in and answer that question for yourself, or I'll have Cal drive you home and you'll never see or hear from us again." He leaned forward a little to make the point.

I was flooded with questions. Questions about questions. And all of them were my typical sitcom reaction questions. Questions that only reinforced me as a confused victim.

"Does us include her?" I asked.

He remained still, his smile bound to some sort of etiquette. He blinked a couple of times then leaned forward. "Just so you know, that wasn't Vijay's real apartment," he whispered, keeping his eyes on me. I met his stare, tempted to laugh at the futility of thinking I had any sway in the matter.

"It's your call, Derrick. I, however, have the maire de Genève waiting for me in another room, and I can barely remember his name, so decide now, please."

I turned toward the doors, spent a second or two taking in their gnarled wrought-iron handles, then reached out and grasped onto one.

"Oh — your will and stuff is still behind the oven, right?"

I didn't budge. I pulled the door open: tall, heavy and stubborn. The lights were off inside whatever room awaited me.

"Open locks, whoever knocks," he whispered. I could sense his smile without seeing it. I took a deep breath and walked inside, realizing it was pitch-dark. The door closed behind me decisively. I waited for my eyes to adjust, hoping they would locate some form of light. I heard Wallace's footsteps turn and walk away on the other side.

I heard him talk to someone in the foyer. Something about...I thought I heard a name. Cathy?

In the pitch-blackness I could smell leather and wood: oiled, rich, opulent. It permeated the entire space, providing the only measurement I could make of the interior. I had no estimate of how large it was. I cleared my throat, hoping the sound would magically dispel the creeping unease inside me. No luck. The sound of my shoes scuffing the floor didn't seem to carry far. I reached into my pockets to see if I had my cellphone, so I could use it as a lamp. Gone. The sunglasses. Gone.

I stepped forward in the dark, delicately, holding blind hands out in front of me. My fingertips touched and recognized the frame of a high-backed wooden chair. I ran my fingers along the edges. It had cathedralesque spires crowning either side. I pulled it toward me and found it didn't scrape against the floorboards, as if there were felts affixed to the legs, allowing it to be both easy to move and quiet. I stepped into the space it had occupied and, as I suspected, felt the curved lip of a table against my thigh. I felt along the edge until my hand made contact with the arm of another chair. Then I saw the shape of my hand, appearing through the blackness like a photograph developing. I looked up and saw a chandelier slowly descending from the chamber ceiling, which seemed, impossibly, four storeys high. The lower the chandelier descended the brighter it glowed. By the time it reached midway between the domed ceiling and my head I heard a short squeak of feedback and then the hum of a speaker system.

"Welcome, Mr. van der Lem," a voice spoke from the rafters. I wasn't sure if it was Wallace's voice or someone else speaking. It wasn't Paul's.

"Please have a seat."

I didn't want to. I wanted a moment to walk around and make sense of what appeared more and more to be the belly of a great hall. I was standing at a massive round table.

"Mr. van der Lem, please sit."

I took hold of the chair I'd pulled away earlier.

The hall was enormous, circular with a recessed stage on one end, complete with thick red velvet curtains. There were crests on the walls. Crests with symbols. Ornate symbols. Vast arching wooden beams...

"Mr. van der Lem, though our organization aids in the creation of formative experiences, our partnership is primarily philosophy-driven. It has been this way since we started sixty years ago. It has been our goal to prescribe philosophical solutions as a means to temporarily stabilize volatile aspects of society. To give pause. To insert ourselves where less rational minds flourish.

"History has shown fascism to be a form of state-sponsored nihilism under the garb of patriotism. Its influence on society is implicitly deconstructive. It is an established charter of our organization to find and, if need be, remedy the beginnings of state fascism, even if perpetrated unwittingly by innocent citizens. We know that when these influences are allowed to merge into the threads of community they become incredibly difficult to uproot, not unlike the spread of a tumour, which, once seated within a host, takes every opportunity to survive and spread."

Something in these words seemed eerily familiar, something that triggered the memory of a day I'd spent with my dad. For a moment I was no longer in the strange hall, but sitting on a Muskoka chair by a lake, the smell of citronella candles...

"There are too many ideas in the world, Mr. van der Lem," the overhead voice said. "Random circuits of ideas and conceptual motifs floating indiscriminately within our every breath. We consume and excrete ideas with every keystroke or blink of the eye. It is only a question of the proper combination of circumstances mixed together in the minds of the right people at the right time. The right composition — economic, social, political — and even a city as equable as yours can become infected.

"Philosophy, Derrick, is the first and last frontier. With the right philosophy, politics, science and even religion can follow single file. Tragically, we learned it is the same with the wrong philosophy.

"Before our brothers and sisters contacted us from the postdated future, we had only begun to understand the value that we could provide to society at large. Until that point we'd amassed a network of localized memberships across North and South America, Europe and Africa. What we were doing then, our experiential psychodramas using props and actors, were very effective in allowing participants to think and see differently. We influenced people with the motivation to change their patterns of thinking, and their patterns of action.

"You may be surprised to hear that nearly everyone who has taken part has come back to the fold, to assist with the management of the Society's membership or take part in its government. It was only when contact with our brothers and sisters in the postdated future happened that we realized how our selection process could take a new dimension, quite literally, and become enriched and influenced by a sharing of perspectives: to direct our energies toward prevention rather than prescription."

"Prevent what?" I asked, staring at the pulsing chandelier.

"Tragedies," the voice answered, growing louder. "Like those which result from the madness of repeated disappointment, from what you call existential heartbreak. But on a scale you couldn't conceive."

I was unable say any more, looking around for a sign of anyone standing in the shadows. Waiting to pounce on me.

"Let us make ourselves clear. You served in two procedures: the first was meant to alter your perspective on your circumstances, which is the traditional role of our organization."

I held my hands against my face, barely allowing myself to listen to the voice. I wanted to scream for help, but I barely understood why. I found it hard to breathe.

"The other procedure was less mechanical: to put our theories as philosophical scientists to a grand test. Our partners matched you with a person in a postdated time. They sent her back to meet you, under the pretext of a somewhat more innocent experiment. We matched you because the experiment was more than just about travelling. It was..."

"No! Stop it! Stop it!" It was me. I was yelling at the chandelier.

From somewhere in the room a projector shone upon the middle space between the massive tabletop and the descending chandelier. Images of newspaper headlines, photos. Pages from an evil little manifesto. I couldn't breathe. I tried to close my eyes, only to shield them when I couldn't close them.

Photo: Explosion.

"It was to stop you from start..."

Words: SCREAMS, FIRE, GIRL.

I sprang from my chair and began screaming, hands clasped over my ears, trying to keep from hearing what was being said, turning my eyes away from the projected images and words. I bent over and grabbed the chair and — barely able to press it to my chest, my stupid weak muscles — tossed it toward the projection. It only managed to go a few feet before crashing pathetically on the tabletop.

"Shut up!" I yelled, cupping my ears. "You don't deserve to tell me my fucking story! You don't deserve it! To tell me things I don't know!" I pointed at the chandelier as it dropped lower. "I don't want to know how it all works, I don't want to know whether it's a fucking stage show or real. I just want to know when I'll see her again!"

The chandelier grew brighter as I caught my breath.

"I just want to know when I'll see her again!"

The sound of multiple sets of footsteps approached the doors behind me. The lights in the great hall erupted and flared with cool light beamed from the rafters. I saw the same little devices from the garage, the luminescent cross-shaped markers. They dotted the interior of the entire chamber.

224

Thousands. The chandelier emitted a piercing beam of light, bleaching my eyes as the PA speakers repeated all the words I'd been told, my responses included, but warped and bathed in feedback, curling and distorting as if sound itself was being torn to pieces.

+ + +

[Excerpt from the introduction to *The Collected Works of Peter van der Lem* | Derrick van der Lem | October 31, 2010]

I remember the most meaningful moment I spent with my father.

In the latter part of our relationship my only memories of him were our intermittent, often impromptu, gatherings for midday drinks on top of the Park Hyatt. But years before, when I was twenty-four, out of school and unemployed, he wanted to get together one weekend. It meant driving to a cottage in Haliburton, the existence of which I'd not known about until the invitation. I assumed it was something he hid from the divorce lawyer or perhaps something my mother hid from me. He invited me over for the day and when I arrived (it would be the last voyage of my '84 Honda Civic) I found that he was the only one there. I knew he had girl-friends, and I just assumed he'd be there with one of them. I saw it on his face when I got out of the car, in his lack of distraction, smiling as I parked on the steep gravel pathway, hoping my emergency brake wouldn't snap and my only means of escape wouldn't roll down the hill into the lake. It was clear that he had been waiting for me. This wasn't the jolly host fetched by girlfriends, greeting me as if a guest on

225

a '60s TV show, drink in hand. His intent this day was clearly different, and it worried me because I suspected it would require that I care.

+ + +

"IS THAT THE Canadian Gibran I see?" a voice spoke from behind me. "Or is it the Danish Hemingway?"

I was at a book signing: my book, my signing. A note informing customers about it hung near the one telling people that the store would be moving. They couldn't afford to renew the lease, so they were moving to the Junction soon. The owners told me earlier how only bars and high-end espresso shops could afford the leases now, how Leslieville and the Junction were the last zones of retail sanity left in the city. It was a shame because Trinity Bellwoods was right across the street.

It took me three years to reach the point where I was invited to sign books. It turned out to be a memoir, albeit someone else's. Shortly after I was abducted, the night the Society raped my mind with truths and hollowed it out, a narrow stream of calls began to come my way for fiction submissions, my name recognition stemming from the few interviews published after Dad's death. I became known as an emerging writer, whatever that meant. It was better than "ungrateful bastard." After a period of intense and surprisingly fresh-eyed revision, I eventually had some work published: an earlier Injured Cowboy piece, and a story about a scientist who gets kidnapped by a secret society, not unlike the Freemasons, posing as a high-concept furniture company. One of the editors I got to know became interested in something more ambitious. The deal I ended up making was with a small publishing house in New York City with a competitive interest in releasing an edited selection of Dad's work. They made me an offer: write the introduction, provide some representation (i.e., editorial input) on the collection, and in turn they would put my name on the front of the book, beneath Dad's, and help me publish my forthcoming novel, *The Embassy*. My deal stipulated that, if the novel sold well, there would be an arrangement in which the Injured Cowboy series would be published either as a standalone trade book omnibus or paired with my other short fiction.

It was a blizzard of development I hadn't been prepared to deal with; yet, overall, an arrangement I would've been foolish to refuse.

Her hair was longer.

+ + +

[Excerpt from the introduction to *The Collected Works of Peter van der Lem* | Derrick van der Lem | October 31, 2010]

I arrived at his cottage early. He made it seem early. We spent the day, this day he had insisted we share, mostly separated. I couldn't write within view of him — that's how special our relationship was — so I ended up reading a mangled copy of *The Gulag Archipelago* while he divided his time between excavating the storage space underneath the cottage and tending to small repairs inside. As for lunch, I expected he would have the barbecue going, but when I poked around the kitchen he called out for me to help myself to a sandwich. As in, make one if you want one. It was at this point that I began to suspect the worst. I had no clue what that might be, and as the day drew its curtains I kept waiting for him to say something, to explain why exactly I had been asked to come out there. Whatever it was, I wasn't sure he realized that I had my own thoughts.

We ended up taking the canoe out onto the lake, without much in the way of reason or discussion. Apart from him asking some disarming questions ("You know how to swim, right?") and providing a colourful editorial on the status of his lakefront neighbours (he hated them), we didn't speak about anything of consequence. I was thankful since I don't think I could have handled another level to the cliché: the vision of us in a canoe, as Canadians, building to some contrived discovery of just how our relationship had disintegrated over the years, wounded loon yelps in the background. I sensed he felt the same. Again, it went unspoken.

Though I am by no means an outdoorsman, it doesn't take a coureur de bois to understand that you don't argue in a canoe in the middle of a lake near sunset.

+ + +

I STOPPED THINKING the moment I heard her voice, stopped thinking about the small group of people milling about my table at the back of the bookstore, the ring, the tone of her voice as clear as when I'd heard it that last morning: young, cunning.

I looked down, as if from a drunken accident or out-of-body experience. I saw the black-tipped Sharpie in my hand, the book — my book — underneath the other hand.

I wondered if she was a dream or if the past was indeed leaking into the present, an artifact of nostalgia. Resonant frequency achieved.

I kept looking down at my hands, at the pen and the book, the book and the pen, unsure if I wanted to keep breathing, or to know what would happen next.

Hearing her voice just now, at this point in my life...

I smiled at the short queue facing my table, cleared my throat and proceeded to rise from my chair, turning around. Somewhere in my head I was still sitting, staring at my hands on the table, with the pen and the book. I'd begun to understand what it was like to have a near-death experience, then realized how many near-deaths I'd experienced.

+ + +

[Excerpt from the introduction to *The Collected Works of Peter van der Lem* | Derrick van der Lem | October 31, 2010]

We got back, alive, through the encroaching darkness and its scrapes and insect bites, smelling of sunscreen and bug repellent. I could tell there was a difference between us, and perhaps it was from having shared the instability of the canoe, but we both felt looser, more prone to talking. We started out with beer and politics, which turned to wine and him telling me about a trip he'd made to Tunisia. The more he talked, the more I talked, and the more I talked, the more I sensed he was listening, and the more I sensed he was, for that moment, my father and not someone being interviewed, which more and more people these days seem to emulate.

"I'm done fighting," he said. It just came out and I can't remember whether there had been a lead-in. It so obviously begged for a response that, knowing his tendency to occupy as much of a conversation as possible, I tried very hard to let it hang in the air without giving in, even though I knew I would have to.

We were sitting on the porch, which, beyond the glow of our citronella candles, overlooked a forest somewhere in the blackness, descending to the lake. Fireflies zigzagged like Nordic Tinkerbells. The Canadianness was nearly lethal.

"Fighting what?" I asked, giving in.

He asked me for a cigarette. It was the first and last time I ever saw him smoke. I swear, he did these things to offset me. If I'd been shooting heroin, he'd have been motioning for me to pass the surgical tubing and syringe.

"Too many, my boy. Your mother. Myself. My career, such as it is..."

Such as it is, I thought, on a lakefront property in Haliburton...

"...Publishing people. Wynona [a girlfriend, not the town]. Canada. And that I haven't seen any change in the course of humanity since I first started looking," he said.

I pulled out a cigarette for me this time: it kept the mosquitoes at bay if not my discomfort with how the conversation was turning.

"Sure, I've seen plenty of changes," he continued, taking no notice of my silence. What followed was a cloud of politico-philosophical rumination that seemed to grow in all directions. He didn't specify about what the change was that he'd expected. This didn't surprise me because he was a romantic, and life is cruel to romantics, so anyone who knew him was familiar with his passions, and those who were very familiar knew of his bitterness. He went on: he talked about the problems with heirs, the historical issues surrounding the relinquishing of power — how the concept of the bloodline wasn't the best way for the human race to engineer this thing he called change. For a second I thought he was going to admit I was adopted (which I'd always suspected).

"This," he said, holding his index finger up, as if it were to be struck by lightning, "is the big fight."

In case you're waiting for a translation, I don't know what the hell he was talking about. I didn't want to listen to half of it. Instead of getting clearer he became more passionately vague. It was the sort of ornate confusion you would expect of him, so it wasn't like I could get angry. I just had to wait for his point to be made, like watching a Greenpeace stunt, the unfurling of a banner with a catchy slogan.

"And so, what is the big fight, exactly?" I finally asked. He had become so good at interviews by this point that he had developed a skill for manipulating others to indulge in his own debates. I would've been happy not asking, but I sensed everything he'd been building up to was being directed down a very intentional path. If not entirely out of exasperation, I wanted to know if there was a reason why he had invited me to be with him here in the first place.

He stubbed out the cigarette and casually looked at mine.

"Keeping society free from those who would use fascism to accumulate power and wealth." An ice cube broke in his glass and I nearly jumped in my seat. He didn't move.

"So, what do you get when you're done fighting?" I asked.

It seemed the natural question to ask, but unlike similar moments in the past, I found myself anticipating what he'd say. He turned to me and smiled. For a moment I was on the edge of incredulity. I thought I'd done the impossible and asked Peter van der Lem a question he wasn't prepared to answer.

"That's a very good question, Derrick," he said, staring out beyond the glow of the candles, as if seeking answers from the crickets in the darkness below. Hearing him say my name — in a tone of voice only a father can use to his son – I cringed, because I knew then that he knew. I was caught in something that seemed pre-scripted. It was then that I realized how much control he seemed to have over me, and how much of it was knee-jerk subservience on my part. How my role seemed pre-assigned to switch between talk-show guest and playing apostle to his messiah.

I hate to break this to some of his readers, but he was not a man with a profound interest in philosophical mystery, though by reading his work you would think this statement odd. He certainly left readers, of which I count myself one, a few bones to chew on. What I didn't count on was how life would become a mystery to me, under his living shadow; how easily convinced you can be about "getting your act together" only to discover that phrases like that are placebos. It took his death before I could eventually walk away from his fires and begin to address mine, long neglected. To put to rest the conflicts, the anger inside of me – things which grew like tumours. As I call it: existential heartbreak.

+ + +

HER SMILE WAS wide and slightly guilty; it was a detail I'd forgotten. Like the jukebox beneath my apartment, it triggered memories; sorting out our self-invested dynamic. Our trip to the CN Tower, where we felt like children fumbling about, discovering each other. Where I fell in love with her. I'd kept so much of this muted.

Her hair looked darker. It was her face though, weathered. The softness still there, but worn. Every time I looked into her eyes there was a depth that intimidated me. Perhaps I'd never noticed it before. Perhaps she saw the same in mine.

By the time I turned around, my hands were already on her waist, as if making sure she didn't drift into the sky like a balloon. Seneca remained, in the flesh, beaming at me, her cheeks flushed. Not yet the cruel dream I feared this would all be. My hands slid up her sides, over her ill-fitting clothes, until I was touching her skin, her neck, the sides of her face with my fingertips, as if handling soft crystal.

"Say something."

I couldn't remember saying it after I said it. Her eyes softened, the blue darkness glimmering with tears, her smile wavering.

"I'm...not leaving," she whispered.

We drew closer and kissed, our lips barely touching, her hands shyly wrapping around my back, pressing her fingers into my shirt, sending shock waves of blood and adrenaline through my system.

She pulled her lips away.

"You've got customers."

I turned around, looking like I'd just had a week's vacation in twenty seconds, and glanced at the puzzled faces in front of the table.

"Finish up here. I'll be in the park," she said, drawing her hand down my chest.

I couldn't remember what exactly I did in the interval between her leaving and my stepping out of the bookstore in an apologetic delirium, save for having authorly little to say or inscribe for the remaining book buyers, who I serviced with the numb efficiency of shell shock.

At some point I just got up, muttered something about getting a coffee and started walking out the door. When I got outside I kept moving, narrowly missing pedestrians, small dogs and commuter traffic as I crossed Queen West. Once I

233

passed the arches of Trinity Bellwoods, my pace quickened. I began to believe I was hallucinating. My speed walking became a jog. Perhaps this would be it: the point at which I inevitably lost my mind. I counted my blessings when I saw her sitting alone at my picnic table in the dog bowl, inconspicuously hunched over a cup of coffee. She caught my stare and smiled in return, biting her lip. It took every source of strength not to run to her.

I was unable to say anything after I sat down, so numb and unbelieving I was of what was happening. Every question that popped into in my head, rational or not, was prefaced by an endless string of new questions.

"I can't speak," I said.

I fought the urge to reach for her, remembering how painfully our experience together had ended years ago. I fought the urge to hold her as tightly as I could. The same guilty smile was on her face, as if tempted to stray from a prepared answer. I wanted to devour her.

"I told them I wanted to come back," she said. "I demanded." She reached over and put her hand on mine. I stared at it, unable to believe either hand was real. Making eye contact was next to impossible. "Cathy pulled a Wallace and didn't answer my messages. Not for a long time. I thought you were gone. Or lost. I know I was lost. So many stupid things came into my head, and they all got compounded by missing you: leaving you without necessarily knowing you or knowing what that meant. Not that I'm saying that I don't have a life or anything. I have a life. Had one. I'm not sure right now." She squeezed my hand, and, whether or not it was a cue, I looked into her eyes. She looked scared. "I put a lot of thought into it, or at least as much as I could. Coming back here, to you. It isn't a surrender of responsibility. Doing this, I'm not running away from something but to something. Someone, as well." She squeezed my hand again. "Independence. I think that's what Cathy was waiting for. They all were, I guess. It probably happened on your end too. I mean, look at you," she said, looking me over, waving her hand in the air, making me want to tell her that the only thing I had accomplished so far was scribbling an introduction to someone else's book.

"They needed to know that I wasn't giving up. She didn't say it, but my guess is that they had it all plotted out. You and me. You doing what you're doing. Me doing...You know, causation points they can map in eleven dimensions. I shouldn't say any more than that." She placed her hand against her chest, holding back. I tried to read something in her face, behind eyes that seemed different from before: a dialogue, an argument. A tear streamed down her face. I didn't know where it came from.

"They stand to the side like they're watching a game from behind glass," she said. "They set out lures and wait while we fight to figure it out. Watching us...watching us pulling our guts out, stuffing them back in again and sewing it up. I'd do anything so long as to prove that...If only so that it didn't seem intentionally cruel. To prove it wasn't a punishment. Cathy waited to see if the choice I was making...Whether the intent was valid, whether I understood it all, what I was getting into. To see if I could be...you know...a citizen of... within the..."

Her face blushed; she was straining to keep her composure.

I leaned forward, smiling wryly: "You should be a writer."

She beamed at hearing my voice. Yet when she squeezed my hand this time I grew cautious. There was something she said which gave me pause.

"Is that what we are now? Citizens," I said. "Have I agreed to something else that I don't understand?"

I didn't know what citizens referred to: the Society, something else? She looked at me with a poker face, the smile that maybe wasn't a smile; blue eyes projecting a mystery.

"You better believe it, Mister Famous Writer," she squeezed my hand reassuringly. "Mister Canadian Gibran."

A chill rose up my spine. I narrowed my gaze.

"And so... Seneca, are you suggesting I'm... That there's this society that has been interfering on my behalf, like an agent? That, in reality, I'm just a half-assed writer? Not that I didn't suspect it, if it's true."

She pulled her hand back and sighed. Hunched over a little, her elbows resting on the table, she rested her chin on her palms, her shoes scuffing the grass below.

"I guess they play a part, Derrick."

She paused to consider her words a little too long for my liking, but I sat listening in a near trance.

"A small one, sure. A small nudge with a stiff elbow," she looked frozen for a moment, staring off with a numb expression. "That's what they do best, after all." She waited for me to say something, but I couldn't speak. I wanted her to keep talking, so that I could know as much as possible.

"Can't you see it?" she asked. There were tears in her eyes. She shook her head irritatedly. "No, I guess that wouldn't make sense. You can't see it yet. Or... I don't know, maybe you won't. Or never will. Fully."

Thoughts racing, I looked away, drained of blood. This thing I thought I had smothered to death — this complicity in something I thought I would never take part in again. I leaned my head to one side, as if hoping all the rationalizations and compromises I'd made over the last three years would roll to one side and spill out of my ear. I opened my eyes and saw Seneca staring at me. I stared back, squarely, with a confidence I didn't have before.

"I know they may have helped, Seneca. I suppose I've always suspected. But I think I'm good. I got this far myself." I nodded in the direction of the bookstore, happy there was some sort of brick-and-mortar proof to point to.

Unless the store owners were...

She tilted her gaze lower, idly observing her coffee cup.

"I think the point is, Derrick," she said softly, "at the end of the day, you're the only one who can answer that question. At the end of the day, you're the only one who can ask that question."

Our eyes met again and our faces danced with an exchange of smiles and blushes. The shorthand of two people who cared deeply for each other without knowing each other.

I cleared my throat. "At the end of the day?"

She grinned, her cheeks flushing.

"There's a nice cliché."

"You know what I mean." She shoved my shoulder.

I let go of my breath as if it were the most vulnerable thing I could do, looking around the park. I saw someone sitting at a picnic table across the dog bowl, a copy of the book I'd been signing earlier in their hands, which served to inflate the absurdity of our situation. I wondered how complicit Seneca was. Even now — as beautiful and cruel as it was to see her, suspecting over these past years that some day it might happen — I still wasn't sure whether she had, like me, been left to fend for herself while the Society watched from a distance.

+ + +

[Excerpt from the introduction to *The Collected Works of Peter van der Lem* | Derrick van der Lem | October 31, 2010]

To be honest, I think I'll always be afflicted. Every time it seems that I can grasp what ails me, I push a little more and uncover a new dimension of uncertainty. And each time, I recoil, for fear of a universe filled with infinite suffering. A suffering I have attempted to avoid contributing to.

When Dad passed away I realized that all of my reasons for or against him were meaningless. In the end it was about me being able to live with myself, without becoming a catalyst for chaos. Every day I am reminded that the world has enough of that.

What do you get when you stop fighting?

I, Derrick van der Lem, son of Peter, have no clue.

In truth, as tempted as I am to gild this lily, my father never bothered to answer the question. But I could tell. I saw that subtle smirk of rebuttal on his face as he sat there, staring out into the darkness. It was something more, more than just a casual show of arrogance.

A lesson I learned that night, as we quietly proceeded to drink ourselves out of our respective funks, is that ultimately it's not losing that bugs me. It's not knowing if I've won.

+ + +

"AND ME?" I ASKED.

"They want you."

She hesitated to match my gaze.

"Not yet, but I'm sure the time will come. They'll come knocking."

I could barely absorb any more information. I swallowed hard and took a long breath.

"And you?" I asked.

She paused, looking down at the table.

"Here's the thing," she said. "When they sent me back, the first time, they told me after we were separated, after Cathy got in touch... They told me that me going back that once... it was only meant to be a start. That they had been searching for someone. Someone who wouldn't just travel there and back once, but who could stay. An agent. Someone who could keep their mouth shut."

I watched a sadness overcome her. I could only imagine: reflecting over a potential life abandoned. A new servitude.

"I took it," she said. "I finally took the job. But it depends on you."

"How?"

"If you can live with someone who can't tell you everything... about me. If you can be with someone who's working for them, which means, yes, you become part of the Society, which means more rules... Sorry, I'm not doing a great job of explaining, I don't think."

I kept my eyes on her. I held my breath.

"You know they're going to keep watching us, right?" she asked, staring at me almost apologetically.

I bowed my head. I struggled to process all of the information presented to me.

"Seneca," I said. "I can't have you in my life knowing that they might take you away some day. I can't have another potential forever without you."

I needed to say it, as much as I wanted to forget the question entirely and reach out my arms and hold her, as much as I wanted to carve a poem in the nearest tree as a testament to the feelings for her I'd nursed these past years.

I expected the worst.

"Me too," she whispered. "I don't want to be taken away. But if we're going to be together I don't have the power to decide that, and neither do you."

I looked at her. And where I expected fear, in the depth of her gaze I instead saw confidence. I saw hope, and it felt authentic. I wanted it too. I was terrified by how she would answer the next question.

"So... What do we do now? I mean, in the meantime? What do we do before things maybe get worse?"

"Well..." she said, grinning mischievously. She reached forward and rested her hands on mine, holding them on the table. "Until then, I guess it's just you and me."

+ + +

ACKNOWLEDGEMENTS

THE GREATEST MOVE 1 ever made was throwing the first novel I wrote into a fireplace (a virtual one). I walked away from the one sure thing I had in hand in order to pursue the book before you, and I have never looked back. I have applied this lesson, with its ensuing waves of terror and exhilaration, to other areas of my life since.

There was a time when I had more certainty that writing was unquestionably an individualistic if not solitary art form. And while the hardest aspects are completed in isolation, I can tell you now that, at least for those who wish to succeed, such is perception only. In the background of everyone's narrative, no matter how self-achieved you might feel, are a multitude of helpers; some of whom are willing partners, while many others assist by virtue of just being themselves. There are plenty of people whom I have learned from, leaned on and found inspiration through.

I would like to thank poet/novelist D. M. Thomas who, through the Humber School for Writers, instilled in me some good habits, and through that experience came a writing

243

group of nine years (Nate Simpson, Meredyth Young, Philippa Dowding, Paul Dore and Siobhan Jamison among others).

For technical advice on the medical front, I would like to thank Dr. Vincent Woo and Dr. Roger Rose for pointers. Some of the first scraps of this manuscript were conceived in Pouch Cove, Newfoundland — for that I wish to thank James Baird and the Pouch Cove Foundation. I also wish to credit Reg Hartt and his Cineforum, whose lecture I borrow a title from. Everything I needed to know about the scientific and literary lineage of time travel was made possible through Paul J. Nahin's *Time Machines: Time Travel in Physics, Metaphysics, and Science Fiction*.

I would like to thank my parents, Marianne Karkkainen and John Cahill, as well as my brother, Darrin Cahill. I would like to thank Stephanie Fysh for providing editorial feedback on the early manuscript, Janie Yoon for taking me seriously and Lesley Grant for presuming I was going somewhere. As well, a parade of stressed-out public school teachers. Dorian Grah for being an early conspirator and a true light in the darkness.

The first draft and subsequent revisions of this book were completed in various bars and cafés kind enough not to kick me onto the sidewalk for exploiting their real estate: Lot 16 (RIP), Squirly's, Last Temptation, Voodoo Child, The Embassy, Tequila Bookworm and Lipstick & Dynamite. Truly fine establishments, all.

The gang at Wolsak & Wynn have been outstanding. Publisher Noelle Allen, managing editor Ashley Hisson and publicity co-ordinator Emily Dockrill Jones all believed in this thing, and boy does that make a difference. Working with Paul Vermeersch, senior editor of Buckrider Books, has been a dream: someone who wants what I've written to be as good as it can be and not someone else's book.

You wouldn't be reading this were it not for the effort of literary agent extraordinaire Kelvin Kong, who, with the help of The Rights Factory and Sam Hiyate, stickhandled this newbie with patience and acumen. The Society would be so lucky to have someone like him.

Most deservedly, this list of thanks would not be complete without making ample space for my partner, Ingrid Paulson. In life, in work, your encouragement, belief and validation have been invaluable to my journey. You are incredible.

Matt Cahill, August 2015
City of Toronto

MATT CAHILL is a Toronto writer. He writes novels, short stories and essays. He's contributed work to *Ryeberg*, *blogTO* and *Torontoist*. His short story *Snowshoe* appeared in September 2014 with Found Press. Matt worked for twenty years in the film and television industry before coming to his senses and training to become a psychotherapist. He now has a private practice and is a member of the College of Registered Psychotherapists of Ontario. Matt reads highfalutin books of all sorts, plays intermediate soccer and occasionally drums. Feel free to visit Matt's website, http://mattcahill.ca. You can also follow him on Twitter at @m_cahill.